Benaud

— On — Reflection

Benaud

—On— Reflection

WILLOW BOOKS
Collins
8 Grafton Street, London W1
1984

Willow Books
William Collins Sons & Co Ltd
London · Glasgow · Sydney · Auckland
Toronto · Johannesburg

First published 1984
© Benaud and Associates 1984

British Library Cataloguing in Publication Data
Benaud, Richie
Benaud on reflection.
1. Cricket
I. Title
796.35'8'0924   GV917

ISBN 0 00 218034 0

PHOTOGRAPHIC ACKNOWLEDGEMENTS

Front cover Portrait by Caroline Forbes; inset by Patrick
Eagar. *Back cover* Press Association (top left); Central
Press (top right); Sport & General Press Agency. *Plates*
Patrick Eagar unless otherwise stated.

Set in Linotron Sabon
by Rowland Phototypesetting Ltd
Bury St Edmunds, Suffolk
Printed and bound in Great Britain by
William Collins Sons & Co Ltd Glasgow

Contents

Acknowledgements 7

1 THE MOST CONTROVERSIAL GAME 9

2 FOUR GREAT CAPTAINS ... AND A FEW OTHERS 19

3 A MEMORABLE FAREWELL SEASON ... AND SOME FURTHER THOUGHTS ON CAPTAINCY 53

4 FOUR OF A KIND ... BETTER THAN ONE ACE 88

5 THE MEDIA TODAY ... CRICKET'S GREATEST ALLY 105

6 ONE-DAY CRICKET, SPONSORSHIP AND THE PAYING SPECTATOR 130

7 THEY DON'T ENJOY THE GAME AS MUCH AS WE DID ... DON'T YOU BELIEVE IT 145

8 UMPIRING, INTIMIDATION AND THE ODD RIOT OR TWO 159

9 SOUTH AFRICA: A CASE OF DOUBLE STANDARDS 183

10 WHAT AM I OFFERED FOR THIS JOB LOT OF ADMINISTRATORS? 196

11 THE BENAUDS – JUST ONE OF MANY CRICKETING FAMILIES 218

Index 250

ACKNOWLEDGEMENTS

One of my great joys of captaincy of a cricket team was that the eleven players were such a diverse lot. It was a fascinating exercise to be part of that team and in the end, hopefully and thankfully, to see order come out of chaos and excitement and of sheer hard slog.

Nowadays I am out of the physical side of the game, but the fascination is still there, working for the BBC and Channel Nine in Australia, writing for newspapers and working in radio. And writing a book.

That has been a real team effort and acknowledgements are due to Daphne, who blanched slightly when I announced the project and yet has checked, double checked and triple checked the copy, but really knows there will still be errors; to Margaret Roseland, who typed 100,000 words of copy in Australia and then flew to London and back to Sydney to type up the final 100,000 words to go to the publisher; to Alan Gardy, for being sensible enough and bright enough to come up with the title of this book when we were dining at his Maroubra mansion; and to Tim Jollands at Collins, for his patience and unswerving devotion to the job in hand. The only task more difficult than being a cricket team manager would be as editor to an author's pride and joy.

My thanks to all and also to the players and characters of the game of cricket. They have ensured in the past and will do so in the future that this remains the most controversial and extraordinary game of all.

Richie Benaud
Sydney
November 1983

1

THE MOST CONTROVERSIAL GAME

The more I observe cricket from a distance, the more I watch at the ground, the more I read about the cricket of years past, the more I'm convinced this is, without doubt, the most controversial game of all. It is certainly the most widely publicised. But no game in my lifetime, and I suspect in the lifetime of many people older than me, comes anywhere near cricket for the sheer diversity of the controversy which surrounds it.

More than 250 years ago there were many in England who felt cricket was merely an excuse for crowds to gather, intent on civil commotion and even revolution, and the law-makers of the land were quick to give consideration to banning the game, or at least banning spectators from the pleasure of watching it. No such problems these days, or at least no such problems in banning spectators, though there are times I believe, because of their behaviour, we would be better off with a minority of spectators kept away from the arenas. The main difficulty though, as always, is to persuade well-behaved spectators to come to the grounds to watch cricket, rather than do something else with their time and their hard-earned money. It has ever been so.

Perhaps in some crowd behaviour we have turned a full circle by way of actions which mirror our society. In 1776, in a match between Kent and Essex at Tilbury Fort, Kent were found to have included a 'ring-in' in their side. In the ensuing fight two were shot dead and one bayoneted to death. In that finest of all books on the evolution of the game of cricket from the early times to the 19th century, *The Social History of Cricket*, John Ford sets the scene of the 1800s with a penetrating observation that cricket then held up a mirror to the times, *to an age of violence, of growing professionalism, of patronage, of foreign travel, of clubs, of jingoism, of drinking and gambling and to a society in which, despite the continuing dominance of London, the majority of Englishmen lived still in villages or in small rural towns.*

The description of cricket in that age could sometimes be applied today to the less desirable happenings in many sports and, unfortunately, those regrettable happenings receive most publicity. We are lucky the good things in sport far outweigh the occasional occurrences which make even the most even-tempered shake their heads and mutter about the good old days . . .

without, of course, bothering to recall that the good old days were sometimes just as bad, as well as just as good.

There is no other sport providing as much controversy as cricket. Football
– never. Athletics – of course not. Tennis – no way. Horse racing – well, the
human element is only part of the sport and I suppose the combination of
man, woman and beast provides controversy from time to time in the Sport
of Kings. But cricket . . . there has been no decade pass in the last 200 years
without controversial happenings which at the time have been the instant
despair, or amusement, for those keeping a watchful, or even baleful, eye on
the game.

In my short span of 36 years as a player, captain and a commentator, there
has been no shortage of events to make a headline in the newspapers, a lead
item on the wireless or television news, or an ear-bashing point at the local
pub or club. No game more lends itself to heated argument, generally
without result. No game has in its following the ability to raise to the highest
level the performances of the players who have now passed from view. I
have seen it all happen over those 36 years yet, in effect, I am only seeing, in
modern-day parlance, a flashback of all which has gone before. That should
not be taken as an indication of a mind tinged with cynicism – rather of a
mind which declines to take for granted the platitudes handed to us by many
who are followers of the sport.

I have been remarkably lucky in those 36 years. I have been able to play
Sheffield Shield cricket in Australia and Test cricket in all the playing
countries of the world other than Sri Lanka. I have been able to work for the
past 24 years for the BBC and *News of the World*, covering Test matches in
England and Australia. At home in Australia I have been able to pursue my
great love of newspapers, work in radio and, latterly, have had the good
fortune to be part of the television revolution of cricket in Australia.

I was extremely lucky to be part of the other revolution, World Series
Cricket, to see at first hand the changes in the game – and in people – in that
period, and to have had the chance to sit back and watch proceedings in the
London High Court for 31 days. This was the case where three players
contracted to World Series Cricket were granted declarations that the
International Cricket Conference and the TCCB had been in restraint of
trade when they barred them from Test cricket. The players were Tony
Greig, John Snow and Mike Procter and a similar judgement was awarded
to World Series Cricket . . . with costs.

Not everyone of course will feel cricket in the past 36 years has been
anything about which one may feel lucky. There are some who would wish
the game of cricket always to be conducted as in the local parish, with the
thatched roof pavilion sheltering the scorers, the scones and strawberry jam,
dainty salmon and cucumber sandwiches and weak tea between innings,
and instant excommunication or possibly execution for the most trifling

misdemeanour. I cheerfully confess not to be in that august company. It is, I hasten to say, a delightful way of life but it doesn't work, and it doesn't work for the very reason Ford highlights in his paragraph wherein he refers to the 18th century.

These days when anyone asks me what cricket books should be required reading I offer, first of all, Ford's book. It gives a fascinating insight into life many years ago. In 1982, when I first met the brilliant American writer Dan Jenkins, he asked me about cricket and how it began. I suggested, whilst he was in Australia and New Zealand on a golf writing tour, he should read this book so he would have a better idea about the origins of the game. He did so and was captivated. Far better to read this book of Ford's and understand those origins than read a history of the game up to the present day, where, understandably, the main theme running through the pages is certain to be that of play up, play up and play the game, cricket is a great character-builder, and so on. Cricket is all of those things and more, but it does have a few warts here and there and, although the old-timers would have you believe otherwise, it has always had a few warts.

They appeared through times when the administrators were keen to change the Laws, when players were rumbustious or so deadly dull attendances fell away, when spectators were jingoistic, players vulgarly dashing, through periods when everyone was saying the game is not what it was. All those things apply today as well. I have seen most of it and I hope I understand it now better than when I was younger and more inclined to take things for granted.

Cricket is a great game. I believe that, so do millions of people. There are other great sports, one of which is golf. In late November 1982, in a short speech to golfers at the Australian Golf Writers' Dinner at the Hyatt Hotel in Sydney, I made the point that cricket has the *reputation* of being the fairest and noblest game of all, but questioned whether this is true or a myth.

The point I was making was that in cricket there never seems to be a season go past where controversy is not with us. There are disputes, with the umpires and administrators of the game coming under pressure for making mistakes and players themselves putting increasing pressure on the umpires. There are constant squabbles between the playing nations, arguments about whether or not a player should have performed as he did on the field, an action regarded by one half of the game's followers as acceptable or even praiseworthy and by the other half as being not in the best interests of the game. I asked if anyone at the dinner could recall the last time a cricketer called a penalty on himself. I wasn't talking about a fielder admitting he hadn't caught a ball – that should be automatic. Golf is supposed to be a selfish game and cricket the bastion of all team and character-building games. If a ball moves when a golfer is addressing it he calls a penalty. Is this not a refreshing change?

I was pleased to see in March 1983, in a farewell address on retiring from the position of Melbourne Cricket Club Secretary, Ian Johnson, the former Australian captain, made exactly the same point. We didn't always agree on everything on the cricket field but we were on the same wavelength there.

Cricket, as I have said, is a great game. It will, I hope, always be a great game and it would have more of a chance of so being if its greatest advocates could spare a moment from burying their heads to appreciate it is played by human beings subject to all the pressures of a society which moves these days at a frantic pace. Just because cricket is regarded as a nice game is not to say it should be forced to move at the pace of the 1900s or the 1920s, or the period up to the Second World War.

It would be a joyous moment were we able to turn back the clock in this way and I hope to be around when our whizz-kid scientists say we are at liberty to step back in time. I suppose we might well be disappointed, for everything which seemed so marvellous years ago is often less so when you get down to the honest task of truthful recall. It is a little like the trip I made in 1966 back to Jugiong, where I lived from 1932 to 1937.

I hadn't been back in 28 years. But I remembered the store-room, the schoolroom, the peach tree where my father killed the snake, the peppercorn tree, the drain where I cut my knee and the place where we used to play rounders. I remembered the school and the house as being enormous. It was a great shock to find they were tiny! So tiny I sat there disbelieving until someone came out to ask if they could help me. I said, 'No thanks,' and drove away. How could you explain your mind had played you false?

Cricket memories are sometimes like that, beautiful but not completely realistic, and we will just have to settle for the game as it is today, warts and all, as indeed it has been since Hambledon Club beat England at Moulsey Hurst over 200 years ago.

The game of cricket has changed dramatically when I compare it with the time I first came into the game. It has changed even in the last five years and it changed in each five-year period going back to the end of the Second World War.

I am always fascinated to listen to my father talk of cricket as it was in the period from 1920 to the start of the Second World War when I was only nine years old. In many ways it must have been a great period from 1920 to 1930 but the Depression years would have been grim. My own memories of watching cricket start in 1939, but they were years burdened with war-time although the structure of cricket was unaltered. The system of playing cricket in Australia then was basically uncomplicated and went in a straight line from cricket played in country areas to Sydney club cricket through the various grades into Sheffield Shield cricket and on to Test cricket. It was the same in England with club cricket and county cricket leading to Test cricket. All these matches were very well attended, some county matches in England drawing as many as 35,000 people on a Bank Holiday Monday and some post-war Sheffield Shield games having Saturday attendances well in excess of 20,000.

The very first game of cricket I watched at the Sydney Cricket Ground was when the match record of 75,765 was established by the clash between Bradman and O'Reilly, with New South Wales playing against South Australia. On the first day, one of 30,400, I sat in the old Sheridan Stand, an ancient monument which has not changed a great deal to this day, my bottle of Blue Bow orange juice in hand and my father alongside me as we ate the sandwiches my mother had made that morning. We had to sit, not in a seat, but in the aisle because of the vast crowd present, but it was a memorable day. To get to the SCG we had caught a bus from North Parramatta, a steam train from Parramatta Station to Central and an old 'toast-rack' tram from Eddy Avenue to the ground. Those lovely old trams! Long gone now but never forgotten, even in the age of the Jumbo jet.

As it happened, I didn't see much of Bradman because New South Wales batted almost the whole day, but I did see Grimmett bowl and take 6 for 118. I went home that evening and started thinking about bowling leg-breaks. To this day I can see Barnes and Chipperfield out lbw to Grimmett playing back to what they thought was a legspinner . . . and being trapped by what I now suppose was the 'flipper'.

30,400 spectators!

So why don't people go to the cricket any more? The short answer is they do, but they go to watch cricket of a different kind because people are different these days. Their lifestyles are different, their thinking is different, travelling is different and there are so many distractions which simply didn't exist in the pre-war days.

In the euphoria at the end of the Second World War, sporting fixtures were resumed immediately between England and Australia and between Australia and India. The Australian teams were Services sides, playing first of all in England and then in India, the team captained by Lindsay Hassett and containing players of the quality of Keith Miller, Cec Pepper and Stan Sismey. Those matches were played in the spirit of men who had just come back from a war which could easily have claimed their lives, and had claimed the lives of thousands of others, and spectators joined in the relief.

Cec Pepper had in fact already made his mark in Sheffield Shield cricket in Australia. Six years before the Services matches, in November 1939, he had impressed Brisbane spectators with the violence of his strokeplay against legspinner Bill Tallon, one of the great characters of Australian cricket. Tallon didn't play in a Test match and wasn't actually a regular member of the Queensland side, playing for them on only nine occasions and taking 21 wickets at 41 apiece, but he was a comedian and, like all the best of the story-tellers, he had a dry sense of humour . . . and a stutter.

In New South Wales's first innings, Tallon dismissed Cyril Solomon lbw and had them on the run when Pepper and Albert Cheetham came together and added 106 for the seventh wicket. Pepper hit seven sixes and eight fours in his 81 and most of them came from Tallon. Bill was bowling from the Stanley Street end and the old tram used to run along that street just outside the ground – a picturesque area it was too in those days, with a lot of wild lantana growing. In the midst of the onslaught Bill Brown, the Queensland captain, came across to Tallon, put his hand on his shoulder and said, 'Spin it, Bill . . . spin it mate!'

'Spin it?' Tallon stuttered. 'It's s-s-so covered w-w-with bloody tram tickets and l-l-lantana thorns I can't grip it, l-l-let alone spin it.'

There was very little else to do in Australia in summer but watch cricket. The motor car hadn't made its impact in 1945, television was eleven years away from Australia and the jet plane was simply a figment of the designers' imagination. This delightful set-up existed in Australia until 1956 when television began and that, combined with the motor car being available to the masses instead of only the wealthy class, suddenly began to change the sports-watching habits of millions.

By the time I became captain of Australia the spectator pattern was established . . . downwards. In Australia we had not been helped by that very slow series which Australia lost to Len Hutton's team and administrators were beginning to worry about the spectators who were turning to other sports, or just staying away from the cricket for a variety of reasons – not in droves, but in numbers large enough to bring a frown to the forehead of any far-sighted administrators.

It was around this time in England similar falling attendances were exercising the minds of those at Lord's and a committee was set up to examine the structure of the game. This was also the time the administrators started looking for new methods to raise money to keep the game going at Test match and grass-roots level. Many people sneer at those who believe money is important to foster the game of cricket, but one only has to look at the cost of staging tours to understand why more and more finance must be arranged if the game is to be self-sufficient and, as well, is to keep at bay many other sports and pastimes.

One of the methods thought of was one-day cricket where a result could be guaranteed for the spectators. This was not exactly original thinking but it seemed likely at the time to be successful thinking. Around the end of the 1950s and early in the 1960s there were televised matches played in England under the sponsorship of the Rothmans' company. These were essentially fun matches played on Sunday afternoon, containing some 'golden oldies' and telecast on BBC2 to a wide audience. In 1960 I played in some of them and they were happy affairs with a high degree of interest in winning the match but also in trying to make sure the thousands of spectators who turned up to see a result in one day had had adequate enjoyment at the end of play. Television viewers loved them, so too the spectators at the grounds.

Traditionalists were not amused when it was suggested there could be a place in the structure of the game for the one-day match. They made their first mistake in this regard 25 years ago and many of them are still making it.

They decried the concept of the one-day game played by first-class cricketers. Now, in the 1980s, they are still at it with all the supercilious snobbishness they can muster, defending what they regard as being *their* game. Cricket is not their game at all, despite the historical notes which make it clear that the game really got under way in England a long time ago.

Cricket is a game for everyone. There are players who are amateurs paying every Saturday afternoon for the privilege of playing. There are players at levels higher than that, playing a professional game culminating in Test cricket, and there are traditional-thinking men and women supporters who over the years have liked Test cricket, county cricket and Sheffield Shield cricket. They might sit as spectators at social matches under the oak trees, sipping tea from bone-china cups or, in the Australian outback, drinking a beer and sharing a barbecue.

Then there are the new spectators, many of whom have been brought to the game by the one-day fixtures of the past 20 years. They are the ones who would never in a million years have been guilty of being found at a boring five-day cricket match or an equally boring three- or four-day county or Sheffield Shield match which may produce no result. They liked cricket but many of them simply did not care for the idea of spending their money to watch one day's play of a match and then only be able to read about the remainder or hear about it on radio. Suddenly these spectators, business-men, housewives and youngsters found there was a game they could watch which would enable them to go home at the end of the day having seen a result. They were captivated. The traditionalists were horrified. It was not proper cricket.

Now in both England and Australia there is great interest in limited overs cricket and there has been, in Australia anyway, an enormous surge of interest in all cricket. Attendances have either held solid or moved upwards because now the season is an extended programme involving matches of both kinds.

There were many who said the concept could not work. When World Series Cricket began, and when it ended, there were those who still were not convinced that in Australia a new type of programme could be used in international cricket, where spectators' interests were to be paramount. Never forget in the end it is the spectators who will always let you know if they disapprove of a programme. They will stay away or they will not watch on television, listen on radio or read about it in the newspapers.

Night cricket at the Sydney Cricket Ground has attracted big audiences,

25,000 attending a match where Australia were not even taking part and often crowds of 40,000 at the ground when Australia play England and the West Indies.

Night cricket?

When it was announced World Series Cricket would play night matches the laughter was intense, and more than slightly mocking. It changed when, on the first evening in Sydney, 52,000 spectators tried to get into the ground and, according to the ground authorities, actually did so.

The doubt was because the gates were thrown open, not because they were closed. Normally with a crowd of that size the gates are shut but, on this occasion, Mr Packer threw them open, having helped man the turnstiles when it became obvious the night was going to be a sell-out. It was a marvellous evening, full of emotion even for the more cynical observers who had watched with interest the comings and goings of the previous 18 months where Establishment cricket and World Series Cricket had been at logger-heads.

There were some very good things to come out of World Series Cricket, and one of them is the international one-day competition now played in Australia on a three-team basis. It is played over 15 matches with each team playing ten games and then a best-of-three or best-of-five Finals' series is played between the top two teams. In 1982–83 in Australia more than one million spectators passed through the turnstiles for those matches and the five Tests against England. The new structure of the game in Australia is now providing an ideal chance for spectators to follow the game of cricket and for administrators to reap the rewards.

You can be absolutely certain it would never have happened without World Series Cricket and the country's enthusiastic sports' followers would have been the losers. Australia would still be playing a Test series and three inconsequential one-day internationals against the one touring team and I am certain that kind of programme will never again be acceptable to paying spectators in Australia. Nor should it be . . . the fact that cricket tours of Australia started over 100 years ago in a certain way should not be binding on present-day administrators.

Elsewhere I have mentioned the Pakistan tour of Australia in 1983–84 where after two Tests there were real problems in interesting the public in buying seats for the matches. They had seen Pakistan in trouble against the fast bowlers in Perth and then in Brisbane and they were prepared to wait and see rather than rush to the booking offices.

The Australian Cricket Board knows now they have a sensible program-me the public wants and agrees with. They are putting on cricket matches the public will want rather than those the old-timers of the game might wish to see. It is one of the most important aspects of the promotion of sport these days: the public must be the first consideration.

If I were to nominate the single most important aspect of the aftermath of World Series Cricket, that would be it; that Australian administrators have come to terms with the fact that they have been given a chance to live with the times and to provide a balanced diet of cricket for the paying public. Those who wish to go to the Test matches can do so, but there are scores of thousands who also wish to see limited-overs matches.

Not all the Board members might like it but at least they have come to terms with it – or at least most of them have. I did hear one quote that it was a case of roll on 1990, so we can get back to the old style tour of five Test matches and the games between the touring team and the Sheffield Shield states. I shall be interested to see if that delegate has his way and cricket in Australia takes a 20-year backward step with the one-day internationals consigned to the scrapheap. I will be even more interested to see what the public thinks of it.

World Series Cricket was fun. It was also just about the busiest time of our lives, and we are not generally regarded as slouches when it comes to work. It was a time of making new friends and losing old acquaintances, a real whirl of organization and a frenzy of determination that it would work. It worked alright. That it did so did not please everyone and there were some of the more perceptive ones who realized instantly that it was nothing directly to do with any country other than Australia. Indirectly all cricket countries were involved. They became more involved when the court case came along, one of the more interesting times of my life.

It has all been well chronicled that the players were recruited months before any announcement was made. The astonishing thing to me will always be that I heard nothing of the venture before I was asked in to a meeting in Sydney early in April 1977. Our firm was made the offer of being sports consultants to World Series Cricket and I'm delighted we had the foresight to accept the challenge. Challenge it was. It was all based around the dissatisfaction of Australian players with their lot and the fact that they considered they were on the wrong end of whatever financial incentives might be available in cricket.

Now those players and the ones who have followed are earning good money for a combination of good performances and pulling spectators through the turnstiles: cricketers in other parts of the world are far better off now than pre World Series Cricket.

There will be some who say that is not a good thing. To that I say . . . nonsense.

The English county cricketer now is able to earn a decent basic wage whereas before he was on peanuts. The English Test player suddenly saw his match fee jump from £300 to £1000. Umpires, the financial outcasts of the game, are now paid in more reasonable fashion, though their payments have again started to lag behind the players. The reason the administrators put up the payments to the latter at the time was that they reasoned correctly there was a shortage of umpires for World Series Cricket on the basis that there are only a handful of really top class umpires in the world.

I am delighted to see players' payments – both Test and county – have risen because of World Series Cricket and I'm even more delighted to see the umpires were given their rightful recognition. They were the real amateurs of what the administrators wanted to believe was still an amateur sport.

There are two other aspects of World Series Cricket that have been of great benefit to the game: the fielding circle devised by Tony Greig and night cricket, which was Mr Packer's idea. The fielding circle was a tremendous success and has since been modified from the original two circles to one. In England it was bitterly resisted because it was a World Series Cricket idea, but now every limited-overs competition uses it. When you see it in the John Player League, the Benson and Hedges Cup and the NatWest Trophy, just gently recall whence it came. It is now an international plus mark for limited-overs matches.

Night cricket is only for Australia. It had been tried in England, but fiddling around with soccer grounds is merely providing a caricature of what it is like.

Night cricket is one of the most exciting things I have seen in all the time it has taken me to graduate from bowling on the back verandah at Parramatta, my teams England and Australia, to this moment where I have the pleasure of commentating on cricket around the world. There are other sidelines of World Series Cricket but they are unimportant because now the game in Australia is handled for the most part sensibly and well since the agreement between the cricket authorities and WSC. But the thing I will never forget until the moment comes to make my way to that great vineyard cum cricket ground in the sky is the first night of cricket at the Sydney Cricket Ground.

Where others were weeping tears of anger and frustration around the country, there were some of us, notably my wife and myself, who were regarding it as one of the most marvellous things we had ever seen.

And for the cricketing public in Australia there has been an additional bonus. The television coverage of cricket matches in Australia has advanced by light years in the short space of eighty-four months.

2

FOUR GREAT CAPTAINS ... AND A FEW OTHERS

Captaincy is ninety per cent luck and ten per cent skill . . . but, for heaven's sake, don't try it without that little ten per cent. There will be many who consider that heresy. To them the captains tagged with the word 'great' are a class above the normal mortals who gambol and gamble around the cricket field, sometimes playing outstanding cricket but often, as players, not quite reaching the greatest heights. As far as I know, there has never been a captain labelled as great who has not been lucky.

It is the ten per cent skill which is brought in at that point. The captain who sees an opening and goes straight for the jugular is the one who is drinking the champagne at the end of the day. The one who muses about it for an over or two before belatedly making the nerve-tingling decision, or taking the incredible gamble, is the one who reads about the next Test series from the comfort of his living-room, sipping from a cold can or an iced glass, according to his habit, and making slightly sarcastic comments on the quality of leadership being displayed by his successor. He has trouble deciding whether to have scrambled or fried eggs with his bacon and is never completely certain in which lane he should be on the motorway. Or he makes it to the commentary box where, I can assure you, it is all much more simple.

The very best captain I ever played under was Keith Miller. When I came into the New South Wales team in 1948–49 Arthur Morris was captain and he would, in my opinion, have gone on to captain Australia instead of Ian Johnson had the New South Wales selectors not decided to make Miller captain of the state. As Australia's administrators regarded Miller as a rebel and not quite the right style of chap to make the speeches on tour, he was never allowed to play his rightful part in Australian cricket. But he was a magnificent cricketer and a great captain. No one under whom I played sized up a situation more quickly and no one was better at summing up a batsman's weaknesses. He had to do this for himself when he was bowling and it was second nature for him to do so as a captain.

Miller became captain of the New South Wales team on returning from England in 1953 and under his leadership the state side began what was to be a run of nine successive Sheffield Shield championships. He retired in

1956 and then Ian Craig and I followed on, with other captains taking over when Test match duties intervened.

There was a story, possibly apocryphal, around the traps that the original reason for Arthur Morris missing out on the captaincy was that he was a little too well up in the menswear fashion stakes. Returning from England in 1948 and 1953, he cut a dashing figure, sporting in his wardrobe a pair of blue and a pair of brown suede shoes which were all the rage in the salons in Piccadilly, Knightsbridge and Park Lane. They were not 'the go' around the dusty corridors of Cricket House at 254 George Street, Sydney. They almost produced a minor coronary. I can quite believe it, for those were the days when you spoke with a touch of reverence and a certain amount of humility to cricket officials in their navy blue suits, white shirts and strong leather shoes. Jack might have been as good as his mate in the outback of Australia in the 1800s but it took a while for the idea to permeate through to the various State Associations and the Australian Cricket Board.

Miller topped the batting averages in his first year as captain of New South Wales and, in his very first match as captain, I was to have some experience of the way he would produce unorthodox thinking to throw the opposition into minor confusion – and, I hasten to say, some of his own players as well, at that stage unused to his methods.

We played Queensland in Brisbane in November 1953, on a splendid batting pitch with the temperature in the 90s, and had the misfortune to lose the toss. Ray Lindwall bowled the opening two overs from the Pavilion or Members end and Jack Clark bowled two from the Stanley Street end. After Lindwall had bowled his third, Miller waved me across to bowl the sixth over of the game. 'Nugget,' I said, 'the ball's still new.' 'Don't worry about that,' he replied, 'it'll soon be old. Just think about the field you want. Now we'll have a slip and a gully and a silly-point. . . .' At that stage he must have caught sight of my face and he said, 'It's all right, it'll spin like a top for an hour. We've got a great chance to bowl them out.' I took 5 for 17 before lunch and we could have had the whole side out if a catch at the wicket and a stumping had not gone to ground. The batsman was Ken Archer, a fine player for Queensland who made a century and, with Peter Burge, saw the side through to 354. When I went in to bat on the second day we were a disastrous 85 for 4 and 'Nugget' said as I walked past him, 'You'd better get stuck into it out there, give 'em a bit of stick.' Arthur Morris and I put on 264 in 180 minutes and it was the start of my captaincy apprenticeship.

With Morris, Miller and Lindsay Hassett, my apprenticeship was always likely to be interesting.

One of the dicta drilled into me over the years has been that you should always obey your captain or vice-captain. Sometimes though you are not quite sure which one should take precedence. I was twelfth man in the First

Test match against South Africa in December 1952 in Brisbane and the game provided me with a marvellous example of that.

It was one of those matches where you don't really want to be twelfth man. It coincided with the worst heatwave experienced in Brisbane for ten years and towards the end of proceedings Keith Miller went down with a throat infection and was unable to take any further part in the game. It meant I was on the field all the way through South Africa's final chase for victory. Before that, however, we had the rest day of the Test and, therefore, the rest night on the Saturday evening – no Test cricket on Sunday in those days.

As the youngest player in the side, I had been given the privilege of rooming with vice-captain Arthur Morris, a man of vast experience and one who had a sound knowledge of what went on on cricket tours and on the evenings prior to rest days. We had a couple of drinks and a quiet dinner with some of the team but when we were on our way upstairs we had to go past skipper Lindsay Hassett's room. A party was in full swing. We looked in for a few moments, said hello, and then reached our own room without too much trouble, whereupon Morris proceeded to give me a very, very stern lecture on what was to happen if anyone came knocking on our door during the evening. 'Just remember this,' he said. 'Under no circumstances are you to open that door to *anyone* during the night, *particularly* if it's the captain who comes along.' 'Why is that?' I asked innocently. 'Well,' he said, 'the captain is a great chap, but at times he has an impish sense of humour and if he decides he'd like to wake up someone in the middle of the evening before the rest day it's not a good thing to be part of that. I'm telling you again, under no circumstances open the door to anyone.'

At 2 a.m. there was a knock on the door, a knock repeated quite loudly a dozen times. But after I had half woken up I suddenly thought, ah, remember what Arthur said: '. . . under no circumstances open the door to anyone.' I dozed off, full of self-congratulation that I had remembered the instructions. Then the telephone rang and instinctively I reached out and picked it up, whilst at the same moment someone began hammering on the door.

I said 'Hello' into the mouthpiece and a voice in my ear stated, 'Someone is knocking on your door.' 'Gosh, thanks very much,' I said. I got out of bed, opened the door and Hassett pushed past me and walked towards Morris's bed – Arthur was now well awake and glaring past Hassett at me. 'I thought I bloody well told you not to open the door,' he remonstrated. Hassett sat on the edge of the bed, held out his hand and said to Arthur, 'Do you have a match? I'd like to talk to you about my golf swing!' After our skipper had left, an hour later, Morris was kind enough only to say, 'Mark it down in your book of experience, son, and never ever open the door to Hassett at 2 a.m.'

Lindsay Hassett was a great character and never one to be parsimonious with property, even if it didn't belong to him. In February 1959, Hassett captained the Prime Minister's XI against MCC at Canberra, a match which the touring side won by four wickets before an excellent crowd of 6500, part of the proceeds going to charity. Also playing with Hassett was Arthur Morris, his former vice-captain, who made a brilliant 79. After he had been dismissed and it came to Hassett's turn to go out, it was suddenly revealed that the former Australian captain did not have his own bat with him; in fact he had only just managed to remember to bring the rest of his gear. Morris generously offered Hassett the use of his bat on the basis it had done the right thing for him; Hassett graciously accepted.

When Hassett had been dismissed and was on his way back to the pavilion he was surrounded by youngsters over the last 30 yards, one of whom asked him if there was any chance of getting a souvenir like a cricket bat. 'Why not?' said Lindsay. 'You take this one. I've finished with it – I've retired from the game and have no more use for it.' When Lindsay arrived back in the dressing-room Arthur held out his hand for the bat but was told, 'Oh, I gave it away to some young fellow who didn't have a bat.' Arthur was out of that dressing-room at about a thousand miles an hour but of course the kid had disappeared. Hundreds of other spectators were still there though. One of them, a gushing lady, put her hand on Arthur's arm and said, 'Oh, Mr Morris, Mr Hassett is such a generous man – I wish the rest of you cricketers were like him. You've no idea how that gesture made me feel.' 'Madam,' said Arthur through clenched teeth, 'I can tell you something – you've no idea either how that makes *me* feel.'

I was very lucky I played with New South Wales when the state was so strong. Morris, Lindwall and Miller were marvellous players from whom to glean experience and the chance to learn captaincy from them was one of the best things which ever happened to me. They knew all there was to be known about the playing side of the game, and the intricacies of blasting or winkling out the batsmen, keeping up team spirit and, above all, winning. Losing captains litter the footpaths of cricketing cities all over the world and I was taught by them very early on that there is no percentage in losing but a big one in being the victor.

The hallmark of Miller's captaincy was that he never did anything ordinary, or rather he never allowed anyone to believe it was ordinary. He had already impressed me with his unorthodox methods that day in Brisbane and, from that time on, I tried to adapt them to my own personality and technique on the field. Sometimes he would try something *very* unortho-dox and he was always prepared to buy wickets. The only thing he demanded was that his bowlers did exactly as he asked and not make him look foolish. Quite right too. When the captain says jump, no matter how it might be phrased . . . then everyone should jump.

One of the most extraordinary things I ever saw Miller do as captain was bowl out a Sheffield Shield team for 27 on a good pitch. We had started the 1955–56 season with a first-innings win over Queensland after Ray Lindwall, who was by then their captain, had put us in to bat. Three weeks later, in November, we met South Australia at the Sydney Cricket Ground and got off to a good start when Warren Saunders and I scored half-centuries. Then came a sensational collapse and, when we had slumped to 215 for 8 with 40 minutes to go, Miller made one of his surprise declarations. Out behind the Members Stand, however, the storm clouds were massing and not a ball could be bowled that evening. Miller had steam coming out of his ears and stalked off the field muttering something along the lines of, 'Just wait until I get these jokers tomorrow.'

It rained most of the night and, despite the pitch being fully covered, there was a 15-minute delay before we could get on to the field. Miller then took 7 for 12 from 7.3 overs and, with Pat Crawford taking 3 for 14 at the other end, South Australia were in again before lunch. They made 252 in their second innings and Miller bowled just six overs of medium pace and took 0 for 19. He had made his point and it was one that the South Australians never forgot.

When they batted a second time Les Favell and David Harris opened the innings and were still together shortly before lunch when two South Australian supporters from Adelaide arrived at the Members entrance to pick up their tickets. 'What's the score?' they asked the gatekeeper, but he didn't answer. When they walked inside and saw the scoreboard on the Hill showing 12 for 0, Favell 5 and Harris 7, there was a long silence and then one turned to the other and said, 'Well, I suppose it's pretty slow . . . but the first-innings points are what matter. They'll push it along a bit more after lunch!'

Favell was a wonderful attacking batsman in Sheffield Shield cricket and a dangerous man in Tests. He never lacked batting confidence, nor did he consider outside influences could have any effect on his run-getting.

In February 1961, desperate for Sheffield Shield points, we played South Australia in Adelaide with the local side winning by three wickets. It was the match where we finally 'nailed' Les Favell – one of the least superstitious cricketers I've ever met – on the unlucky number of 87. We were bowled out for 158 in our first innings and 'Favelli' was cock-a-hoop when his side got away to an excellent start. When he was 87 Ian Craig and I walked past him and I said, 'Have you seen the scoreboard, Les?' He looked up, saw the unlucky 87 on the board and said, 'We'll soon fix that' – and the very next ball hooked Barry Bates straight down Warren Saunders's throat at deep fine-leg. Out for 87 and off he stalked, far from pleased.

South Australia had a handy lead of 239 runs over us and then we made 415 in our second innings to set them a target of 177 to win. Les and Murray

Sargent walked out to open the innings, Les to take strike against Gordon Rorke. I said to him from gully as he was taking block, 'You do realise you're still on 87 Favelli?' 'Not for long,' he snapped. He immediately holed out to Barry Bates and as he began to storm off the ground I was able to call to him through muffled laughter, 'And what's more you're still on 87!' I suppose these days what happened would be called 'sledging' for trying to disturb the batsman's concentration, and I would be reported to the Board and the Players Committee.

Favell was also a fine captain of South Australia and he set a great example of attacking leadership down there for many years.

In that period when Miller was being looked at as the possible Australian leader, one of the things which stood between him and higher captaincy honours was the fact he was an outstanding bowler. I first saw him when the Services team returned to Australia in 1945 and he bowled against Sid Barnes at the Sydney Cricket Ground. Barnes made 154, having been dropped by Hassett in the gully off Miller before he scored. From that season, Miller was always bracketed with Lindwall as Australia's fast-bowling pair and they were the equal of any fast-bowling combination the game has seen.

As a captain Miller was no great theorist. Some of the captains I have seen over the years have had more theories than an Australian bullock driver had vocabulary, but Miller believed the game was played best by those players who were natural cricketers rather than forced cricketers. There was no better example of this than Miller himself, nor was there ever a better example of a cricketer who could have played in any era and been an eye-catching favourite with everyone who followed the game. He taught me many things either by word or by example.

Two things stood out though in all the time I was serving a self-styled apprenticeship. The first was never allow the game to fall into a routine – as soon as it looks like doing that, pull something out of the hat which will surprise the opposition, even if it surprises your own players as well. The second was . . . *win*.

Miller was one of the greatest competitors ever to step on to a cricket field and he never allowed the opposition to forget it, whether he was batting, bowling or captaining the side. He saw plenty of losers in his time, even backed a few of them among the winners he had on the racecourse, but he was always desperately keen to avoid looking at the dressing-room wall and thinking of what might have been.

He was, for all his flamboyance, fairly shy when it came to things like making speeches or what one might loosely term good deeds. In fact, he would be horrified if anyone thought that under the brash man's exterior there lurked a generous heart. But the idea of having him stand up at Fishmongers Hall in London to make the speech, as captain of Australia, in reply to Lord Justice Birkett was too much for our administrators. What a waste!

* * *

If Keith Miller was the best captain *never* to lead Australia, then Ian Chappell was certainly the best I have ever seen occupy that position. He came to the job in 1971 for the final Test against Ray Illingworth's touring team after Bill Lawry had been given the boot in ugly fashion by the Australian selectors.

Lawry took over from Bob Simpson for the tour of England in 1968. That series was drawn, with Australia winning the opening Test at Old Trafford but then going down in a thriller in the final Test at the Oval. After winning the home series against West Indies 3–1, he took the Australian team to India and then South Africa in what was an astonishing and, from the point of view of results, disastrous second-half tour. Although Australia beat India decisively – no mean feat when playing on Indian pitches – the playing of nine Tests in two different countries and in contrasting conditions was too much for the Australians. I don't wonder. Playing six Tests on one tour is enough, but the Australian Cricket Board somehow managed to talk themselves into believing the players would handle nine without difficulty.

On that tour Lawry had plenty of problems and put himself high on the list of unpopular captains (with the Board) when he wrote them a letter, scathing in its content concerning the Indian section, at the conclusion of the tour. His note criticised the concept of the tour and other administrative matters and barely concealed his anger at the various situations in which the players found themselves placed. Riotous behaviour was high on his list, though at least he managed to retain his considerable sense of humour whilst it was all happening.

It is difficult for a captain to know what to do about rioting crowds. Len Hutton, when he was in the West Indies in 1953–54, refused to leave the field during the Third Test because he was convinced it was a ploy on the part of the spectators to give West Indies breathing space. Quite right too. Ray Illingworth had different ideas in 1971 and I am not too sure what my reaction would have been because I have been fortunate enough not to have been in the centre of a riot in any cricket ground anywhere in the world – nor would I wish to be.

Lawry in 1969 was vilified by the Indian press for slapping a photographer with a bat – what the photographer's business was in the centre of the ground alongside the two batsmen I've absolutely no idea, but to hear Bill and Keith Stackpole, who was with him, tell the story is something of a party piece. So too is the story which Ian Chappell relates of the same match. Australia were in the field at the time and the spectators were trying to have the match delayed; a delay which would have been to India's benefit. Smoke was coming from the stands and Chappell says, although he understood very, very little of the Indian language, he knew enough of the English language to realise 'Kill Lawry – Kill Lawry' was not good news. There was no shortage of bottles coming over the fence and no shortage of people trying to push over the fence which, although designated riot-proof, looked at that stage as though it was about to belie the description. Chappell wasn't vice-captain of the Australian side, he wasn't even third selector, but he did have some common sense. He went up to Lawry and said, 'Phanto, at stumps I reckon we should all go off as a team rather than have everyone race off individually.' He says he looked at Lawry to see whether his rather shaky voice had made any impression and, not being sure that he had got through, queried, 'What do you reckon, Phant?'

He was right. Bill hadn't heard him. He stared over Chappelli's head and, raising his voice a few decibels to defeat the noise, said 'We've just got to get a wicket. . . .' He couldn't get the wicket and at the close of play on that fourth evening, amid the din and smoke and hurtling bottles, India were 125 for 9. They were all out for 137 the next day, giving Australia a win by eight wickets after they made 67 for 2.

Lawry had summed up that particular situation perfectly, but when Australia lost the Third Test at Sydney in 1971 under his leadership the signs were visible that the selectors, who now had the nomination of the captain in their hands, were unlikely to look kindly on any further setbacks. Lawry batted bravely in the second innings of the match, carrying his bat for 60 not out, with only his Victorian team-mate, Keith Stackpole, making double figures in a dismal team display of batting on a pitch providing plenty of uneven bounce. John Snow took 7 for 40 against a batting side which included Ian Chappell, Ian Redpath, Doug Walters, Greg Chappell and Rodney Marsh. Not a bad line-up and yet only Lawry and, to a lesser extent, Stackpole, were able to stand firm.

What Lawry's thoughts were as the rest of the team crumbled about him can only be imagined. They would, however, have been nothing compared with his thoughts when he stepped off the plane in Melbourne after the Adelaide Test had been drawn. England played so well in that match they could have enforced the follow-on, but Illingworth declined to do so, on the basis that his bowlers were weary. Australia in their second innings made 328 for 3, with Stackpole and Ian Chappell hitting centuries. England, going into the final Test, led 1–0 with Australia holding the Ashes.

The Australian selectors then dropped Lawry. That is the nicest way to put it. Actually, they gave him the selectorial axe right at the base of the skull, in one of the most unfeeling acts I have ever seen from any group of selectors.

They brought into the team Ken Eastwood, Lawry's Victorian team-mate who had been scoring prolifically in Sheffield Shield cricket but who had no previous Test experience. To do that, with Snow in the opposition line-up, was like attacking the forces of Hannibal with a hundred conscripted unarmed men. Poor Eastwood, a likeable and talented player at the lower level, found the assignment daunting. He made only five and nought, did not play again for Australia and few people, other than the selection committee, were surprised.

To replace Lawry as captain they chose Ian Michael Chappell, the eldest of three brothers, all of whom were to represent their country. Chappell and Lawry at the time were locked in a battle for the Sheffield Shield which in the previous season had been won by Victoria. After England won the final Test in Sydney, South Australia and Victoria clashed in a vital Sheffield Shield game which Lawry's team won, but it was not enough to win the Shield. South Australia finished ten points ahead to complete a great summer for Chappell.

He was, however, never to forget the manner in which he came to the captaincy. A bald announcement of the twelve names for Sydney was made to the media the day after the Adelaide Test, not the slightest attention being paid by the selectors to the possibility of speaking to Lawry beforehand. Words to the following effect might, perhaps, have been a reasonable gesture: 'Thanks . . . but we want to try something new for the final Test which must be won. It's our judgement we need Chappell to captain the side – we're doing you the courtesy of letting you know so the first you hear won't be from the media before you step on the plane.' That is the background to Chappell's appointment and, from that moment on, if he seemed rather preoccupied with keeping one eye on the match in progress and one eye on his own back then one need not be unduly surprised. 'They won't get me the same way as Phanto,' he was heard to say immediately after his appointment – and he was not referring to the famed comic-strip character who, with Lothar, was engaged at the time in yet another battle with the dark forces of a different world.

Chappell's first brush with England as captain brought plenty of excitement, much controversy and a loss. It did little good to tell him it had been a fine match and that Australia had almost pulled it off. They were beaten and the Ashes were gone and he approached it in the same way in which he was to continue. 'There's no prize for running second, pal,' he said. 'In years to come, when people look at the scorecard of that match, they will only see Australia lost by 62 runs.' Chappell had started the match by winning the toss, sending England in and bowling them out for 184. He had in his side two legspinners, Jenner and O'Keeffe, and two bowlers short of Test cricket experience to take the new ball, Tony Dell, making his début, and Dennis Lillee, in only his second Test.

Timing is one of the most crucial aspects of cricket captaincy. So is the luck I mentioned earlier. No better example of the two could be found than the transition from Lawry to Chappell in the Australian captaincy. At the end of the series in Australia in 1971 Dennis Lillee was just beginning to fire. He had already been to New Zealand with an Australian 'B' team but had given no indication that one day he would be considered as the greatest fast bowler ever to play the game. An arguable rating in some circles, but nevertheless a view held by many people, myself included.

Lillee caught the eyes of the selectors with his early season promise in 1970 but Lawry had the benefit of his services for only one match. That was in Adelaide where he took five wickets in the first innings against England but none in the second. From then on he was almost the exclusive property of the Chappell brothers, Ian and Greg. Lawry would have loved to have had him in an Australian side but, instead, had to make do with bowlers big in heart but not as fast and less likely to win Test matches.

When Chappell took his team to England in 1972 it was after the Australia v Rest of the World matches in Australia staged by the Australian Cricket Board when the South African tour had been abandoned. Lillee made his mark in that series by taking 8 for 29 in the second representative match in Perth, on a pitch true enough for the Australians to make 349. He was looking good now, his action was holding together, his run-up less sprawly and his pace correspondingly improved.

When Chappell and his team arrived in England, Lillee was immediately an eye-catching force in the nets. It wasn't necessarily the pace he was showing but also his flowing dark hair and Zapata moustache which brought back memories of either a Mexican brigand or Frederick Robert Spofforth, whichever you had in mind at the time.

Chappell was also catching the attention of many cricket followers with his slightly unorthodox handling of events. If there is one thing Chappell cannot abide it is people who are two-faced in their attitudes. He made it clear to all he was going to run things without any humbug and he didn't expect any from inside or outside the team. His initial press conference was hard-hitting and it was brief: he preferred being in the nets or on the golf course to speculating about a game which should be decided on the field.

His first effort of captaincy had not worked out in 1971, although Illingworth had beaten him only by a small margin. Now they were to be opposed again, but this time he had Lillee and a swing bowler named Massie plus some steady fast-medium bowlers in David Colley, Graeme Watson and Jeff Hammond. As it happened, Massie was injured prior to the First Test at Old Trafford and the match was lost – not because of Massie's absence but because of batting frailties. The selectors might have given him a fine bowling attack, with Mallett and Gleeson providing the spin back-up to Lillee, but some of the batsmen were well short of hard Test match standard. Forced to bat at number three, all too often he found himself having to come in against the new ball, the opening partnerships realising only 68, 9, 1, 20, 16, 15, 10, 5, 24 and 16.

In the course of the Old Trafford Test, I looked out of the back of the BBC commentary box and Massie and Ross Edwards were practising in the nets at the extreme left-hand side of the Colts ground. Chappell was laying his plans for Lord's. Because of Massie's injury, he had been forced to play John Inverarity in the Old Trafford Test although the pitch suited pace rather than left-arm spin. Massie was bowling around the wicket in the nets to Edwards for part of the time and the ball was swinging prodigiously, both ways.

In another ten days Massie was to join Lillee at Lord's to rout the English batsmen by bowling over and around the wicket and, with Chappell leading the way with tough, aggressive captaincy, Australia were on their way back to being a force in world cricket. When that match at Lord's was won it broke a depressing sequence for Australia. It was the longest period in the history of Test cricket that Australia had been without a victory: Chappell was to see them through the next three years undefeated in a series.

I thought his finest effort in the early part of his captaincy career was not so much the bowlers' match at Lord's but the game at the end of that series at the Oval where Australia had to win to square the rubber. The Ashes had been retained by England at Headingley where there was served up to the two teams a strip of turf which was a disgrace to the name of Test cricket. Derek Underwood had been brought back into the team and England thoroughly outplayed Australia, Chappell having won the toss and having had the advantage of batting first. Fuserium was blamed for the state of the pitch but, fortunately for Yorkshire, a remedy was immediately found for the disease and their County Championship matches were able to be played on decent surfaces. The rest of the square for this Test was brilliant green, the pitch a dull grey, shorn of its grass.

The Oval Test was, on the other hand, played over six days and was a credit to the groundsman. Both teams played splendid cricket and Australia were left to make 242 runs, with part of the penultimate day and all the last day in which to make them. It was a fine ending to the tour for Chappell and even though Ray Illingworth has always been of the opinion that his injury cost England the match, Chappell does not even consider the possibility.

'I was batting with "Stacky" the second-last afternoon and we were going along very well. After tea it was "Illy" and Underwood sharing the attack and we handled it with no more trouble than you would expect against two spin bowlers on the fifth afternoon of a Test. When Ray sprained his ankle he had bowled almost nine overs without taking a wicket and although the ball was turning the pitch was still very good.

'Our biggest worry was not that "Illy" might come back but that

John Snow might make a miraculous overnight recovery from the injury to his left arm where Dennis Lillee had hit him, or that Derek Underwood would suddenly discover the ability to bowl on a hard dusting pitch, the same way as he had bowled on the one at Headingley. When we lost three quick wickets on the final morning we had problems, but one of the most enjoyable things I had seen in my short time as captain was the way Marsh and Sheahan batted that afternoon.'

The other thing about the match was the way Dennis Lillee bowled. Anyone who saw him bowl in that game could not fail to have been convinced he would eventually become a great bowler. Lillee took five wickets in each innings, in a bowling display as good as anything I had seen since Miller took ten wickets at Lord's or when Davidson bowled so superbly in the Tied Test.

I thought Chappell's captaincy top-class in this match. Whereas in the Old Trafford Test he had not always appeared completely sure of himself, he had by now grown in stature and every move seemed to fit in perfectly with the situation of the game. He continued to attack throughout, even when Alan Knott was smashing the Australian bowlers all around the ground, and there was never a moment when the match really seemed to be slipping away from him. He led from up front with the bat, making a century, and his field-placings always gave the bowlers the chance to attack. I had never doubted that he would be a great captain and the confirmation came in the final Test match.

I thought the selectors missed the bus with Chappell as an allrounder in the early part of his career but I was hoping then he would concentrate more on his bowling than eventually proved to be the case. I thought he should have gone to England with Bob Simpson's side in 1964, particularly after he hit a dashing double-century in Queensland and made 600 runs at an average of 64. He missed the tour, also the one in 1965 to the West Indies, although that may not have been too disastrous. Hall and Griffith were at their most dangerous on that tour and it was no place for a young player to make a name for himself. That was in some ways a slice of luck, as was the manner in which he was later to become national captain.

I asked him in December 1982 what he had felt about his elevation to the captaincy, having been just a player, though a valuable one, in the team the previous day.

'The whole thing was very strange. I hadn't been given the slightest inkling of what was about to happen. I heard the news sitting at the counter-lunch section of the Overway pub near where I was working. I had dashed in there for a quick bite to eat and a beer and suddenly the news broadcaster announced it in the bulletin. I was stunned for a moment, then I thought, "Jeez . . . Phanto," and the phone rang and it was "Sheffield" [Alan Shiell, cricket writer for the Adelaide *News*] saying, "You've been made captain of Australia." I made some reply and he repeated the news. I can't recall what the conversation was then but I walked back to work in a daze.

'The next thing was to have a look at the team I had been given. The selectors had done the right thing by me there because I had Lillee who was fast, Tony Dell who was big and could be lively and had the advantage of coming from left-arm over the wicket. Then they had given me two legspinners in Terry Jenner and Kerry O'Keeffe so I couldn't really have asked for much more than that.

'When we got to Sydney there was no great change in my attitude at the team meeting because I still had to convince the players I could handle all the pressure to which they would be subjected over the next six days. Whether or not I managed it at that first meeting I don't know but I doubt it. What I did say to them was they could come to me with any problems or ideas and I would think about them. Whether or not I put them into practice was another matter, because in the end I was the one who would have to stand or fall by the decision.

'On the day before the game we were able to practise although there had been heavy rain in Sydney throughout the early part of the week. When Rod Marsh, "Stacky" and "Redders" asked me if I wanted to have a look at the pitch I very quickly declined. It was the start of a principle I never abandoned – don't pay the slightest attention to the pitch on the day before the match. It's what's out there when the game is about to commence which matters. On the morning of the match the papers were full of the fact that the pitch looked to have a greenish tinge about it and perhaps it would be a surface favouring the pace bowlers.

'That wasn't why I sent England in to bat however. I reckoned there was so much moisture in the outfield the side batting first would lose something like 50 runs in the day. If my reasoning were correct then things should be much better for us when we batted on the second day. Sometimes things like that don't go to plan but, on this occasion, it all worked. We bowled England out for fewer than 200 which should have been a winning performance. It was very disappointing to make only 264 in our own first innings and then England, with some very good cricket, got away from us. If we had batted well enough in the second innings we still would have won but, even with the nasty injury to John Snow, we couldn't make the 223 needed. It was a lesson for me and one which stood me in good stead when we were at the Oval 18 months later. We were by then a tougher combination and I was a tougher and more experienced skipper.'

He certainly was. Not only tougher but less amenable to the rigid discipline the Australian Cricket Board used to seek to impose on players and captains. Cricket teams are always, in the eyes of Board members, 'The Board's Team'. That was the case in 1961 when I was captain in England and I have never known it not to be the case since that tour. Chappell now had a team with him able to take on the very best in the world and, in the case of England, finish all-square with them.

I watched him with great interest in the following summer of 1972–73 in Australia as the team built up strength against Pakistan, with the batting proving, for the most part, too strong for the Pakistan bowlers. Chappell himself was in excellent form with the bat and his captaincy was strong and purposeful. My brother played in the first two Tests of the series making 24, 13 and 142, the latter innings played after he had been informed he was not chosen for the final Test in Sydney. He made the tour to the West Indies, however, and came back full of admiration for Chappell's leadership qualities.

One of Chappell's most remarkable captaincy efforts was in the final Test at Sydney in 1972–73 against Pakistan where Australia crashed in their second innings, making only 184 – and that almost entirely due to an improbable ninth-wicket stand of 83 between Bob Massie and John Watkins, the latter playing in his first and, as it turned out, only Test match. They came together when Australia had lost 8 for 101, Chappell and Redpath alone reaching double figures.

That evening Mushtaq and some of the other Pakistan players came for dinner at our Coogee flat and, while chatting about cricket, I mentioned that the next day should see Pakistan beating Australia in Australia for the first time. Whilst I had no doubt 159 should have been, if not a 'cakewalk' then at least a readily attainable target, there was no such confidence in the Pakistan camp. They were apprehensive about what Lillee, Massie and, to a lesser extent, Walker, the new bowler in the side, might be able to do on a pitch where the ball was moving off the seam a little more than normal.

Chappell the next morning gave them no respite. Ross Edwards had sent Sadiq back to the pavilion with a magnificent catch the previous evening and now Chappell applied relentless pressure. Lillee was showing the first signs of the back trouble which was temporarily to suspend his career, but for Chappell he came out on the last morning to bowl off a shortened run and at reduced pace. Massie swung the ball both ways and Walker, judiciously used by Chappell, was magnificent. The field-placings to back up the three bowlers were not only attacking but also thoughtful and aggressive, whilst Chappell never lost sight of the fact he was defending a small target.

It was one of the best exhibitions of captaincy I had seen in many years, the true test of a man who can defend no total at all with bowlers and fieldsmen who were right behind him. It was a superb preface to the tour of the West Indies where the cricket followers of the Caribbean were waiting in anticipation for the team led by Chappell. Beating Pakistan in Australia was not necessarily the ultimate in cricket ratings but to draw with England, then beat Pakistan and West Indies, would set up the 1974–75 battle against England as a magnificent contest.

I didn't cover the West Indies tour but my brother John was one of the players chosen and he came back with his confidence in Chappell's captaincy at an all-time high. I asked him in 1982 who he thought was the outstanding captain he had seen.

'The best was undoubtedly "Bertie". He made sure everyone fitted in well in the team and he looked after us superbly. When I was obviously on the boards against Pakistan in Melbourne in 1973, he was good enough in the second innings, because he knew I was to be dropped for the Sydney Test, to promote me to number three in the batting order which is where I was batting so successfully with New South Wales.

'The thing which lives most in my memory was in the West Indies – we went there with a good squad, Lillee broke down, Massie broke down, we had Johnny Watkins in the side, who was performing as well as the selectors would have hoped, and Sheahan and Mallett had been unavailable for the trip anyway. It's tough, that West Indies tour. We were down basically to twelve fit men for the Test in Trinidad and we got up and won, after West Indies needed 60 for victory with six wickets in hand. I'll never forget Ian at lunch that day – he didn't say a word, he just lay down on the dressing-room bench and you only had to look at him to feel what was going through his mind – what a fight we had on our hands – and you could sense the dressing-room atmosphere charging all the time by Chappell not saying a word. When the umpires came in and said, "Right you are, out you go again," he got up, slowly looked around at every player, put his cap on and said, "It'd be a good one to win." No unreal and insincere rhetoric.

'That team went out there in a fantastic mood, determined and charged up, and we took a wicket first ball. He would never hear of defeat. I remember Kerry O'Keeffe in Melbourne. The Pakistanis had to get 300-odd to win the Second Test against us and Sadiq and Zaheer were going along well. Kerry expressed to Chappelli some doubts as to whether or not we might win and he said, "Listen here 'Skull', have you ever heard of a team getting 300 in the fourth innings – it doesn't happen, and it won't be happening here." We got back on top and won quite easily. Undoubtedly a great team captain – I played under others for short times but he was far and away the best.'

On that West Indies tour a ten-wicket win in the next Test match in Georgetown was just as surprising, with Lillee having returned to Australia because of his back problems and the captain forced to use Doug Walters and Jeff Hammond as his strike bowlers. Walters and Hammond? Not much strike about that, but they did the job, aided by some shrewd, tactical planning of field-placings and some inspired catching. A 2–0 win in the series was a tremendous boost for Australia and, when a six-Test series against New Zealand was won 3–1 in 1973–74, there was great anticipation that Australia, with dynamic leadership, were in with a real chance of regaining the Ashes in 1974–75. The only problem was that Lillee, who had been undergoing a strenuous fitness programme in the off-season, had about a 50–50 chance of playing.

There did not seem to be another pace bowler around capable of allowing Walker to play in his correct spot of third pace bowler, although there were some interesting stories circulating about one young fast bowler, Jeff Thomson, whose only Test match experience so far had been to play against Pakistan in Melbourne and take 0 for 112. My brother telephoned me at home one day in November 1974 to tell me he had the previous Saturday played against Thomson in a match at Bankstown Oval. He had no doubt about him being the fastest bowler in Australia: one 'bumper' John had faced had hit the ground first bounce just in front of the sightscreen. Still, no one was absolutely certain about his ability at Test level, even though it was conceded he had plenty of pace and a lot of fire.

I was in England commentating on the Pakistan and India series against England when the Australians were making their preparations for the English team to arrive. England's matches against bowlers of fast-medium pace might have seemed at the time to be adequate but, with hindsight, they were like organising for a major battle with a preparation involving a Boy Scout jamboree.

With little idea of which bowlers he would have at his disposal in the Test series, Chappell took more than usual interest in the early Sheffield Shield match against Western Australia at the Adelaide Oval where Dennis Lillee was making his comeback. Lillee did enough there to convince Chappell he had a really good chance to be fit for Brisbane, and the Australian captain laid his plans accordingly. He knew, barring accidents, he would have Max Walker in the team and Ashley Mallett, with Doug Walters there as a change bowler. Lillee, if fit, would head the attack and there had been some indications in the previous season that Thomson might be worth a gamble.

Lillee's lead-up performances to the First Test were nothing out of the ordinary but by now he was full of confidence. This was where the luck ran for Chappell: to have both Lillee and Thomson firing at the one time was a real stroke of fortune, the equivalent of a captain like Bradman having Miller and Lindwall, or Armstrong having McDonald and Gregory.

Chappell was confident about Lillee. After the 1974–75 season he said: 'I batted against Dennis in both innings at the Adelaide Oval in that match and I felt, although he was taking it easy, there was a progressive build-up in speed and confidence with him. He knew what he was doing the whole time and he got me out with a bouncer in the second innings. I think it was simply to let me know he was still around and firing, if not on all cylinders then on most. The bouncer was a really good one, so fast and awkward I could only miscue it to mid-on. Yes . . . there was no doubt he was back, and the best thing about it was the English team and their press corps didn't seem overimpressed with what they had seen. Mike Denness's players were practising at the nets at the back of the Adelaide Oval but they made a point of having people watching the entire time to see what Dennis was doing and how he was going. I don't think they believed they had any real worries.'

When the team was announced for the opening Test match, Chappell realised he had a potentially top-class side at his disposal and, if the Englishmen showed any distaste at all for pace bowling, Australia had a good chance of winning. England, with Mike Denness leading them, had their own pace battery and two fine spin bowlers in Fred Titmus and Derek Underwood. Before long they were to be reinforced by the burly figure of Colin Cowdrey.

Chappell led the side splendidly in the opening Test, keeping up the pressure on England right through the game and then, in Perth, his pace bowlers really got at the English batsmen. Amiss and Edrich, with thumb and hand injuries respectively, were unavailable for the Second Test in Perth and the Australian batting, bowling and fielding were quite exceptional.

This had not come about by accident. Having spoken to some of the team members, it was clear Chappell had produced a spirit of extraordinary quality. The basis of it was that he was going to be in charge of the team and would make all the decisions and take the blame if they went wrong, although anyone in the side was at liberty to make suggestions either to him or his vice-captain, preferably to him. At the same time, there were never, under any circumstances, to be any cliques in the team, particularly state cliques, where there is always a tendency for players, without knowing they are doing it, to form groups simply because they know their team-mates better than the players from other states.

This team-work had begun in 1972 when Chappell had had his first taste of captaining a side overseas. It was now a natural part of his leadership, as was his abrasiveness. He was never averse to speaking his mind, particularly if it were to do with some bungle made by an administrator, or if his players were being harshly treated by the Australian Cricket Board. He was a prime target for snipers and he gave them plenty of opportunities to criticise him: sometimes he had himself to blame, sometimes he was blameless but blamed anyway.

One of the stories which had hung around the cricket dressing-rooms for many years concerned Chappelli's brush with Glenn Turner in New Zealand in 1974.

'It was in Christchurch, when Brian Hastings was batting at the pavilion end and Ashley Mallett was the bowler. He bowled a ball of full length to Hastings who swung it away towards the mid-wicket boundary. There was an odd rule in force at the time that to be four the ball had to roll into the gutter, and for a six it had to pitch either into the gutter on the full or go right over the fence. This time the ball hit the wire and bounced back on to the field.

'Umpire Bob Monteith signalled six and, as I could not see how it was six, I trotted up the pitch to question the ruling. "Bob," I said, "that looked to me as though it hit the wire . . ." – or rather that was what I wanted to say. I only had time to get out the, "Bob, that looked . . ." and Turner interrupted. I said I wasn't talking to him and then, when I tried to talk to Monteith twice more, he interjected again. I gave Turner a very brisk series of four-letter conversation pieces which I should definitely not have done and received the explanation from Bob Monteith that he had made a mistake.

'Doug Walters said to me later Turner was only trying to tell me the umpire had made an error and it was four runs and I was too hasty. "If he had minded his own bloody business," I said, "Bob Monteith and the Australian captain could have sorted it out very quickly and that was the way it should have been." There was a call from the New Zealanders for an apology from the Australian captain, a courteous request to which I gave an equally courteous reply in even less time than I had spent on Turner on the field that day.

'It is quite correct the language I used to Turner was a bit rough – as he was so fond later of telling anyone who would listen. Glenn, in fact, is very fond of offering his views on any matter under the sun which could be considered helpful in putting the world to rights, ranging from the economy of Tierra del Fuego to the way cricket and television should be run in New Zealand.

'There was, though, a delightfully amusing aftermath to the happenings of that afternoon in Christchurch. During the 1976 tour of South Africa by the International Wanderers (Turner and I were both team members), my former wife Kay and eight-year-old daughter were guests at a cocktail party to which Glenn was invited. He was holding court to a mixed group of half a dozen people and when Kay and Amanda joined the group continued with his story which included – would you believe – the same four-letter word I had used to him in Christchurch.

'It was a funny story and when he had finished, to laughter and nods of approval, Kay said to him, "I'm astonished to hear you use the same language you complained about Ian using in Christchurch." There was a muttered reply and she was able to add, "and ... with Ian's eight-year-old daughter listening as well!" Perhaps the most astonishing thing about the whole episode was that Kay was able to keep a straight face.

'New Zealand caught us on that tour just as we were on the way back, at a time when we were toughening up for the MCC tour of Australia. They too were toughening up and that win in Christchurch was the start of a very competitive era for New Zealand when Geoff Howarth took over the captaincy from Bev Congdon. Turner went into self-imposed exile because of differences of opinion with the New Zealand Board over matters of principle which included whether or not he should be paid as a professional or an amateur, and whether the amount should be enough for his family to live on. As many of my complaints with the Australian Cricket Board centred around whether Australians should be paid as club players or as professionals that is one point, possibly the only one, on which I am in complete agreement with Glenn. That New Zealand tour, though, and the three matches against them in Australia, gave us the chance to get our game together for the following season in Australia, 1974–75, which was the really important one as far as we were concerned.

'That was a great moment, to beat England in Australia, and to do it with an attack based on fast bowling, in the same way as they had beaten us four years earlier. When Rodney Marsh came hurtling across to me in Sydney and shouted, "We've got the bastards back ..." I realised I'd forgotten about the Ashes in the tension of trying to win the match. One thing at a time I guess, but when we were walking off the SCG I was able to come to terms with the fact we had indeed got them back. And it was as good a feeling as the actual winning of the match.'

* * *

Chappell captained Test teams against Ray Illingworth, Mike Denness and Tony Greig but did not come up against Mike Brearley in the Anglo–Australian matches. Brearley is one of the greatest captains I have seen, not from the example he set as a great run-getter, a fine bowler or a brilliant fielder, but from the point of view of being a clear thinker, courageous and ... having that share of luck so essential for any successful captain.

Brearley came into the English captaincy when Tony Greig was sacked by the English cricket authorities in the aftermath of World Series Cricket. In 1977 he regained the Ashes easily against a team lacking Dennis Lillee and

Ian Chappell and then toured Australia, beating a second-string Australian team 5–1. After that he was beaten 3–0 in a series of three matches in Australia, where England had the foresight not to put up the Ashes, and, as a highlight to his career, held the Ashes against Kim Hughes's team in England in 1981.

Brearley obeyed the first rule of captaincy in that he was a clear thinker on the game. He was not always in accord with traditionalists; indeed, while he was in charge of the Test team there were those of his detractors who considered him to be a little too 'socialistic' in his outlook on life to be in charge of an England XI – whatever that might mean. At least he was English 'through and through', which was more than Tony Greig – as we were told in a rollicking English explanation of why Tony didn't think twice about joining World Series Cricket.

I first came into contact with Mike Brearley in May 1961 when the Australian team played against Cambridge at Fenner's. I was having problems with my shoulder at the time and had no intention of bowling against the University side, but late on the third day, when the other bowlers were having trouble getting rid of Brearley and Minney, I came on and tossed up some leg-breaks to try and buy a wicket. Jarman stumped Minney off me and we won the match but we certainly filed Brearley away in the little black book as a possible player of the future. His 73 and 89 and a neat exhibition of wicket-keeping were surely the work of a potential England Test player.

The difficulty in England though was to be able to strike a balance with the good players you saw on a tour and the type of pitches on which they played. Brearley had batted well against us on a superb Fenner's pitch where the bowlers had little chance. Would he play as well on a green-top pitch at Lord's or one of uneven bounce at Headingley? We were not really destined to find out, for although Brearley made it into touring teams they were more of the 'B' variety than the full Test side, and at that stage he did not show any signs of forcing a place in an England team at home.

What he did do, though, was establish himself in his 1963 year at Cambridge as an outstanding captain, acting as an inspiration to a team which included Richard Hutton, who later played for England and toured Australia with the Rest of the World team in 1971–72. When Brearley took over the Middlesex captaincy in 1971 he brought the same urgency to the job. 'Purposeful cricket' was what he promised and Middlesex jumped from sixteenth to sixth in the Championship table after being on top at one stage in the middle of the summer.

In 1976–77, he was vice-captain to Tony Greig on England's successful tour of India and Sri Lanka and then took over the captaincy at Lord's in June 1977. He came into the match with Championship scores of 51, 50 and 123 not out so his form at that time was worthy of a place in the team. When he became captain of England it was, looking from the outside, almost as though an amateur had returned to the fold of English cricket, not that his views were those of an amateur. He was established as a certainty in the minds of his players as captain for the series, almost irrespective of performance with the bat.

When he was recalled in desperation at Headingley in 1981 it was with Australia one up after the opening Test at Trent Bridge, the Second Test at Lord's having been drawn. Botham at this stage was learning just how difficult captaincy can be. He had been thrown in against West Indies for ten consecutive Test matches – a daunting assignment for anyone to handle, or try to handle – and had returned from the tour of the West Indies with the critics hammering him and calling for yet another change in the English captaincy. When he lost the First Test against Australia at Trent Bridge and then bagged a 'pair' at Lord's in the Second, Botham got in first and stepped down from the captaincy, but it would have been wrenched from him in any case. It was too much for the selectors and, as a loser, he took the blame. So should all captains, based on the premise that they take the credit as well when things go right.

It was ironic, when Mike Brearley was asked to take over for the Headingley match, that throughout the early part of the game his captaincy was no more outstanding than Botham's, and it was Botham who eventually saved him with an astonishing batting performance which allowed Brearley to set the Australians a target, albeit a small one. Australia had won the toss and batted on what looked to be on the first day a good pitch. It played accordingly and Kim Hughes's side, with 401, seemed at the very worst to be safe from defeat. When they bowled out England by the third afternoon and, with plenty of uneven bounce available, made them follow on 227 runs behind, it seemed the rest of the match would be a mere formality.

I was musing on this at the back of the commentary box on the Saturday afternoon, pleased for Australia and cursing the luck which, from the commentators' point of view, had almost certainly destroyed the series as a spectacle. From the nationalistic viewpoint, it was great to see the touring side giving England a rare old shellacking. So much so, the banter around the commentary box gave very little thought to the fact that England had a chance of making a game of it. Jim Laker, as a matter of wishful thinking, did say it would have been nice, because of the unpredictable bounce of the ball off the Headingley pitch, to have seen Australia forced to chase 150 and to have seen what pressures could be placed on them. Wishful thinking it may have been but, as things turned out, the words were prophetic.

On the Monday morning the English players checked out of their hotel. It was clear no one had any real idea that a match could be made of it, let alone making Australia fight for 150 runs. The game, to all intent, was gone and forgotten. With Gooch already back in the pavilion, England began the fourth day at 6 for 1, requiring a further 222 runs to avoid an innings defeat. At lunch they were 78 for 4, and when Dilley joined Botham at 135 for 7 in the middle of the afternoon, life for an English captain was grim.

There was absolutely nothing Brearley could do about things now. He had tried everything on the field when Australia had batted, but some indifferent catching from his team had not helped him and there had been an inability on the part of his pace bowlers to break through with the new ball. Botham, as usual in England, had turned up trumps and bowled just on 40 overs to take six wickets – he had also taken them at exactly the right time because at one stage Australia, at 332 for 4, looked certain to reach something like 500. Hughes in the end had declared and now here he was only three wickets away from a famous victory.

It wasn't difficult for me to picture the inward misery Brearley would have been hiding with his usual sensible approach to life. 'What the hell am I doing here?' must have been the theme clanging away at the back of his mind. The move by the selectors to bring him back had failed, or seemingly so, and his own batting had contributed a mere 24 runs in two innings.

He was in a position not too far removed from the one I had found myself in at Old Trafford back in 1961, where I had not taken a wicket until the last day of the Test and had made three runs. Came the last day of that match and the quick fall of the three Australian wickets, and life really became desperate for the Australian captain of the moment. It all ended at Old Trafford in a fairy-tale story later in the afternoon and here, at Headingley, it was about to do the same for Brearley, although at the time he had no idea it was to happen.

The pulsating stand which was to follow (117 off 18 overs) marked the turning-point in the fortunes of the respective captains. It also underlined that a captain must seize every chance *before* it comes along. It's no use being late with your thinking, slow with your decisions. The game must be planned all along the way, bearing in mind a captain must change with the circumstances. It seemed to me that the Australians had no real plan for bowling to Botham and the left-hander Graham Dilley. Botham is always at his best when he is given room for the stroke outside the off stump, never quite so certain when he is cramped for room with the ball moving in at him from short of a length and slightly outside off stump. At the same time, Dilley simply cried out for a pace bowler to come round the wicket at him, making certain there was no chance at all of him flinging the bat at the ball well outside off stump. Neither of these points were tried soon enough by the Australians; when eventually they tried, they were not good enough to land the ball in the right spot. Brearley would have sensed this in the dressing-room and his heart, after a while, would have started to beat a little faster.

With both men laying about them to such effect, cracks began to appear in the Australians' fielding – certainly they began to appear in the captaincy and in the advice seemingly given by the senior players. Now in the dressing-room Brearley would have been starting to think about the vague possibility of setting Australia a target, however insignificant it might be. That was definitely in Brearley's mind when Botham later reached his century off the 87th ball he received, for the England skipper was out on the balcony making it quite clear to his champion that he wanted him to stay there.

When Dilley was out the lead was only 25 and then came what I thought was a brilliant piece of captaincy. Brearley sent in Chris Old, who was on a pair, *with orders to play his own game* and try to hammer the bowling . . . if he could! Other captains, with Botham going so magnificently, might well have told Old to play defensively and, had he done so against the pace bowling, I am convinced he would have been out very quickly. The Yorkshire allrounder was no great shakes against the 'quicks'. When Dilley had joined Botham at the crease, everything had seemed lost and Dilley really had to go out there and pick up whatever runs he could. Old's departure from the dressing-room was in very different circumstances and required the bravest of decisions to be made.

There were other decisions Brearley had to make on the final day when Australia needed only 130 to win. He had no runs with which to play and he had two pace bowlers to lead his attack, neither of whom had taken a wicket in the Australians' first innings. How much pressure could he apply to take wickets and at the same time give away no runs at all? The answer was that he handled it perfectly, even when Australia, at 56 for 2, seemed to be coasting. He handled it perfectly when those two experienced campaigners, Bright and Lillee, added 35 for the ninth wicket, and he handled it perfectly in psyching up Bob Willis on the way to his best-ever Test haul.

Even so, I did not rate that exhibition of captaincy as highly as the one he pulled off at Edgbaston in the following Test. There was some magnificent cricket played at Headingley, but there was an element of luck for Brearley in the way the latter part of the game unfolded. There was no such element in the Edgbaston Test where it was sheer hard slog for the captain who had no runs with which to play after some more indifferent English batting. Brearley himself was the top scorer for the match – with 48.

There seemed to me to be nothing really wrong with the pitch yet Australia's first innings total of 258 was far and away the biggest of the game. The ball came off the pitch slowly enough although there was sufficient bounce for the Australian captain, Kim Hughes, to be caught on the fence hooking; and for him to feel the necessity to protect Graham Yallop from the pace bowlers. The latter was as curious a captaincy decision as I have seen, considering the fact that Yallop was a Test batsman.

At one stage in England's second innings Australia had them, in effect, at

46 for 6 but a great partnership between Emburey and Old gave Brearley a final lead of 149. Not much of a lead I can tell you. Very few captains I have seen in international cricket could twice defend such leads as at Headingley and Edgbaston and, in the end, do it in relative comfort. Of course, you must have the players in your team able to rise to the occasion in situations such as this, but they have no chance of rising to the occasion unless pushed and pulled and cajoled and bullied in the right directions.

What I liked most about Brearley's leadership on the last day at Edgbaston was his clever use of offspinner John Emburey. It would have been easy to give the ball to Willis and Old who bowled so well at Headingley and tell them to get on with it. Instead, he used Emburey for more overs than anyone else and had the satisfaction of seeing him claim the wickets of Border and Yallop, the two Australians who were threatening to take the game away from England.

Their partnership was broken on the Australian unlucky number of 87 and then Brearley whipped Botham back into the attack. Now, not every captain would have done that at this stage of the match. Botham had made 26 and 3 and, in the context of the scoring of the match, had taken something of a hammering in the first innings with 1 for 64 from 20 overs. His reaction when Brearley called him up was to say he thought someone else might be more suited to the conditions. 'The others are bowling better,' was his remark.

Diffidence from the world's greatest allrounder? Well, diffidence or not, Brearley knew how to handle him, as captains must know how to handle all players with their different personalities and psychological hang-ups. Botham took 5 for 1 from 28 balls. It was hard to believe watching from the commentary box but it had happened again, and this time there was not an ounce of luck involved.

It was brilliant captaincy, an exhibition showing Brearley had correctly gauged the strength and weakness of the opposition, which is one of the vital things in cricket leadership. Another is to be game enough to play your hunches. I have seen a lot of captains unwilling to take with their minds the risk which they know in their hearts is worth the gamble. Brearley was never like that even in defeat and he deserves full marks for it. He won the next Test at Old Trafford in more straightforward fashion, simply setting Australia 506 to win after another remarkable innings by Ian Botham. He then had the pleasure of saving the final Test by batting well at the Oval when the pressure was on in the second innings. Australia had plenty of time in which to dismiss England and, in fact, had them at 144 for 6 when Brearley and Knott came together. He could hardly have wished for a better partner than Knott at such a crucial time and their joint efforts kept the Australian bowlers at bay.

In this match there was a good example of a captain needing to be quite ruthless with his players and yet not being prepared to be so. In the second innings, young Dirk Wellham was on his way to a century in his début Test, a fine innings which was to establish him as one of only two players, the other being the Indian batsman Gundappa Viswanath, to have made a century on his début in both a first-class match and in a Test. Sitting in the pavilion was Kim Hughes, desperately wanting runs quickly enough to declare, and standing out on the ground was Brearley, leading in the series and wanting the runs to come slowly so the declaration would have to be later than Hughes wanted. Brearley closed the game right down to his own pace and then had the satisfaction of seeing the Australians forced to bat on past the time the closure should have been made, Wellham being pinned on 99 for 25 minutes. Hughes, with everything to play for, should have been making all the running, but Brearley shrewdly kept pushing him into a corner. Wellham's century was of far less importance at that stage than the chance to have an extra 10 or 20 minutes at the English openers.

These were all plus marks for Brearley and added to his stature as a skipper, a stature which had grown in recent years with his top-class performances with Middlesex in the County Championship. Quite rightly he was highly regarded for his management of men. Some called it having a degree in people – a rather flowery way of saying he knew his players very well and knew how to get the best out of them.

It is essential a captain has the regard of his players, and their respect as well. If he is liked by them it is a bonus, although it does not necessarily have to be the case so long as he is a winner. Respect for a winning captain comes easily, for a losing captain it is only too simple to see where he made his blunders. Mike Brearley had plenty of experience of this in 1981 and so too did Kim Hughes as each went through the range of captaincy emotions.

Life on the captaincy circuit was not always as pleasant for Brearley. After he captained England against Australia and won back the Ashes in 1977, he took the English team to Australia in 1978–79 and beat Graham Yallop's team 5–1. It was a victory achieved against a second-class Australian line-up which had been brought about because of the banning of the top players after they joined World Series Cricket. When England came back to Australia in 1979–80, however, things started to go wrong for Brearley.

The English team were at full strength but England had vigorously declined to put up the Ashes for the series, on the basis that the series was only being played over three Tests rather than four, five or six. The many years of Test cricket had produced matches of two days through to timeless Tests, and not always in the past had series been of four, five or six Test matches. It was as well that England decided to record their displeasure at the return of the Australian World Series cricketers to the national team by declining to let the little urn be put up as the prize. Australia hammered them in Perth, Sydney and Melbourne, with England having to wait until the final

Test for any semblance of batting form from champion allrounder Ian Botham. He made a century but it was not a happy series for Brearley who found, in defeat, he was struggling tactically as well as with the bat. It often happens that way.

* * *

One of the most successful MCC tours of Australia was that of 1965–66 when Mike Smith was captain and S. C. 'Billy' Griffith the manager. Smith was a very good captain – one of the best England had – but his Test match performances in Australia were moderate. When he went to New Zealand at the tailend of that tour he made runs in the three Test matches, but English cricket followers were already talking about his successor. At least they were talking about it publicly, which was more than happened to poor Bill Lawry when he was sacked in the 1970–71 Australian season.

Smith made the mistake of losing the First Test match to the West Indies by an innings and 40 runs at Old Trafford in 1966 and Colin Cowdrey took over. His first effort at Lord's produced a drawn match and the West Indies won the Third Test at Trent Bridge by 139 runs and the Fourth by an innings and 55 runs. Then, in the final Test at the Oval, Brian Close was introduced to the English captaincy for the first time and made such an astonishing success of the whole thing that the home side won by an innings and 34 runs with nearly ten hours to spare.

It was one of the most incredible games I have ever seen because at one point, with England 166 for 7 in their first innings in reply to West Indies' 268, you would have bet anything that West Indies were going on to another big win. Graveney was still there but it was not until John Murray joined him that the English innings started to show any kind of recovery. Those last three wickets produced 361 runs, the first time this had happened in a Test match; it was also the first occasion when the last three men between them had scored a century and two fifties. Close's captaincy, to some, was a revelation, but to others, who knew him to be a fine skipper, it was just his normal type of leadership. What it did was to show that England had a captain who was prepared to carry the attack to the opposition.

In 1967, Close recorded a 3–0 victory over the Indians and was one up on the Pakistanis after the Second Test ended on 15 August. At that time it seemed certain he would be taking the team to the West Indies the following year. Then on 18 August it was alleged that Close, in leading Yorkshire, had wasted time in the match against Warwickshire at Birmingham. Yorkshire in 100 minutes bowled only 24 overs, with Warwickshire making 133 for 5 and falling nine runs short of victory in the match. It was also reported that Close had pushed a Warwickshire member who was abusing him as he made his way between the boundary fence and the dressing-room.

On the last day of the Oval Test, which England won, Close was sacked – wrongly in my opinion – after an orchestrated campaign to get rid of him, on the hypothetical basis that if he were to become involved in a similar incident in the Caribbean it could lead to fighting, violence and, for all one knew, a cast of thousands lying in pools of blood on the field of play. It was a very good and successful campaign and it left poor Brian Close, a fine captain and a tough campaigner himself, lamenting on the fact he came from Up North and not the Deep South. That, however, is often a complaint in the north, where they are still not certain the home of cricket should be in London rather than Pontefract or Wigan. It was added that Close, because of the time-wasting incident for which he had been censured by Lord's on the eve of the Test match, might well have been a liability in the light of the volatile West Indian situation, a sentiment which caused a great deal of hilarity in other parts of the world when one considered some of the time-wasting which had gone on in Test cricket in previous years.

As it was, Colin Cowdrey led England well on the tour and, what was more, led them to victory with a win at Queen's Park Oval after Garry Sobers had set England a target of 215 in 165 minutes. It was one of the more generous declarations of our time, for Sobers was without Wes Hall and Charlie Griffith had been injured in the first innings. The bowling attack thus consisted of Sobers himself, Gibbs, Willy Rodriguez and Joey Carew. In some quarters, particularly with the English team, it was regarded as a marvellous declaration for the game of cricket, but in others, including some sections of the Caribbean, it was considered a piece of captaincy in which the skipper hadn't got his sums right. There aren't many Test teams able to be bowled out in 165 minutes.

I had no idea when I captained Australia against England in 1961 that one of the more experienced members of the home team, Ray Illingworth, would ten years later be taking the Ashes back to England. 'Illy' was a useful cricketer at Test level, although he had done little to catch the eye of the historians of the game up to that point. His batting was always courageous, his bowling tight in the tradition of Yorkshire offspinners, and, at gully, he was a very safe catcher though never really spectacular. He was a deep thinker on the game, without having any of the theories which sometimes produce woolly thinking from captains. He was also one of the cricketers Yorkshire decided to dispense with from their playing staff which, in cricketing terms, was a decision something along the lines of Decca turning down the Beatles 22 years ago.

Yorkshire is a fine cricket county and of course always has been. It is a beautiful place and the citizens are sometimes more like Australians than southern Englishmen. Loyal as they come, they love their cricket and their traditions. They argue like Australians, do not gladly suffer fools and have the most awful problems in deciding who should captain the county cricket team. Len Hutton couldn't get the job when he was captaining England and Illingworth couldn't get it when he was negotiating terms, not for the captaincy but for whether or not he would stay on as a player. He went to Leicestershire.

Now, of all the moves made by the Yorkshire committee, that had to be one of the least understandable. Here was a man who was far better than normal county standard, though not of star quality as a Test player, and his cricket knowledge was beyond dispute. Yorkshire needed a firm, strong skipper to handle the firm, strong and often outspoken members of the team but, instead, Leicestershire got him. They certainly made the most of it and, with Mike Turner, one of the cricket world's finest administrators, in charge, it proved to be a splendid combination.

Ironically Illingworth's captaincy of the English team came about when Yorkshire were going through even more dramas and the captaincy of the England team was in the hands of Colin Cowdrey, who had taken over from another Yorkshireman, Brian Close.

Colin Cowdrey is one of the most pleasant men I have ever met on or off the cricket field but he had a small problem as regards captaincy: he always had difficulty in quickly and decisively making up his mind. No one who has played Test cricket had more courage than Cowdrey, though his brand was the diffident type, rather than the brash, extrovert style exhibited by Close. Neither man ever flinched from a fast bowler, both were bruised over the years, but Cowdrey was simply not a great decision maker – either as captain or player. He was one who needed a strong captain to guide him along the right lines.

Illingworth was a proposition quite different from Cowdrey. He was a shrewd psychologist and one who left his team in no doubt as to what he required from them. He was always prepared to give his players an explanation of the plans of the day and he had their complete confidence. Above all though . . . he made his decisions before the critical moment. It was never a case of thinking for an over or two about whether or not a move should be made. If he had a hunch it would work, and if it seemed remotely within the carefully laid-down plans of the series, then he would do it. He was by no means regarded by all as a generous captain; he worked on the basis that the first aim was to win the Tests and then the series, and would anyone blame him for that? Illingworth was never really forgiven in some quarters for beating Colin for the job, and for hanging on to it, and there were many ever at the ready for him to make an error. He was well aware of that and took care not to provide the opportunities.

For most of the time he was too good for his detractors. His opening Test match skirmishes were against West Indies and New Zealand when he did well, but his eye was on Australia and the 1970–71 tour. The Ashes had been with Australia since February 1959 and England's players were hungry for success. In Illingworth they sensed they had the man to lead them to that victory. Cowdrey was vice-captain on the tour, a disappointment for him which he bore with his usual calm and good grace, but it was almost wrist-slashing time for some of his supporters who lacked his equanimity. Illingworth knew he was not universally popular in the upper echelons of English cricket and he knew failure would mean an invitation to return to the hustle and bustle of county cricket. He decided no one would have the pleasure of offering the invitation. There was no doubt in my mind prior to the tour that Illingworth would give Bill Lawry's team a tremendous battle.

That 1970–71 side was tough and professional in outlook and perform- ance. There was no room for the *approach* to the game being the most important aspect and *winning* not mattering at all. Illingworth, to my mind, had the right idea. Throughout the tour, he pursued a single-minded approach and he had the pleasure of seeing the Australian administrators in complete disarray towards the end of the summer when Bill Lawry was so brutally removed from the Australian captaincy and Ian Chappell substi- tuted. Illingworth, without knowing it, was to have a direct influence on the next decade of Test cricket by the manner in which England defeated Australia 2–0. The Australians had a very high regard for Illingworth's team and a great respect for the tough and arrogant way they went about their cricket.

They had complete confidence in everything they did. Australian players have told me they had the feeling when Illingworth's men walked on to the field in that series they knew they were better than Australia. They weren't, but there was no diffidence about their play and certainly there was no diffidence about their leadership.

The players knew Illingworth would back them up if they were right, that he would tell them if they were wrong, and the same went for his attitude towards the administrators. When the latter decided to put on a limited- overs international fixture sponsored by Rothmans after the abandoned Third Test in Melbourne and then in addition play a seventh Test, 'Illy' had plenty to say because the tour management had not taken into account the wishes or fitness problems of his players.

It was an unusual arrangement made by the ACB and representatives of MCC. Illingworth had every right as captain to query the whole thing and, as well, to ask that his players receive extra payment for a match for which they had not originally contracted. He was widely regarded as (a) a rebel for so doing and (b) yet another example of the perils of allowing a man of professed hard professional attitude to handle the side in lieu of one with amateur principles. I thought it all rather amusing but I doubt if Illingworth did. He was having enough trouble with the handling of the side and the regaining of the Ashes, and the surprise addition of an extra Test was superficially endangering that chance.

When Ian Chappell became captain, England still had a 1–0 lead in the series and the last match could have gone either way although, to be fair, England over the last three days gradually asserted their superiority. It was in the later stages of the match there occurred the walk-off incident where, after John Snow had been assaulted by a drunk on the Paddington Hill, cans were thrown on to the field in an ugly and potentially dangerous scene and the game was held up.

In taking his men from the field Illingworth was doing exactly the right thing by a team which had been the target for a disgraceful piece of behaviour by a small group at both ends of the Hill. When play recommenced it was in a far better and more subdued atmosphere. Australians who had sneered over the years at the fact that in India, Pakistan and West Indies there had been stoppages of play due to riots now had some practical experience to go with their knowledge of cricket history. It was not at all pleasant. Those who are alarmed at spectator violence these days should remember it all began many years ago. West Indies, India and Pakistan have been the worst countries in that respect, but nowadays they no longer have a monopoly on the situation.

Illingworth was pilloried in some quarters for his action and the umpires hustled him and his team back on the field with the implied threat that the game would be forfeited if they did not make it back to the centre in quick smart time. I question that now, as I did then. Is it seriously suggested a match at Test level would be taken away from England because there was a crowd demonstration and the captain rightly feared that his players would be assaulted? That's the only point where I thought Illingworth wrong. He didn't indicate strongly enough to the Australian Board, the umpires and the ground authorities that this was supposed to be a sporting event and his players had not come 12,000 miles to play against their traditional foe to be insulted and face the possibility of injury.

England won the series and I arranged an interview with Illingworth at the Gazebo Hotel after play on the last afternoon. In the course of it he talked of his plans for the future and, when we had finished the interview, he asked, 'I've two choices, haven't I? Retire at the end of this tour from the Test captaincy or go on for a couple of years. What do you think?' 'Ray,' I answered, 'there are a lot of people out there waiting for you to make a mistake and there are others who will never really forgive you for having slipped into the captaincy. Make up your mind and if you think there is no greater height you can reach then this is the time to give it away. Get out when on top. Never stay on until people are saying you should retire – that's the worst possible thing you can do. But in the end you are the only one who can make the decision and I suspect you'll probably go on.'

He did choose to go on and was removed from the captaincy in 1973 after being beaten by the West Indies 2–0. Mike Denness was chosen in his place, although Tony Lewis was the man who was favourite in many quarters. No matter which man had been chosen for the series against India and Pakistan in 1974 in England, the tour of Australia was likely to be a rude shock.

Illingworth, in my view, made two errors in his captaincy life. He didn't retire from the England captaincy at the right time thus allowing himself to be sacked; and then he moved into the managership and later the captaincy of Yorkshire when they were going through yet another crisis. Nothing, however, can overshadow his Test captaincy and, for me, he was one of the best I have ever seen in the Test arena. They're tough characters these Yorkshiremen: he was still captaining Yorkshire and managing them in 1983 and, what is more, took them to the top of the John Player League table.

Illingworth was quite different from Peter May, although both of them were equally ruthless as skippers. Steel in the soul! May's was the amateur approach but he was tough as they come in an extremely cultured way. That trio – May, Illingworth and Brearley – were the best English captains I saw over 37 years, through Hammond in 1946 to Willis in 1983. Hutton was very good because he won, but the way he deliberately slowed down the game lost him a lot of marks with me compared with those he gained for his tactical knowledge of the play. If that over-rate trend had continued we would have had 70 overs a day bowled in cricket these days – it's bad enough as it is only getting 90 a day from the law-makers and the players.

Hutton was a shrewd skipper and he had a few scores to settle with the Australian fast bowlers who posed many problems for his teams over the years. His greatest merit though was that he was a winner and he showed good commonsense in retiring when he did – right at the top. He was the first professional cricketer to captain England and in 1953 it was a considerable achievement to come from the pros' dressing-room to the leadership of your country. Hutton did a tremendous service to his fellow professionals by setting the example that you didn't have to be an amateur to be able to put ten words together in replying to a toast at a luncheon or dinner; and you could certainly have just as much knowledge of the game. It was a far cry from the day in 1925 when Lord Hawke, in speaking to the Yorkshire Annual General Meeting, said 'Pray God, no professional shall ever captain England. I love and admire them all but we have always had an amateur skipper and when the day comes when we shall have no more amateurs captaining England it will be a thousand pities.'

Hutton, a superb batsman, was very quick to spot the weaknesses of other batsmen and he had a big advantage over some of the others being advocated for the job in that he was a great player. Some of the others were good, but Hutton was one of the greats and could lead by example. These days he writes a perceptive column for the London *Observer* and, to his credit, he has resisted the temptation to criticise the over-rates of modern-day cricket.

*　　*　　*

West Indies have had two great captains in the history of the game, Frank Worrell and Clive Lloyd. Frank Worrell turned West Indies from being the most magnificent group of individual cricketers in the world into a close-knit team. No one else could have done it. Many tried but the island system was too much for them and bickering, plus a general lack of enthusiasm to be anything but brilliant, proved too much.

Worrell was named to take the West Indies team to Australia in 1960–61, succeeding Gerry Alexander who decided to retire from the captaincy after the 1959–60 MCC tour of the Caribbean. I met Frank at the airport on the day of his arrival in Australia and he wasn't well, having eaten some shellfish to which he was allergic. We had a short chat and as I was leaving I said, 'I hope it's a great year . . .' 'Well,' he said, 'we'll have a lot of fun anyway.' We certainly did. Worrell by that time was slightly past his peak as a batsman yet he played some splendid innings for his team and, even though this was his first major tilt at the captaincy, he managed it magnificently. From some points of view this was one of the greatest exhibitions of captaincy I ever witnessed. He finished up with a ticker-tape farewell through the Melbourne streets and was eventually knighted for his efforts on the tour and elsewhere.

In the early stages of the tour there were few signs that it would develop into such a memorable series. Indeed, when the West Indies came to the opening Test in Brisbane, after playing around the states, they had a dismal record. I captained New South Wales against them and we beat them in three days. Their champion batsmen were either brilliant or disappointing – the last thing they were was solid, with the exception of Worrell himself, Hunte and Alexander.

Worrell knew it would be a very unwise thing to go back to the West Indies with a beaten side, the history of cricket there suggesting that losing captains were not highly regarded as tacticians or future leaders by the West Indies Board. He concentrated on building up a team performance rather than one from a series of outstanding individuals, though he wanted the individual efforts also. How well he handled the whole thing was shown later in the tour when, under a variety of pressures, the West Indies never collapsed as had been their habit.

When things threatened to get out of hand, Frank was there with his calm air of authority, his smile, and the husky laugh which was instantly recognisable at a distance by anyone who had played with or against him. I saw all of this at first hand in the Tied Test on the final afternoon because I had to bat for much of the time with Alan Davidson in what was akin to a limited-overs situation. We knew roughly how many overs we would receive, even off Wes Hall's longest, longest, longest run, and how many runs were needed, and we made our plans accordingly.

Frank made *his* plans which involved the new ball, taken at 200 runs in those days, and the careful use of Wes Hall and Garry Sobers mixed in with Ramadhin and Valentine. You could tell the West Indians were under pressure by some of their throwing in the field and from the tension in the centre. You could also tell there was little likelihood of them crumbling under that pressure because of one incident. When Joe Solomon threw down the stumps to run out Davidson whilst Sobers was bowling, Alexander was up over the stumps for the throw – not on the run but actually over the stumps – and there were two men backing him up.

After that dismissal Worrell kept telling his men to concentrate and relax. It is not all that easy to do both at the same moment, but the idea was right. 'Relax fellas, relax' came the call time after time. When Wes Hall made a nonsense of catching Wally Grout at square-leg – square-leg mind you next to the umpire – off his own bowling, knocking over Rohan Kanhai at the same time, Frank never for one instant allowed annoyance to show through. Instead, he walked over to Hall, put his arm around his shoulders and told him . . . to relax. Talking with Wes a few years after the event, he told me this was one of the worst moments of his life. He thought he had thrown away the Test match for his country and it was Worrell's calming influence which again got him back on the rails.

That match set up the West Indies as a force on the tour, yet they were well beaten in the following Test in Melbourne, only to come back in fine style in Sydney and again square the series. It was a great thing that Worrell went back a hero to the West Indies. To return otherwise would have set back for a long time the lot of the black cricketer. As it was, he went from strength to strength, never losing the calm, generous approach so badly needed by his cricketers at that time.

I played my first Test against West Indies in the final Sydney match of the 1951–52 series when they were captained by Jeff Stollmeyer, who had taken over from John Goddard. I saw Stollmeyer at close quarters in that game and then I watched caretaker captain Denis Atkinson, a marvellous character and man, who was appointed over the heads of Worrell, Weekes and Walcott at a time when he was only beginning to learn the trade of Test cricket. After Worrell there came Sobers and Kanhai and Clive Lloyd, the latter being West Indies' nearest equivalent to Worrell.

Like Worrell, Lloyd is a father figure to his team and it is not meant in any way to be disrespectful if I suggest that is exactly what they need. When they are captained otherwise they tend to move back to the excitable individual state of years gone past and there is less responsibility in their cricket. With

Lloyd there and Viv Richards waiting in the wings, they play with that brilliant mixture of exciting strokeplay and calm authority. Several times Lloyd has rescued their batting with marvellous displays, attacking almost from the moment he has gone in to bat. There have been times when he has tended to let things on the field run themselves, but then, when you have four or five fast bowlers, you can afford to do that, on the basis that at some stage one of them will achieve the breakthrough.

3

A MEMORABLE FAREWELL SEASON ... AND SOME FURTHER THOUGHTS ON CAPTAINCY

There was nothing at all dreary about my extraordinary last captaincy season in first-class cricket in Australia, 1963–64. I started off playing for New South Wales against Queensland in Brisbane early in the season in October and it was one of the most astonishing games in which I ever took part. We lost the toss and Queensland made 613, with Peter Burge hitting a magnificent 283 before he ran himself out. We lost two wickets straight-away, Grahame Thomas and Norman O'Neill, and then came one of the most remarkable innings I have seen – Bob Simpson made 359 in a total of 661 to give us first-innings points.

Ten days later in Sydney we played Western Australia and this was the last time I captained New South Wales in a Sheffield Shield match. Western Australia, with Barry Shepherd making 149, totalled 420 after we had had them at one stage 69 for 4. Then Grahame Thomas and Bob Simpson batted brilliantly and rattled up 308 for the first wicket, and we passed Western Australia's score with only one wicket down. At that point I made a surprise declaration. I couldn't really see the need to go on and it was going to make it a much better contest if Western Australia thought they had some chance of victory. We could probably have bowled them out a second time had we batted on and then closed but it would have been a boring business. In our second innings Brian Booth made 169 not out in the victory and already in the 1963–64 season I had taken part in two wonderful games of cricket.

Ten days after the Western Australia match, New South Wales played South Africa at the Sydney Cricket Ground and South Africa won by an innings and 101 runs, the first time New South Wales had been beaten by a touring team since Douglas Jardine's 'Bodyline' tour in 1932–33. I had realised by now that this was going to be no run-of-the-mill year.

As soon as that match was completed, the Australian selectors announced the team for the First Test against South Africa to be played on 6 December at Brisbane ... and included in the 12 players was Ian Meckiff, whose bowling action had aroused so much controversy some years earlier. This was a dramatic decision by the selectors – Sir Donald Bradman, Jack Ryder and Dudley Seddon – who had not chosen Ian for the Test side against Ted Dexter's English team in 1962–63, despite him taking 47 wickets, the most in the Sheffield Shield. Neither had he been chosen for the Combined XI to play South Africa in Perth early in November, nor for the Australian XI against the South Africans on 15 November.

Even more extraordinary, though pure coincidence, was the fact the South Africans had not seen him bowl that year because there was no fixture against Victoria in the early part of the season. What had happened was the cricket authorities had agreed to the Australian XI match being played in between the South Australia and New South Wales fixtures. Whilst the Combined XI match was being played in Perth against the South Africans, Meckiff was playing in the Victoria v South Australia Sheffield Shield fixture in Melbourne where he took five wickets in the game which Victoria won on the first innings. Then, in another match in Melbourne on 22 November, whilst New South Wales were going down to the South Africans, Meckiff took 5 for 59 and 1 for 47 against Western Australia. For that effort, he was nominated for a return to the Australian side.

When I heard the announcement of the team I reckoned there must have been one of two things happen on the selection committee although, 20 years on from then, I've never had a whisper as to exactly what went on at the meeting. First, the selectors must have received a guarantee from the umpires standing in those two Sheffield Shield matches, Smyth, Collicoat and Sheehan, that at no stage had there been the slightest doubt about Ian's bowling action. One would think that to be implied anyway, otherwise they would have called him after the very strict instructions given by the Australian Cricket Board in regard to throwing, following the ICC meeting at Lord's in 1960. Either that or there had been some kind of disagreement on the selection committee which had resulted in a split vote on the final 12 to go to Brisbane.

It must seem strange now but throwing was a very big subject in world cricket in the late 1950s and early 1960s. There had been the ICC meeting at Lord's and lots of other conferences to try to work out a solution – and even politicians coming into the matter at different times, so great was the feeling about it. I had seen from the commentary box the cricket in England in 1960 when Griffin, the South African, was called for throwing and I had a fair idea of the nasty business which could be the lot of any captain so embroiled. I was about to see it first hand.

The previous summer, 1962–63, when England played Australia in Adelaide, Sir Donald Bradman had all the Sheffield Shield captains to his home for dinner and afterwards showed us some very interesting films he had gathered over the years to do with various bowlers who either had suspect actions or actions slightly out of the ordinary. Present at that social get-together, because of playing in the Test, were Bill Lawry of Victoria, Barry Shepherd of Western Australia, Ken Mackay of Queensland and myself from New South Wales. Because Les Favell lived in Adelaide he was there also, so we had every current Sheffield Shield skipper. At the end of the evening I had said that in future I would not continue to bowl anyone called for throwing by an umpire and I intended to go a step further and not continue to bowl anyone *I* considered to have a suspect action.

Five days before this meeting I'd had every opportunity to put my actions where my mouth was in the game against South Australia, where New South Wales won by ten wickets in three days. Gordon Rorke had played in it and, in my opinion, had let go a couple of deliveries which looked unusual. He hadn't bowled much in either innings, just three overs in the first and four in the second. Neil Harvey and I had each gone to stand out at square-leg near the umpire and were convinced that, every so often when he really bent his back, he was letting one go without his arm being perfectly straight.

Later in the dressing-room I had had a discussion with New South Wales's Chairman of Selectors, Dudley Seddon, and he'd wanted to know why Gordon hadn't bowled more. The reason, I told him, was simple. Most pertinent was the pitch was taking a lot of spin and I hadn't needed Gordon; and secondly, I thought there were one or two occasions when his delivery hadn't been completely legitimate. The answer I got was the selectors would nominate the side and *they* would make sure the bowlers in the team were completely legitimate – my job was simply to captain, so would I remember that in future? My reply was if I found in the New South Wales side in future any bowler I thought had in any way a suspect action then I wouldn't bowl him at all, but, to make my point, I would open the batting with him and they could do what they liked about it.

Five days later, in January 1963, came the dinner at Bradman's house and now here we were in Brisbane on 5 December, 1963, attending a cocktail party at Government House with the three selectors, both teams and some local dignitaries. It was, as they say in the trade, 'a queer 'un'. The only captain, apart from me, present at the cocktail party in Brisbane from that dinner at Bradman's house was Bill Lawry, Ian Meckiff's state captain. In the room, as we sipped our drinks and nibbled our prawns and Moreton Bay 'Bugs', it seemed to us players that the selectors were having a problem either in communication or navigation: if you had drawn a triangle each of them would have been standing on one of the corners.

In the match we had the splendid good luck to win the toss on a perfect batting track and, with Brian Booth making 169, we put on 337 for 5 at the close of the first day. It was exciting stuff and late in the afternoon I shared a partnership of more than a hundred with 'Sam' Booth, one of the most pleasant and cultured cricketers Australia has ever put in the field. We finished with 435 on the second day and then I threw the ball to Graham McKenzie to bowl, with a nice breeze coming from over his right shoulder from the Stanley Street end, against Trevor Goddard and Eddie Barlow.

The bowling plan, in theory anyway, was to use McKenzie and Meckiff with the new ball and then I had myself, Alan Connolly, Tom Veivers and Bob Simpson, plus Norman O'Neill, as extra bowlers. Connolly and Veivers were making their Test match debuts so they were likely to be a little on the nervous side and this was very much a new-look Australian combination.

Then came the calling by umpire Colin Egar on the second, third, fifth and ninth deliveries of Ian's opening over and I had to make a decision on what I was going to do about continuing to bowl him. There really was no choice, in the light of the statements I had made to the other captains and to the chairman of selectors that, as soon as anyone was no-balled, I would instantly remove him from the attack, which is exactly what I did with Ian Meckiff.

It was very sad because it had a most detrimental effect on one of the nicest men ever to step on to a cricket field. Ian never played first-class cricket again. It had an effect on his family because it put enormous pressure not only on him but also on his wife and his children and it left a hollow feeling with everyone who had taken part in that game – it was an awful day and it all seemed slightly unreal.

It was also, I can tell you, a very strange way to captain your last Test match. It underlined for me my feeling earlier in the season that this was going to be no mundane summer. I had already gone through those other matches and now here I had played in a Test match with one of my main bowlers and team-mate of years called out of the game for throwing. A violent thunderstorm with green clouds and vicious lightning had ended proceedings that day before we could get a result and I was anxiously waiting for the next thunderbolt to strike. It didn't take long.

Play was washed out on the Monday of the game and we had nothing to do but sit around and watch the rain belt down. There were many reports in the local Brisbane newspapers and on radio stations and television channels concerning police protection being offered to the umpires, but no one had considered the captain might like some as well.

There is nothing worse in the cricket world than not being able to get out on the field, particularly if there is some sort of pressure weighing you down. I was sitting in the luncheon room next to the dressing-room, musing on life in general and wondering if it were all worth it, when suddenly a strangely-garbed figure appeared in front of me. It was Jock, the team masseur. He had on his masseur's clothes but over the top he had a plastic raincoat and he was wearing a hat, something I had never seen him sport previously. He was also carrying a copy of a pink newspaper, the Melbourne *Sporting Globe*, which in banner headlines asked why I hadn't bowled Meckiff from the other end, with a secondary story of police protection being provided for the captain.

Jock looked a bit strange. The whites of his eyes were showing and he said, 'Why didn't you bowl him from the other end?' 'Jock,' I said, 'please go away, I've got enough problems at the moment.' All of a sudden he whipped away the pink *Sporting Globe* from . . . the gun he had in his right hand . . . and said, 'You should have bowled him from the other end.' The story of my life went before me as he pulled the trigger of the gun producing a bright flash from the barrel.

It took me a couple of seconds to realise nothing had penetrated the area adjacent to my heart and, as I slumped in a wave of relief, I caught sight of the figure rolling around on the floor outside the luncheon room. It was Bill Lawry. He had pulled off one of the greatest practical jokes of a cricket lifetime, although at that particular instance I didn't really feel like chuckling too much. It took me a few seconds to pull myself together and then I could see the humour of it.

We had no more Sheffield Shield matches until 26 December, 15 days away, and the only game of cricket I had coming up was a grade match for Cumberland against Mosman at Mosman Oval. In trying to take a catch off Doug Walters's bowling at third slip early in the morning, I broke in three places the third finger of my bowling hand – my spinning finger. I looked down at my hand and said, 'Would you bloody well believe it?' I walked off the ground, drove myself to the hospital for confirmation of the break, phoned Dr Brian Corrigan and told him I wanted to play again as soon as possible – and started squeezing a squash ball 2000 times a day.

This meant Bob Simpson skippered New South Wales in the Christmas Match in Melbourne against Victoria, making 135 in his début innings as New South Wales's captain, although it wasn't enough to gain first-innings points, Victoria coming out on top by 138 runs. Then, because of my broken finger, he captained Australia in the Second Test match on the same ground a few days later. I went down and covered the match for newspapers and it turned out to be a resounding victory for Australia and Bob Simpson. He made nought in Australia's first innings – in a total of 447 against South Africa's 274 – but he led the side well and Australia needed only 134 second-innings runs to win, a victory they gained on the final morning of the match with Simpson not out 55 – a great moment for him.

In the course of the penultimate day of the match, when it looked certain, barring another thunderstorm, that Australia would win, I went around to the executive room of the VCA and asked to have a word with Sir Donald Bradman. During a Sheffield Shield game in Sydney the previous year, when we'd been talking about the captaincy and my own plans, I agreed I would let him know when I thought it was the right time to step down for Bob to take over as Australia's captain. I reckoned, seeing the way the game was going in Melbourne, this was the ideal time. What better way for Simpson to start his captaincy career than with a victory, and it would have been pointless if I had then come back to take over, particularly as I had announced that I would not be available to go to England with the Australian side at the end of the season?

Sir Donald was in full agreement with the timing, Bob Simpson remained captain of the Australian side and I came back in for the Test in Sydney where I made 43 in the first innings and top score of 90 in the second. Wickets were much harder to come by and the match finished in a draw, but this was a summer I shall never forget, even though the rest of it passed in less eventful fashion. The first half was the most controversial in which I had ever taken part, but I suppose it was better to go out with a bang than a whimper.

Prior to that season I had played in a Commonwealth team with Bob, the 1962 side organised by Ron Roberts to the Far East, India, Pakistan and Africa. In one of the matches played at the old Hong Kong Cricket Ground we managed to keep everyone's interest going, including our own, by fiddling the game a little. Suddenly, though, the two batsmen put on enough runs to make things slightly difficult for the captain who happened to be your correspondent. We arrived at the point where the opposition needed two runs to win and they had three wickets in hand. Derbyshire fast bowler 'Dusty' Rhodes was in the side and he gave a bit of a grin and said, 'Okay, let's see you get out of this.'

I threw the ball to Neil Adcock who proceeded to take a hat-trick – I caught two of them at first slip and the third one had his middle stump cartwheeled back near wicket-keeper Harold Stephenson. We walked off the field with me chuckling and 'Dusty' Rhodes shaking his head. 'You know, Benord,' he said, 'if you put your head into a bucket full of slops you'd come up with a mouthful of diamonds.'

Walking off the field with us that day was Bob Simpson who, in two years time, was to go on to captain Australia. Fifteen years later he was again to take over the captaincy of the Australian team when there came the split between Establishment cricket and World Series Cricket. I was televising one of the WSC matches the day Bob, to celebrate his appointment, was guest of honour at a Sydney Journalists' Club luncheon. I had received an invitation from the man in charge of proceedings, Pat Farrell. I did however send Bob a telegram wishing him well in his new captaincy jaunt and added a rider at the bottom of the telegram: 'Always remember, diamonds are a skipper's best friend!' He read it to the assembled company and it gave him the chance to relate the full Hong Kong story which brought the house down.

*   *   *

The attitude of a cricket team on the field and the entertainment the players provide for the public is directly connected to the attitude of the captain. No team could possibly have a good attacking attitude, and one geared towards entertainment, if it is led by a stodgy captain whose thoughts are solely concerned with not being beaten and who cares little whether or not the public are entertained.

In turn, the captain needs to be bolstered in that attitude by the administrators who, theoretically anyway, should be backing him with everything they have. The classic example of this during my own captaincy career occurred in 1960 in Brisbane when we played West Indies in the Tied Test and where, on the last day at tea time, Alan Davidson and I had come off the field with the Australian score 111 for 6. The sixth wicket, that of Ken Mackay, had fallen at 92 and we'd had a few close shaves in the remaining 20 minutes before tea – but we were still there.

I always found one of the great pleasures of captaincy was the added dimension it gave to the game. Whereas the other players must concentrate on their own batting, bowling and fielding, as captain you must also continually be thinking about your players, what has previously happened to them, what is happening at that moment to the game and what might happen in the immediate future. The plans you make must be influenced by a line of thinking, attacking or steady, and it matters whether or not you are backed in that line by administrators.

Before the start of this Test match we had held our normal team meeting and dinner at which there were many things to discuss, notably the on-the-field tactics for five Test matches when the West Indians were batting. There were also the overall tactics to discuss in regard to the series itself and those, in the end, were influenced by Sir Donald Bradman, at that stage Chairman of Selectors and of the Australian Cricket Board, who came to the team meeting and addressed the players. It was, in a sense, a curious business. Administrators and players rarely got together in Australia then and never before in the history of the game in Australia had a Chairman of Selectors or Chairman of the Board addressed the team as a whole in order to make a plea for a *certain type* of cricket to be played.

That Sir Donald should feel it necessary to visit the dressing-room was a reflection on the state of cricket in Australia over the preceding five years. In the 1954–55 series against Len Hutton's England side, the over-rates, by the standards of those days, were so appalling that it was almost impossible to provide a decent day's run-getting for the people who paid their money. Ian Johnson, as Australia's skipper, did his best but he wasn't even met quarter way, the result being a lot of dreary cricket for the spectators, though for England it was a marvellous series because the Ashes were retained. Much the same applied in 1958–59 with, once again, over-rates very, very slow and, consequently, few runs made in the day. Between the end of that tour and the start of the series against the West Indies, Sheffield Shield cricket had been interesting without being dynamic. In fact, in the previous season the Test stars had missed the Sheffield Shield matches due to the tour of India and Pakistan.

Sir Donald's main concern when he talked to me about addressing the team before the Test match was that it was desperately important for Australian cricket not to have a third successive Test series at home which could, in the eyes of the public, be a disaster, even if we won. There was nothing to be done of course about the matches themselves, in the sense that either side in the Tests could finish up winning 5–0, even though this was rather unlikely. But, from the point of view of attitude, there was a chance at least for the home side to set the pattern – this was the message he wanted to convey to the team.

Organising something like this might be very simple these days but 24 years ago it wasn't quite as easy. Sir Donald wasn't saying he was coming to the meeting, he was asking if I would check up with the players and find out if it would be all right for him to come along and talk to them. There was that fine difference in wording, indicative of the attitude of the times – nowadays Fred Bennett, with the democratic set-up of the team, would simply say to Kim Hughes or Greg Chappell, 'I'd like to pop in and have a few words with the lads.' At any rate, when I had a few words with the lads in 1960, they were all intrigued by what it was about and the answer I conveyed back to Sir Donald was that we'd be delighted to pour him a drink and everyone was interested to hear what he had to say.

His message was simple and it amounted to that one word, *attitude*. He made a plea, and a very strong one too, for the Australian attitude in the Test series to be one of attack and enjoyment and he wanted that enjoyment to be conveyed to spectators sitting on the boundary's edge. Irrespective of the final result in the series, the selectors would back the players if they did the right thing.

At this stage the tour was looking anything but a complete success from any point of view, other than enjoyment. The West Indians had played some fine individual innings and turned in several excellent individual bowling performances. Their fielding though was a mixture and they had already been beaten by Western Australia by 94 runs and by New South Wales by an innings and 119; had played three draws; and had one victory against Victoria when Sonny Ramadhin took ten wickets in the game. Not the ideal background for the start of a Test series.

Nowadays it is commonplace for administrators to offer their views directly to the players on the way a Test series should be conducted and to make a plea for bright or attractive cricket, but I can assure you, back in 1960 in Australia, it was anything but commonplace. The whole thing was to have a marked effect on the way the Australians conducted themselves on the field throughout that series. It made no difference to our planning at the meeting after Sir Donald had thanked us for our attention and had left the room, because our planning remained exactly the same: when the West Indians were batting we intended, as far as possible, to attack them on their strength which was their strokeplay. In a way this was going to fit in with Sir Donald's ideas. We would not try to contain them in negative fashion but give them the opportunity to play their shots and we reckoned, on average, we would have more success than failure. In the end it may not always have worked out as we planned, but it certainly had something to do with the fact it was such an entertaining series of cricket. It *was* a question of attitude.

The match in Brisbane was a high-scoring affair with, in the first innings, West Indies making 453 and Australia replying with 505. In previous Test matches in different countries there had been only five other teams to make more runs than the West Indies had in their first innings and then be overtaken by the opposition. All those matches finished in a draw. Ours didn't produce any more decisive a result but I expect everyone at the ground and around the cricket world was perfectly happy with a tie rather than a draw.

Sitting in front of our dressing-room at the tea interval on the last afternoon of the match, with the score 111 for 6, it was a time for courage. We still had to score 122 at around four runs an over and against the West Indian attack it was not likely to be easy – we also had the problem of only having four wickets in hand. All these things were going through my mind because I needed to have a battle plan to offer Alan Davidson when we walked back on to the field. I have never been one for saying a Test player should automatically know what to do without his captain telling him. Otherwise why have a captain? It was no good saying we would take it as it came; there had to be either a concerted effort to win or a concerted effort not to allow the West Indies to beat us.

My reasoning was simple and I suppose, in one sense, even a trifle negative: I believed if we played for a draw we would have no chance of saving the match. First of all, needing only four wickets, I thought West Indies would bowl us out if we played defensively because it would be foreign to our natural game. Just as important for the rest of the series, it would go against what had already been agreed at the pre-Test meeting. You deserve little respect if you cannot even get over the *first* hurdle.

Consequently, when Sir Donald walked along, sat down and asked what was happening after tea, whether we were going for a win or a draw, I was able to say to him clearly, 'Well, we're going to try and win it.' His expression didn't change but he said, 'Good, I'm delighted to hear it,' and I'm quite certain it fitted in perfectly with his own plans. Even someone as astute as he though would hardly have envisaged the end result of his team meeting chat and my afternoon tea decision!

There is no point in a captain being anything but positive, irrespective of whether he is right or wrong. It's a little like being navigator for a rally driver, when one of the things you must do is to retain the confidence of your driver. If he asks you whether to turn right or turn left at the next T-junction, it's no good at that point saying, 'Look pal, hang on a few minutes – I'll get the map out and have a check.' You need to be very positive and give him a turn left or turn right – and it is better if you are correct rather than incorrect. In the same way, you need to have your cricket team working with you and be able to say to them turn left or turn right, or do this or do that – the key to it is you must never appear to be indecisive.

Australians have a reputation for playing the game of cricket hard and indeed playing every sport hard. Well, I'm probably one of the people who have given Australia that reputation because it was drummed into me right from the time I was a youngster and all the way through my formative years in first-class cricket: no matter what you're doing on the cricket field you try your best and never give up. It's quite easy to say no one should give up, but if you ever feel that way, and if you ever carry it through and actually give up, then you are finished. There's no point in you playing cricket, or whatever the sport might be or working in business, if you are not out there prepared to try to win and to do your best one hundred per cent of the time. I found it so as a player, as a businessman and find it so now as a commentator.

*   *   *

Captaincy was always a great challenge to me and it provided more mental stimulus than anything I did until World Series Cricket came along. I believe the man in charge of a cricket team, or any team, must have the conviction that he can, at the very least, do anything he sets out to do; on top of this, he needs to believe that occasionally he can achieve the impossible. This will never come about without your players being one hundred per cent behind you, so one of the first things you must do is to establish respect from those players. Likewise, you must have respect for them and an enormous amount of faith in them.

All this adds up to the need for a good captain to have an air of tremendous confidence about him and that is one of the yardsticks for which I would look. In addition to the attributes already discussed a captain must give visible signs of deriving pleasure from the game. It's no good – no matter what you're feeling or what might have gone wrong at home or at work before you set out for the ground – going around the field with a face as long as a wet week. It doesn't have to be contrived but it should be there – that impression of deriving pleasure from being out on the ground for six hours every day. It's not always easy because, in adverse circumstances, there is the temptation to grouch about things, no matter how sunny your personality might be. The temptation must be resisted.

Personality has a good deal to do with leadership of international teams but, even more than that, honesty plays an enormous part in successful captaincy. If you are not honest with your team, and if you are not able honestly to examine your own performance as captain, then you might as well give it away right from the start. It is not the slightest use telling your team something is likely to happen on the field if in your own heart you know that, if not impossible, it is the next best thing to it. Certainly if you have any misgivings about what you're saying to them, you can bet your life they are looking at you and having equal misgivings. As soon as that permeates through a team then a captain might as well step down. He must make certain at all times that he thinks carefully before opening his mouth because, although his team members are his greatest supporters, it only needs them to start raising an eyebrow occasionally at some of the extravagant dressing-room or on-the-field statements and the captain's authority is undermined.

At Manchester in 1961 on the last afternoon, when tactics played a big part in the fact Australia won the match against England, I was in the fortunate position of having every member of the team, on and off the field, right behind me. Desperation perhaps? Will to win? It was my job to think out the tactics, theirs and mine to carry them out. It was no time for faint hearts that afternoon. The decision had to be made that, as far as we were concerned, at a given moment the match couldn't be drawn and the only possible result was a win or defeat. The summing up at that point needed to be conveyed to the players and, when I called for drinks, it was only partly because we were thirsty on a gloomy Manchester afternoon and partly because it was the best way to call a halt for a moment to the havoc being created by Ted Dexter's flashing sword.

Neil Harvey and Wally Grout were the lieutenants on that occasion and I had already told them of the decision to go for a win. Colin McDonald was not playing in the match because of an injured wrist. There was one hundred per cent agreement the team would get stuck in exactly on the tactical line I was espousing. There was a great deal of luck in the fact it came off, as indeed there is in all forms of cricket, but at least when you try something and it comes off it does give you a very good feeling.

Whether the side is great, good or even mediocre, one of the most rewarding experiences for a captain is to lead an unselfish team in which the team spirit is high. I was lucky I inherited this aspect of an Australian team in 1958 because Ian Craig had taken us through two series against New Zealand and South Africa (the latter one official) and a fine team spirit had been built up.

There was a day in Lahore during the 1959–60 tour where that was underlined for everyone. We had bowled out Pakistan in their second innings for 366 after they had made 146 in their first. We needed 122 to win and we had two hours to bat. That should have been a very simple task but the problem was to force the Pakistan bowlers to bowl the ball. Fazal

Mahmood was unfit for this match so Imtiaz Ahmed took over as skipper. He was one of the most pleasant men in the game, but he had been given a real ear-bashing before going back on to the field by officials who wanted him to try to bowl as few overs as possible – presumably none would have been the ideal. As things turned out, the two pace bowlers bowled 15 overs between them and the three spin bowlers with short runs bowled 10.3 . . . and all that took almost two hours.

Mohammad Munaf took the first over, Israr Ali the second and each took a wicket, removing Les Favell and Gavin Stevens. Then Neil Harvey and Norman O'Neill shared a partnership of 62 before Harvey deliberately stepped away and allowed Munaf to bowl him. Quite deliberately. What was happening was that Haseeb Ahsan and another fielder had been put at cover on the boundary for both right- and left-hander and they were *walking* across the field each time a single was taken by O'Neill or Harvey. I had promoted myself to five in the order and when Harvey walked past me he said, 'You'd better do something about that, mate, otherwise it'll finish up a farce.' What I said to Imtiaz as I went past him would these days bring a red card and a letter from the Chairman of the Board. One thing it did though was have him act as though someone had threatened summary execution: the over-rate came back to normal and we were home safely by ten minutes.

Many players and captains fail to understand, even in 1984, that those coming through the turnstiles will simply not tolerate negative and unimaginative performances. You can produce many kinds of new-style cricket, you can change the Laws with an eye to pleasing the people who come through the turnstiles but, I promise you, without the backing and goodwill of the captains you are wasting your time. There is absolutely nothing wrong with cricket in the 1980s which cannot be put right by the captains. It is useless in Australia if the Players' Committee meet with the Australian Cricket Board and decide to adopt some new, dynamic approach to the game and then find, when the players get on the field, the captain goes to water and doesn't carry out those ambitions.

Before World Series Cricket started in 1977, and in many ways changed attitudes towards the game, players could get by pleading they were only part-time cricketers and were paid accordingly. Nowadays, in England and Australia, with the increase in basic payments to cricketers at Test, County and Sheffield Shield level, as well as in the West Indies, India and Pakistan, cricketers can't get away with that any more. They must remember they are paid entertainers, particularly that they are visible on television and, if they fail to produce the goods as regards entertainment, the time must come when they will not be given the chance to play but will be forced to look elsewhere. Their attitude must be correct or they will find themselves on the outer whilst the selectors nominate others who can get it right.

One of the worst things selectors or administrators could possibly do in the nomination of a captain is choose someone simply because he might happen to be the best player. I have seen many occasions in cricket teams where the best player would be about number eight on the list of those who should lead the side. However, because a player is outstanding in ability is no reason why he should *not* have a chance at captaincy. I do not go along with the idea that an outstanding batsman, bowler or allrounder will have too much on his plate without worrying about the added responsibility of making all the tactical decisions. I regard that as a challenge rather than a deterrent and, whilst the selectors need to be careful to make certain their choice has all the attributes required, they should not be put off by the fact it might be giving him a little bit of extra work.

A captain must make certain he has a mental picture of the capabilities of every player he is likely to meet in the summer. I captained New South Wales for just on six years and Australia for approximately the same time, and one of the things I made a point of doing was to keep a mental file on every player I ever came up against. Perhaps this was partly because I was a bowler and it was necessary from the point of view of bowling tactics to know the strengths and weaknesses of the opposition. This is one of the reasons why I believe a bowler often makes a better captain than a batsman because the bowler must know the weakness of every player he sees walk out through the gate to the centre of the field.

Not always will that knowledge take a wicket for you but certainly you should start off in that manner. For example, if you know someone is particularly strong on the leg stump and you see him coming out to bat against one of your bowlers who, in the last couple of overs has been inclined to slant the ball to round about line of leg stump on the batsman's pads, then you need very quickly either to change the line of your bowler or change your bowling. There's nothing worse than to see a fellow come in and a few minutes later you look up and almost without trying he's already made 20 and his confidence is sky-high.

It is often said a bowler should not captain a team at Test match level yet there are so many arguments in favour of bowlers captaining the team the minus marks pale into insignificance. It is a shame that Bob Willis, in Australia in 1982–83, set back by approximately a hundred years the idea of bowlers captaining Test match teams. Not because he wasn't a nice guy, which he was; not because he wasn't a fine bowler, which he was; but because he didn't actually captain the team.

It was all done by committee. Bob had been brought in as what the selectors seemed to believe was likely to be an interim appointment between the deft removal of Keith Fletcher and the introduction of someone like David Gower to the job. Willis's appointment coincided with P. B. H. May taking over the chairmanship of the English selection committee and it was said, in part, that Willis's appointment was to re-establish the values of Test cricket and behaviour. No quarrel with that. And no quarrel with the way Bob handled himself in Australia because he was always very courteous and pleasant with the public and media. Bearing in mind some of his statements about the fourth estate when he was merely a player, his attitude to the media must have required a good deal of self-control.

In Australia though it was commonplace to see Willis, Gower, Botham and Taylor all having a go at changing the field or having a conference in the centre of the ground. When the decision was made to put Australia in to bat in Adelaide – an extraordinary decision if ever I've seen one – Willis went as far as to allow himself to be *overruled* by the majority decision, as he has documented in *The Captain's Diary*.

'The pitch had dried completely by this morning. When we gathered on the ground at 9.45 a.m. I could not move the surface at all with my thumb. Nothing suggested it would be other than a perfect batting strip and, although silently regretting my forthright remarks about damp wickets and insertions at yesterday's press conference, I decided we should certainly bat first if I won the toss.

'It would be an understatement to say I was surprised when I discovered I was in the minority, but every player I consulted came up with the same view – we should bowl. In my heart I knew we should be doing it for all the wrong reasons, negative reasons because the batsmen plainly did not fancy batting first against the pace bowlers. That disappointed me. I had hoped there might be more appetite for the battle. I wondered whether to use my authority and overrule everyone, but what frame of mind would the batsmen have gone out in then?

'Sometimes I have premonitions about things, and today I was quite certain I would win the toss. In my mind I could plainly see that old penny of Greg's coming down on heads, and I almost dreaded it. But I called "heads", for the third successive Test, and of course I was right.

'The usual pitch interviews, immediately after the toss, were a strange experience this time. I had to adopt a tongue-in-cheek attitude to explain my decision. Already, I fear the rest-day press conference is likely to be the most unpleasant, and bizarre, of the tour.'

Captaincy by committee never works as far as I am concerned. The captain should either lead the side on his own and take all the blame for losing and all the credit for winning, or let someone else get on with the job and move back into the side merely as a player. If he wins then he can pay full tribute to those who have helped him in the back room; if he loses it's no good him saying it's David's fault, or Ian's fault, or Bob's fault, or even, for that matter, Doug's fault.

In being critical of what went on in Australia in 1982–83, I am critical merely of the principle of the thing and I was delighted to see that Bob handled the side so much better, and with a great deal more authority, when England played New Zealand in 1983. Willis, Botham and Gower are intelligent men. Is it impossible for them to captain a cricket team on their own? Captaincy by committee is a recent England method and one should therefore let the players and selectors get on with it if that's what they want to do, but it wouldn't do for me. I would have hanging over my head in the field and dressing-room all the time the knowledge that I had been talked into doing something which hadn't come off and in which I hadn't really believed. I would have found that intolerable.

I repeat, there can only be one captain out in the centre of the ground or in the dressing-room. You can *ask* for advice from your senior players, and indeed I used to ask for advice from Neil Harvey and Colin McDonald when the former was vice-captain and the latter the third selector in the side. Occasionally they used to offer it on the field as they walked past me and it would then be my job to evaluate what they said in the knowledge that, if I decided not to accept the advice, there would be no hard feelings. But we never engaged in 'talk-ins' on the field and they would have gone pale at the thought of moving fielders for any captain of Australia.

The one thing you couldn't say about any of the four English captains on the field in Australia in 1982–83 was that they were lucky. Not much went right for them. The decision to allow Allan Border to take runs at will in the Fourth Test in Melbourne was a collective job and, as such, it almost cost Bob Willis his head. In the end England lost the series 2–1 but it was within a whisker of being 3–0, and it would have been no good Bob turning around at the end of that and saying, 'Well, it was a collective decision, and although I've got to stand by it, the others were the ones responsible for it as much as I was.' Life as a captain doesn't work like that.

Peter May was the best captain I played against and perhaps that rating ties in with what I've said about a captain needing to do the job on his own. May was much more of a dictator than, say, Willis in 1982–83, and he was well aware he would live or die by the decisions he made on the field.

My first experience of May's captaincy came in 1956, in England, when I was a member of Ian Johnson's team. Aided by Jim Laker's record bag of 46 wickets at 9.60, May never missed a tactical chance and gave us a real thrashing. He then went on to draw the series in South Africa in 1956–57 and record convincing victories over West Indies and New Zealand at home in 1957 and 1958. His reputation was deservedly high, so much so that *Wisden*, as a preface to the tour of Australia in 1958–59, stated the following:

'Peter May's achievements as captain are without parallel. Never before has the same man led England through a series of Test matches and his county to the top of the Championship in the same year. Clearly England stand at the top of the cricket world. Rarely has our prestige been so high. There are some who aver that England have never possessed a better side, but in making comparisons one must remember conditions have changed. Pitches are certainly very different in this country and in Australia compared with 20 years ago. Tactics, too, have changed with a leaning on occasions towards defensive bowling. The reason for England's present success is possession of a grand captain, a fine array of bowlers suited to all types of pitches and the way these men have been brilliantly supported on the field. Also adequate reserves have been available when first choices have withdrawn.'

At a time when some of his players, ability-wise, were on the way down rather than on the way up, May was ill-served by the pre-tour publicity which listed his team as the greatest ever to leave English shores. They had an enormous amount to live up to and sometimes that kind of adulation can be worse than fierce criticism. Both obviously are a problem for any skipper, but the main thing he must do is evaluate his team realistically for himself and pay little attention to what is said about them outside the confines of the dressing-room. If, for example, I had taken notice of people saying the 1961 team was the worst ever to leave Australian shores, then that may have infiltrated into the dressing-room and resulted in a loss of confidence on the part of the players. Correspondingly, if you have this feeling in the dressing-room you are unbeatable, because you've been reading about it or listening to backslappers, it comes as double the jolt when things start to go wrong.

Plenty of things did go wrong for May on that tour and we won back the Ashes 4-0. We had them on the defensive for much of the series and, whereas May had handled his bowlers and fielders faultlessly against us in 1956, his field-settings in 1958–59 were dictated by the fact that his bowling attack was nowhere near as strong as in previous years.

I didn't play cricket before the war but, in talking with those who did and captains who led teams at that time, I am in no doubt that field-setting and tightening-up tactics have been much improved since then. That doesn't necessarily mean the art of captaincy has also improved. When I talk about the tightening-up of field-settings, on some occasions that can produce straight-out negative tactics in the centre, although we do seem to have got away from the days of six or seven players on the onside which used to be so much of a bugbear. It was difficult to find any excuse for negative or very defensive field-settings. That is not so much because I vehemently disapproved of them. but more because I liked to find some other way of winning a match.

I could never see how playing negatively was going to win you a game: it might draw one for you, but the actual winning of it was likely to slip away. By contrast, attacking the batsman with close-in field-settings, and quick bowling changes which made him constantly think about what might happen next, always seemed to me to be offering an opportunity to the fielding side to come out as victors in the shortest time possible.

Captaincy is an art. Believe that, but also believe it is unwise to get too technical about the whole thing because you always come back to the situation of a game being a contest where you are in charge of only one half. *Keep it simple* is the key.

I don't think there is much doubt it was easier captaining a cricket team in the old days, and perhaps that is partly because of less attention then being paid to the techniques of field-setting or bowling changes. There was less pressure then on teams to win, not that there was any less endeavour in the field or any less skill shown. But the worst that would happen to a captain before the Second World War was that his on-the-field tactics might be queried; they wouldn't be blasted unless they happened to be something quite reprehensible like Jardine's 'Bodyline' effort.

I am sure some of the old-time English captains like Lord Hawke, Lord Harris, Percy Fender, G. O. Allen, and others who skippered Australia through from 1900 to the start of the Second World War, found it much easier to be in a position where they could be autocrats rather than what these days is more the shop steward. There are modern-day exceptions to this. Ian Chappell was one who was very much his own man, so too Ray Illingworth and Mike Brearley, and that is one of the reasons I list them as the finest captains I have seen in modern-day cricket.

I know England believe they have the best system of nominating their captain, that is to choose him first and the rest of the team later, but I have never been able to come to terms with it. I suppose it's a hang-up from believing if you have to pick 12 players to assemble the morning of a Test match on a given ground, one of them at least should be able to captain the side and captain it very well.

I reckon one of the bad things to have come out of the compromise between World Series Cricket and the Australian Establishment was that the players, in their bargaining, managed to organise themselves into a position where the captain of the side sat on the selection committee.

The greatest ever Australian selection committee was a threesome, Sir Donald Bradman, Jack Ryder and Dudley Seddon. I didn't want to be part of their discussions because I reckoned it might have prejudiced my thinking on certain players. For example, if I had been at a two-hour meeting with the selectors and I'd held out very strongly for a particular batsman or bowler to come into the side, I refuse to believe I would not be thinking of that when the actual game was in progress. Would I be prepared to push that batsman

Season	Opp	ENGLAND Captain	T	W	L	D	Opp	AUSTRALIA Captain	T	W	L	D
1945–46							NZ	W. A. Brown	1	1	0	0
1946	I	W. R. Hammond	3	1	0	2						
1946–47	A	W. R. Hammond	4	0	2	2	E	D. G. Bradman	5	3	0	2
		N. W. D. Yardley	1	0	1	0						
	NZ	W. R. Hammond	1	0	0	1						
1947	SA	N. W. D. Yardley	5	3	0	2						
1947–48	WI	G. O. Allen	3	0	2	1	I	D. G. Bradman	5	4	0	1
		K. Cranston	1	0	0	1						
1948	A	N. W. D. Yardley	5	0	4	1	E	D. G. Bradman	5	4	0	1
1948–49	SA	F. G. Mann	5	2	0	3						
1949	NZ	F. G. Mann	2	0	0	2						
		F. R. Brown	2	0	0	2						
1949–50							SA	A. L. Hassett	5	4	0	1
1950	WI	N. W. D. Yardley	3	1	2	0						
		F. R. Brown	1	0	1	0						
1950–51	A	F. R. Brown	5	1	4	0	E	A. L. Hassett	5	4	1	0
	NZ	F. R. Brown	2	1	0	1						
1951	SA	F. R. Brown	5	3	1	1						
1951–52	I	N. D. Howard	4	1	0	3	WI	A. L. Hassett	4	4	0	0
		D. B. Carr	1	0	1	0		A. R. Morris	1	0	1	0
1952	I	L. Hutton	4	3	0	1						
1952–53							SA	A. L. Hassett	5	2	2	1
1953	A	L. Hutton	5	1	0	4	E	A. L. Hassett	5	0	1	4
1953–54	WI	L. Hutton	5	2	2	1						
1954	P	L. Hutton	2	0	1	1						
		D. S. Sheppard	2	1	0	1						
1954–55	A	L. Hutton	5	3	1	1	E	I. W. Johnson	4	1	2	1
	NZ	L. Hutton	2	2	0	0		A. R. Morris	1	0	1	0
							WI	I. W. Johnson	5	3	0	2
1955	SA	P. B. H. May	5	3	2	0						
1956	A	P. B. H. May	5	2	1	2	E	I. W. Johnson	5	1	2	2
1956–57	SA	P. B. H. May	5	2	2	1	P	I. W. Johnson	1	0	1	0
							I	I. W. Johnson	2	2	0	0
								R. R. Lindwall	1	0	0	1
1957	WI	P. B. H. May	5	3	0	2						
1957–58							SA	I. D. Craig	5	3	0	2
1958	NZ	P. B. H. May	5	4	0	1						
1958–59	A	P. B. H. May	5	0	4	1	E	R. Benaud	5	4	0	1
	NZ	P. B. H. May	2	1	0	1						
1959	I	P. B. H. May	3	3	0	0						
		M. C. Cowdrey	2	2	0	0						
1959–60	WI	P. B. H. May	3	1	0	2	P	R. Benaud	3	2	0	1
		M. C. Cowdrey	2	0	0	2	I	R. Benaud	5	2	1	2
1960	SA	M. C. Cowdrey	5	3	0	2						
1960–61							WI	R. Benaud	5	2	1	2*
1961	A	M. C. Cowdrey	2	0	2	0	E	R. Benaud	4	1	1	2
		P. B. H. May	3	1	0	2		R. N. Harvey	1	1	0	0
1961–62	I	E. R. Dexter	5	0	2	3						
	P	E. R. Dexter	3	1	0	2						
1962	P	E. R. Dexter	4	3	0	1						
		M. C. Cowdrey	1	1	0	0						
1962–63	A	E. R. Dexter	5	1	1	3	E	R. Benaud	5	1	1	3
	NZ	E. R. Dexter	3	3	0	0						
1963	WI	E. R. Dexter	5	1	3	1						
1963–64	I	M. J. K. Smith	5	0	0	5	SA	R. Benaud	1	0	0	1
								R. B. Simpson	4	1	1	2
1964	A	E. R. Dexter	5	0	1	4	E	R. B. Simpson	5	1	0	4
1964–65	SA	M. J. K. Smith	5	1	0	4	I	R. B. Simpson	3	1	1	1
							P	R. B. Simpson	1	0	0	1
							P	R. B. Simpson	1	0	0	1
							WI	R. B. Simpson	5	1	2	2
1965	NZ	M. J. K. Smith	3	3	0	0						
	SA	M. J. K. Smith	3	0	1	2						
1965–66	A	M. J. K. Smith	5	1	1	3	E	R. B. Simpson	3	1	0	2
	NZ	M. J. K. Smith	3	0	0	3		B. C. Booth	2	0	1	1
1966	WI	M. J. K. Smith	1	0	1	0						
		M. C. Cowdrey	4	1	2	1						
1966–67							SA	R. B. Simpson	5	1	3	1
1967	I	D. B. Close	3	3	0	0						
	P	D. B. Close	3	2	0	1						
1967–68	WI	M. C. Cowdrey	5	1	0	4	I	R. B. Simpson	2	2	0	0
								W. M. Lawry	2	2	0	0

Season	Opp	ENGLAND Captain	T	W	L	D	Opp	AUSTRALIA Captain	T	W	L	D
1968	A	M. C. Cowdrey	4	1	1	2	E	W. M. Lawry	4	1	1	1
		T. W. Graveney	1	0	0	1		B. N. Jarman	1	0	0	1
1968–69	P	M. C. Cowdrey	3	0	0	3	WI	W. M. Lawry	5	3	1	1
1969	WI	R. Illingworth	3	2	0	1						
	NZ	R. Illingworth	3	2	0	1						
1969–70							I	W. M. Lawry	5	3	1	1
							SA	W. M. Lawry	4	0	4	0
1970–71	A	R. Illingworth	6	2	0	4	E	W. M. Lawry	5	0	1	4
	NZ	R. Illingworth	2	1	0	1		I. M. Chappell	1	0	1	0
1971	P	R. Illingworth	3	1	0	2						
	I	R. Illingworth	3	0	1	2						
1972	A	R. Illingworth	5	2	2	1	E	I. M. Chappell	5	2	2	1
1972–73	I	A. R. Lewis	5	1	2	2	P	I. M. Chappell	3	3	0	0
	P	A. R. Lewis	3	0	0	3	WI	I. M. Chappell	5	2	0	3
1973	NZ	R. Illingworth	3	2	0	1						
	WI	R. Illingworth	3	0	2	1						
1973–74	WI	M. H. Denness	5	1	1	3	NZ	I. M. Chappell	3	2	0	1
							NZ	I. M. Chappell	3	1	1	1
1974	I	M. H. Denness	3	3	0	0						
	P	M. H. Denness	3	0	0	3						
1974–75	A	M. H. Denness	5	1	3	1	E	I. M. Chappell	6	4	1	1
		J. H. Edrich	1	0	1	0						
	NZ	M. H. Denness	2	1	0	1						
1975	A	M. H. Denness	1	0	1	0	E	I. M. Chappell	4	1	0	3
		A. W. Greig	3	0	0	3						
1975–76							WI	G. S. Chappell	6	5	1	0
1976	WI	A. W. Greig	5	0	3	2						
1976–77	I	A. W. Greig	5	3	1	1	P	G. S. Chappell	3	1	1	1
							NZ	G. S. Chappell	2	1	0	1
	A	A. W. Greig	1	0	1	0	E	G. S. Chappell	1	1	0	0
1977	A	J. M. Brearley	5	3	0	2	E	G. S. Chappell	5	0	3	2
1977–78	P	J. M. Brearley	2	0	0	2	I	R. B. Simpson	5	3	2	0
		G. Boycott	1	0	0	1	WI	R. B. Simpson	5	1	3	1
	NZ	G. Boycott	3	1	1	1						
1978	NZ	J. M. Brearley	3	3	0	0						
	P	J. M. Brearley	3	2	0	1						
1978–79							P	G. N. Yallop	1	0	1	0
								K. J. Hughes	1	1	0	0
	A	J. M. Brearley	6	5	1	0	E	G. N. Yallop	6	1	5	0
1979	I	J. M. Brearley	4	1	0	3						
1979–80							I	K. J. Hughes	6	0	2	4
							WI	G. S. Chappell	3	0	2	1
	A	J. M. Brearley	3	0	3	0	E	G. S. Chappell	3	3	0	0
	I	J. M. Brearley	1	1	0	0	P	G. S. Chappell	3	0	1	2
1980	WI	I. T. Botham	5	0	1	4						
	A	I. T. Botham	1	0	0	1	E	G. S. Chappell	1	0	0	1
1980–81	WI	I. T. Botham	4	0	2	2	NZ	G. S. Chappell	3	2	0	1
							I	G. S. Chappell	3	1	1	1
1981	A	I. T. Botham	2	0	1	1	E	K. J. Hughes	6	1	3	2
		J. M. Brearley	4	3	0	1						
1981–82	I	K. W. R. Fletcher	6	0	1	5	P	G. S. Chappell	3	2	1	0
	SL	K. W. R. Fletcher	1	1	0	0	WI	G. S. Chappell	3	1	1	1
							NZ	G. S. Chappell	3	1	1	1
1982	I	R. G. D. Willis	3	1	0	2						
	P	R. G. D. Willis	2	2	0	0						
		D. I. Gower	1	0	1	0						
1982–83							P	K. J. Hughes	3	0	3	0
	A	R. G. D. Willis	5	1	2	2	E	G. S. Chappell	5	2	1	2
1983	NZ	R. G. D. Willis	4	3	1	0	SL	G. S. Chappell	1	1	0	0
Total			345	122	78	145			262	109	68	85

*includes Tied Test

up into a dangerous situation, say as one who had to go in at ten minutes to six, or would I, in good light and good conditions, put in a night-watchman? The same would apply to bowling. If I had insisted on that player being chosen and eventually I had the deciding vote, would that affect my captaincy in regard to the time of the innings in which he came on to bowl? I was also much happier to be in a position where I could study the team with a fresh mind – as was the case when the 1961 team was announced to go to England – and *then* I would prepare my tactics.

It is an indication of the different style of administration in those days that in 1961 I had no idea beforehand of what the team might be. I was at Mornington races the day after the conclusion of the last Test in Melbourne against the West Indies and Bert Bryant, one of the great race broadcasters in Australia, was able to give me the list of names announced for the forthcoming series against England some few minutes previously. The only thing I had known about the team was that Sir Donald Bradman thought I might like it. He told me so in the morning, but that was all he told me. That is the way selectors should be.

The other aspect which led me to believe it was much better to be separated from the selection committee was that once they chose their side, and I had not had any heavy hand in deciding which players would be in it, I could then go out and captain the side as I wished. I was not beholden to the selectors to do exactly what they might want. I found that worked perfectly.

At some stage before a selection meeting Sir Donald Bradman would ask me if I had anything in particular I would like to put to the meeting – and it was always phrased in that way rather than 'anything I wanted' – and I might offer an opinion about the way someone had played. Bear in mind though, this was my opinion from the centre and sometimes a quite different view could be gained from the perimeter by the selectors who weren't as wrapped up in the game as I was out in the middle. When they sat down and chose their side they would have paid courteous but little attention to what I had said, particularly if my views had not accorded with what they had seen for themselves.

When I received the nominated 12 players I sat down and worked out my tactics, batting order, bowling strength, what type of back-up strength I had, and I might come to the conclusion it wasn't exactly the side I would have chosen. But at least I knew I had a free hand in the way it was going to work. The selectors weren't able to come along and put any pressure on me and I believe that's the way captaincy should be.

You are more likely in England than Australia to have a captain who is a successful leader but whose performances are not quite up to Test standard. For a long time Mike Brearley, on form, was hardly worth a place in the England side, and there were plenty of batsmen who must have looked longingly at his position and wondered what they had to do to gain the nod for the national team. Greg Chappell had a run of outs in 1981–82 which would have destroyed a lesser player and yet he was able to come back from that and still play very well. I had experience in 1961 of being captain and, up to the second innings of the Old Trafford Test, not doing very well because of my shoulder injury. That was particularly annoying and depressing and at one point, no matter how much steely resolve there was to keep going, there was also a little mental problem coming into my cricket.

Cricket captaincy though is great fun. There is no doubt, in modern-day international cricket, a captain has everything to gain and, if anything, more to lose. It has applied to Australian cricket right from the time the game began more than a hundred years ago. There were no amateur captains in Australia, nor were there professionals, because in that country we've always only been cricketers and Australian captains have been able to go back to their job of work after a Test match and, in a sense, treat the whole thing as a lot of fun – which it was if you won the match. Captaincy is a great challenge and the captain, if he has sufficient good material at his disposal, will turn out to be a hero. That is if he is able to do something worthwhile with the material, but, if he fails in that endeavour, then he generally finishes up on the scrap-heap of captains.

Captains come in all guises, even the non-playing variety. In 1964 I went with E. W. Swanton's team to Malaya and the Far East and then on the way back to England we stopped off in Calcutta to play one match.

It was very hot at the ground where we played the Combined Indian XI, 106 degrees in the shade and approximately 146 degrees out in the centre. A captain always needs a sense of humour in situations like this and Colin Ingleby-Mackenzie's was tested as we arrived at the ground on the first morning. Two of his top bowlers, Garry Sobers and Sonny Ramadhin, reported ill. Ingleby's good humour wasn't quite equal to persuading them to become 'un-ill' but the manager, E. W. (Jim) Swanton, in his best and most imperious manner, explained to them the problems associated with them not turning out. I was intrigued by this storming performance from the non-playing captain but I was also delighted because I knew, if either or both of them didn't play, there would be a lot of extra work for the remaining bowlers, Richard Hutton, Ken Taylor, Dan Piachaud and me. As it was, Sobers played an enormous part in the game, taking 6 for 63 from 22 overs and 3 for 78 from 24 overs and then making a brilliant 123 when we batted.

Jim Swanton's finest captaincy hour that match came from having Sobers play and from a change in the batting line up he ordered in the second innings when we were chasing 242 for victory in three hours. I was pushed up the batting order with the instructions to take care of Bapu Nadkarni who had put a brake on things in the first innings to the tune of 22–9–40–2. Seymour Nurse, the splendid West Indian batsman, at the other end smashed one lot of bowlers out of sight, I did my bit with Nadkarni and it goes down in Calcutta as one of the great autocratic captaincy triumphs of our time by a non-playing captain of the golden age.

* * *

Life is never dull for the captain and not always does he control his own destiny. There is always the toss.

On many occasions over the years, when the flip of the coin comes down favouring one side throughout a Test series, or almost throughout the series, there comes a call for the toss to be decided alternately, on the basis this would be the fairer approach. In 1953, on my first tour of England, Len Hutton won the toss in all five Test matches and that revived suggestions the toss should be alternate. But none of those suggestions came from Australians. Lindsay Hassett claimed things worked out evenly over the years and statistics showed him to be correct. Furthermore, I'm sure the people who are suggesting alternate tossing in a Test series would be the first to be up in arms once the ramifications became obvious.

Take as an example an Australia–England series in Australia where the home side won the first Test match in Perth and they did that after winning the toss and batting. Now it is England's turn to choose in Brisbane and somehow, after reluctantly deciding to bat first, they are bowled out for 140 on the first day on what turns out to be a fiery pitch. I don't think the idea of the alternate toss would last past that point because no one in the world would be convinced the green-top pitch, soft underneath, had not been deliberately provided for England, with Australia having a surfeit of fast bowlers. There would also be the obvious case of Australia or England, as the home team, one up in the series and the pitch for the final Test is a batsman's paradise, with the toss the turn of the home team.

There's no question tossing is important, but it would never work to have alternate tosses for the reasons already advanced. And there is always Bill Tallon to fall back on if there is any problem at all with the toss – he maintained it was a tremendous advantage to be a stutterer. He told the story of playing in the country in Queensland in one match where, by the time the coin was flipped up and by the time it hit the ground and rolled away, he was able to walk across to it and say, 'Th-th-th-that's the one!'

Sending the opposition in to bat these days is the most popular tactic in modern cricket. Perhaps it is to do with the full covering of pitches but it is definitely different from the way I was brought up when I was starting in first-class cricket. Very rarely would anyone even dream of putting the opposition in to bat. My first experience of it at Test level was in July 1953 in the Fourth Test at Headingley. It was a miserable chilly day and the pitch was so green it could hardly be distinguished from the rest of the square when Lindsay Hassett won the toss and put England in – the first time an Australian captain had done that in 44 years of Test cricket. The last time had been Monty Noble at Lord's in 1909 in a game Australia won by nine wickets. On that occasion, in the early 1900s, Lord's had been under water two days prior to the start of the match and the English selection committee had left out Gilbert Jessop and Walter Brearley. The match took only three days and at the end of it Noble was a hero.

It was said in England at the time the performance of the selectors that year was the worst ever known in the history of English cricket – criticism of selectors is nothing new. It was also said the same year that the whole of the English team would need reorganising and, in fact, England would want practically a new XI for the Test matches to be played in 1911 or 1912. In the 1909 side were players like R. H. Spooner, Wilfred Rhodes, A. C. MacLaren, George Hirst and S. F. Barnes, plus Colin Blythe. There were also J. B. Hobbs and George Gunn and, as well, Tom Hayward. Warner, Hobbs, Rhodes, Barnes and Gunn managed to hang in there for a couple of years: at least until MCC went to Australia in 1911–12 and they slaughtered the home side.

The Fourth Test at Headingley in 1953, where Hassett put England in, was the one where time-wasting saved England. My second experience of a captain winning the toss and putting in the opposition was in Brisbane in 1954 when Len Hutton put us in and easily lost the match. Of the two, I thought Hassett had best reason for the decision, in the light of the conditions at Leeds, but I couldn't see the purpose behind Hutton's move and I think he knew by tea time on the first day he was in real trouble. You must always have good reasons for putting in the opposition and I feel in recent times that doesn't happen with some of the captains – they do it more as a defensive measure so their own batsmen don't have to face a little bit of life in the pitch in the first session.

I did it three times, the first against England at the end of the 1958–59 series. The selectors had chosen six batsmen for this final Test (we had already won the series and regained the Ashes), McDonald, Burke, Harvey, O'Neill, Mackay and Favell. Meckiff, who had been out of the side in the previous Test when the Ashes had been regained, was back in the twelve and when the selectors gave me the name of the twelfth man it was Les Favell. I said to Sir Donald Bradman, 'That's four fast bowlers – I'm just going to have to put them in to bat.' 'Well,' he said, 'that's your job. We've done ours and you can make up your own mind.' The conditions were very much in favour of bowling. There had been heavy rain during the week, the outfield was slow and lush, batsmen were unlikely to gain full advantage for their strokeplay and the pitch had a decided tinge of green about it because of the rain and humidity. It all worked out well, with a lot of life in the pitch in the first session and the game barely went into the fifth morning.

The other occasion I put the opposition in in Australia was in the final Test of the series against the West Indies, and that was for almost precisely the same reasons. There had been heavy rain earlier in the week and once again the outfield was slow and the atmosphere was heavy. Although we had three spin bowlers in our team – Johnny Martin, Bob Simpson and myself – I was banking on Davidson and Misson plus Ken Mackay being able to use the conditions on the first morning. This one only just worked out, with West Indies starting moderately, recovering in the middle and then finishing up with 292. We won the match but not by much.

Then in Pakistan, in 1959, I fielded first but this time for entirely different reasons. We had been assured before leaving Australia the Test matches in Pakistan would be played on turf rather than on matting and when we reached Dacca for the first of the Tests we asked for transport to take us to the stadium to have a look at what had been provided for us by way of a pitch. By the time we arrived we had been told by local administrators that, owing to problems with too much rain, it had been decided to play the match on the mat. We were far from happy about this, particularly when we saw the square was covered with the most beautiful dark green grass and the only bare part of it was where the pitch was being prepared so the mat could be put over it.

The reason for putting Pakistan in on this occasion was so our players, who had little experience of playing on the mat, would at least be able to see how the ball performed. Part of my planning included Ken Mackay as a bowler – 'Slasher' was always accurate and able to move the ball a little off the seam on turf but I had a feeling he might be a trump card for me on this artificial surface.

Pakistan were dismised for 200 runs, Alan Davidson and myself taking four wickets apiece, and we ended up 25 runs ahead on our first innings after some brilliant batting from Neil Harvey (96) and Wally Grout (66). Enter Ken Mackay, who put in a tremendous match-winning performance with 6 for 42 off 45 overs. We went on to win by eight wickets.

For the captain, though, the unsung hero of the two matting Test matches in Pakistan (the Third at Karachi was also played on the mat) was Lindsay Kline. Every morning of the match his job was to go down to the ground well before the rest of the team arrived and superintend the laying of the mat. There was nothing physically demanding about this but his instructions were clear. By the time we arrived at the ground to start play, that mat had to be as tight as a drum, both lengthways and widthways, and the morning we were batting in our first innings there was no doubt Lindsay had taken his duties quite literally and very much to heart.

'Pull, you bastards, pull,' was ringing out across the ground as we walked through the gate and no one out in the centre was sweating more than L. F. Kline. Having a mat as tight as a drum may not seem very important. But old cricketers who recall having played on matting surfaces in Pakistan will know exactly what I mean when I say it made the world of difference to our performances, and to those of the opposition bowlers. The mat was so tight you could have strummed a tune on it!

That tour of Pakistan and India was, in many ways, a real eye-opener. As manager we had S. J. E. Loxton, MP, and it was a lucky choice.

It was a funny tour, not always funny ha-ha, although there were plenty of humorous moments, but funny peculiar with the pitches and some of the official administration happenings. We had managed to get through the early matches without Sam going too berserk about the umpiring, although he did have a short, sharp conversation with one of the Pakistan umpires who asked after the match at Dacca if Sam thought he'd be umpiring at Lahore. The reply was, 'After my report, if you start walking now pal you might just get to Lahore in time for your next umpiring appointment.' I don't think Sam would get away with it now, but he was regarded as something of a god in India and Pakistan in those days because of his associations with the various Commonwealth teams which had played there.

When we arrived in Bombay we had the problem of organizing the tour finances, in the sense that before a ball was bowled in any of the Test matches $7000 had to be deposited in the bank and the deposit slip had to be placed in Sam's hands. It transpired that the Secretary of the Board had been too busy, or not quite interested enough, to do this. So there we were, an hour before the start of play, with Sam saying the tour rules stated that if he didn't have the deposit slip in his hand, then the match wouldn't start. The administrators made the mistake of saying to him, 'But Mr Loxton, if the match does not start the 50,000 people in here at the moment will be very displeased and there is no telling what they might do.' They should have known better. Sam looked them straight in the eye and said, 'That is going to be your problem because I'm going to tell them it's your fault.' The deposit slip was in his hands inside 20 minutes and the game started on time.

It did have an interesting aftermath though because of the happenings at Kanpur in the previous Test match where Australia had been beaten and Jasu Patel had taken 14 wickets in the course of what was a marvellous Indian victory. The late Maharaj Kumar of Vizianagram had written a local article in Kanpur praising the Australian team to the skies for everything, including sportsmanship. But then in another newspaper a few hundred miles away at the same time had been published an article under his name saying exactly the opposite – we were terrible sportsmen and it would be better if we didn't come back to India.

Unfortunately for everyone concerned a friend of mine, an Indian journalist, sent me a copy of that article and I put each alongside the other and showed them to 'Vizzy' when we saw him in Bombay in the dressing-room.

As usual he marched in as if he owned the place (which he probably did), and at the end of our short, sharp discussion demanded an apology because I'd besmirched his good name by suggesting he could possibly have written that second article which had obviously been rewritten by some sub-editor up on the furthermost part of the Indian border. We came to a compromise which was fairly one-sided. I told him, former Indian captain or not, I didn't want to see him in the dressing-room again until I had a proper explanation and an apology for what he had written, and he said he wouldn't come back into the dressing-room until the Australian team apologized to him. So it worked out perfectly all round.

I still have a memento of the tour which has its connections with the late 'Vizzy'. When we were in Kanpur we had been told there was an official function to which we should go, but when we checked up with the Board's Secretary he said he knew nothing of any official functions there and we certainly weren't required to go to any dinner. 'Vizzy' eventually prevailed on us to turn up, on the basis that first of all it was official and, secondly, it was for the benefit of a charity. But when we arrived, in a very suspicious frame of mind, we found all the menus and brochures indicated the function was a 'tribute to the Maharaj Kumar of Vizianagram' for all the great work he had done for the community and for Indian cricket.

As I had been the one, with Sam, who had conned the players into going, you can imagine I wasn't very popular when I caught the eyes of my team-mates scattered around the room. I was even less popular when it was announced I would be the recipient of a magnificent tiger skin and head, and it was the hardest job of the tour to prevent that tiger skin from being cut into 17 pieces – one small piece for every member of the team who reckoned I must have known what was going to be my pay-off for making them sit there through four and a half hours of speeches extolling the virtues of a former Indian captain.

Playing cricket in Pakistan and India has always been a fascinating task. They have had some wonderful players in both countries and, on their own pitches, they were extremely difficult to hold, let alone defeat. Sometimes it was necessary to indulge in a little off-beat exercise to boost the adrenalin of our players.

Neil Harvey was one of the greatest and most entertaining batsmen the world has seen and a prime reason for this was that he was always prepared to carry the attack to the bowlers. Not for him the stilted defence which can drive away the spectators: even on bad pitches, his one aim was, if possible, to get on top of the bowler.

On this tour, Subash Gupte was the main spinner for the local side and there have been few better leg-break bowlers over the years. He had good flight but was just quick enough through the air to make it difficult for the batsmen to get to him and he had a great 'Bosey'. I won't say it was impossible to detect but it was the next best thing and there was no likelihood of Harvey being able to 'pick' him. The little left-hander rarely tried to do this with any bowler, preferring to dance down the pitch and in that way break up the length. He used to say, 'If the ball doesn't have time to turn, there should be no problem for the batsmen.'

Subash, to reach his 100 wickets in Tests, needed five wickets at the start of the three-Test series. A local newspaper ran a story on the morning of the first match that he would almost certainly join the ranks of the greats this day and would probably get another five as well against batsmen like Harvey and others who had shown recently, against Laker and Lock, they could not play spin.

At breakfast we were very careful to place the newspaper alongside 'Harv's' plate and waited for the inevitable outburst which duly came. He reasoned later, on the way to the ground, that Gupte, not having bowled against him previously, would almost certainly let him have the 'Bosey' first ball.

He didn't pick it, of course, but as it was a good length 'Bosey' on middle stump, spinning sharply away, what more reasonable than to step back and punch it to the cover-point boundary? And, at the same time, he took a few paces down the pitch and called to his batting partner . . . 'Nice wrong 'un but it's easy to pick.' Harvey saw few 'Boseys' from that moment on. After all, why bowl it to someone who found it 'easy to pick'. He made 37 and 140 before Subash managed to get his hundredth wicket in Tests.

Nowadays you would call it 'sledging'.

Another memory of India and Pakistan in 1959–60, though not necessarily the greatest one, was the taste of Foster's Lager. The Foster's Lager taste came about through the expertise of Sam Loxton, our manager, who had an arrangement with the Brewing Company that they would ship to India several thousand cans of the amber fluid for drinking after the game when the players were relaxing.

Pakistan was in the 'too hard basket'!

The various Australian High Commissioners and their assistants were the recipients of the crates and, after we had signed forms confessing we were alcoholics, we were allowed to have a drink. The local beer in those years was a real problem because of the glycerine type liquid used in the neck of the bottle as a preservative. The soft drinks were bloating, fresh fruit juice was impossible to obtain in quantity, and so the after-match relaxing was done with approximately two cans per man per day of Foster's which added up to something like 250 dozen cans shipped from Australia. Some managers finish with a trademark for one activity or another . . . Sam will never be forgotten by the beer drinkers on that tour.

For me, though, the most memorable part of the tour was that win on the matting Test at Dacca where I had the pleasure of seeing a captaincy hunch come off. Ken Mackay was superb in Pakistan: not unplayable but very accurate, and the movement either way off the seam on the mat was one of the prime reasons we were the only team ever to beat Pakistan on matting. I take pride in that as one of the most rewarding achievements of my playing days.

*   *   *

Whatever hunches you play in this game must be geared to the strength of your team. It's no good using tactics applicable to a team containing Sobers, Miller, Botham, Kapil Dev, Imran Khan and Hadlee if, in fact, you have at your disposal a group of enthusiastic but rather moderate players. A reasonable example comes in whether or not a team captain should enforce the follow-on and, these days, with pitches covered, I can see no reason not to enforce it in normal circumstances.

Kim Hughes, for instance, did the right thing at Headingley in 1981 when he made England follow on, even though Botham in the end turned the game and the series upside-down. This was only the second time in Test history a team had won a match after following on and it had taken 87 years for it to happen again.

There is always the fear in the back of a captain's mind that something like this could happen. When Australia played England in Adelaide in 1959, we had won the first two Tests and drawn the Third and therefore only needed to draw the Fourth Test to regain the Ashes. A win would be even better.

It was the match where Peter May sent us in to bat and we made 476 and, having bowled out England again for 240, had the chance to make them follow on. I could see 3-0 coming up and was on my way into the English dressing-room to tell them they could have another go when I met at the top of the steps 'The Don', who was Chairman of Selectors. All he said was, 'It's the only way you could lose you know . . .' I didn't actually give it the old Australian expression of, 'She'll be right mate', but the reply was cheerfully along those lines and, even though we had to bat again, we made it in comfortable fashion.

Providing all things are equal, it is the psychological aspect which should be the final arbiter in decisions of this kind. Psychologically England could not have wanted to bat a second time that day, particularly as they had Fred Trueman batting seven, followed by Tony Lock, Frank Tyson, Brian Statham and the injured Godfrey Evans.

Captains should always be prepared to talk to other members of the team if there is in any way a chance of improving performance. I had Neil Harvey to chat with on tactics, Colin McDonald was very good and down to earth and so too Wally Grout. There were many little points discussed with them and others and filed away for future reference. Or even immediate reference.

When MCC came to Australia in 1958–59, my 'Bosey' was working just about as I wanted it. It wasn't a great 'Bosey', because it only spun a couple of inches, but sometimes that was enough to find the inside edge of the bat which was possibly better than spinning a foot and missing the edge. When we played MCC in Sydney, in the return state match, Peter May gave me a tremendous hammering and every time I bowled the 'Bosey' he kept on stepping into the ball and smashing it against the fence at long-on or deep mid-wicket.

What had gone wrong? Up to now no one really had picked it more than fifty per cent of the time, and here was Peter picking it all the time and giving it an absolute pasting. No one in the team at first could come up with a solution. Doug Ford was our wicket-keeper in those days in the New South Wales side and he was a good, thoughtful cricketer. Feeling sorry for ourselves, we had a few beers in the dressing-room that evening and eventually he reckoned, after much torso swinging, I had been dropping my shoulder at the instant of delivery, instead of keeping it high. This triggered instinctive diagnosis of the ball as a 'Bosey' and Peter made no mistake about the treatment.

When play resumed again in the match, Peter and Trevor Bailey were the not-out batsmen and I bowled immediately from the Southern or Randwick end at the SCG. I bowled three overs, each of eight balls, all 24 were 'Boseys' and all were delivered with a high shoulder action. The ploy caused enough consternation in the camp to have Trevor march down the pitch for a consultation. He knew what I was trying to do . . . confuse the issue by deliberately showing the proper 'Bosey' to Peter 24 times.

Different countries and different sports bring different methods. I always believed I could get the most out of a player by co-operation rather than domination. I would have had far less chance if I sat in the hotel lobby waiting for players to return to bed by 9 p.m. So long as they turned in a one hundred per cent effort for me on the field I was satisfied. And if they didn't, they were well aware there could be problems.

Not all captains and managers adopt the same methods. In fact, there are some rigid disciplinarians who insist on everyone going to bed early and not having a drink, not just during the match but at any stage of the tour. There was an American baseballer a few years ago called Hack Wilson who had that sort of problem with his team manager. Hack was a great player and a great gin drinker, one of the best ever seen on the American baseball circuit. He had the misfortune one evening to be drinking gin in a bar the night before a big game at the New York Yankees' Stadium when in walked not only the team manager but also the owner of the baseball club. They both looked at Hack Wilson and walked over – and kept looking at him.

The owner told him that, unless he could produce a good reason for being there drinking gin the night before the match, he'd be in the front office the next morning and there'd be real problems. Wilson looked at them and said, 'I drink gin so I don't get worms.'

There was a stunned silence.

The owner remarked, 'I think you'd better see me in the front office tomorrow morning.' Wilson turned to the bartender: 'Bring me a large gin on the rocks.' There was no conversation until the gin arrived and was plonked down on the table in front of Wilson. He reached into his jacket pocket and pulled out two live, wriggling worms and dropped them in the gin, whereupon they immediately expired. Wilson got up off his chair and over his shoulder as he made for the door said, 'That's why I ain't got worms.'

Not even the hardest-hearted owner or manager could have carpeted him after that.

Cricketers always know how much sleep they need and how much roistering they can manage. Like all sportsmen they have it in their own hands to stay in the team: if their performance suffers from over-indulgence the selectors will soon get rid of them. The captain has to keep his eye on this and, at times, decide how to tackle anyone stepping out of line or, indeed, if to tackle them at all. An isolated incident might need no discipline.

There was a day in England during the 1961 tour when I sensed in the dressing-room that there was something amiss – 'Wrong vibes' as they say nowadays. There was plenty of merriment, as there always was before we went out on the field in a minor match, and there was plenty of good-natured chaffing, but something was up. It took me until we were on the field to work out what it might have been . . . and even then it was only a guess.

'Come and have a bowl,' I called out to the figure on his way down to deep fine-leg. 'Bowl?' he said. 'Give someone else a go if you like – I'm happy to field.' 'No, come and have a go at the pavilion end – you haven't done much bowling so far on the tour and you were saying the other day I didn't bowl you enough.'

I'll say this for him, he never flinched until the end of his tenth over and then he said, 'If you make me bowl one more over there is going to be a big problem . . . I'm feeling very ill.' 'Late night?' I ventured. 'I actually came straight to the ground from the party,' he replied, 'but I can assure you I will never do it again because there might be some other bloody sadistic captain who'd bowl me ten overs on the trot just to find out if I'd had a late night.'

This, we all agreed later, was a better, lighter and certainly more humorous way of handling it than hauling him over the coals in front of his mates who, incidentally, had been trying hard to shield him in the dressing-room. That was what had produced the unusual vibes.

Don't be over-smart but keep your sense of perspective and, above all, keep your sense of humour. Even better, find yourself a team with a sense of humour. It's handy also if they're good cricketers and, if you can combine the two, then you have just about the ideal combination for any class of cricket from club to Test. Ashley Mallett and Doug Walters were good friends, each with a droll sense of humour, and occasionally they came into conflict on or off the field, but only in a very light-hearted way.

Back in March 1970 the Australians were touring South Africa and not doing it very successfully, after they had had a very good run in India where they won the series fairly easily. Mallett and Walters were in the Australian team to play against Western Province and they were doing very well against the local side until the brilliant allrounder Mike Procter strolled in at 68 for 3. He proceeded to hit a magnificent 155 and Ashley Mallett bowled 27 overs and took 2 for 166.

Procter didn't fool around. He hit sixes off each of the last five deliveries of one over from Mallett and, when the last one had disappeared into the railway yard alongside the ground, there was a delay whilst they tried to find the ball. In the end the umpires called for another one from the dressing-room and, as they were waiting for it to be tossed on to the field, Doug Walters strolled across to Mallett who was looking into the distance longingly, possibly at the Brewery next door, and said, 'Okay Rowdy, that's the end of the reds . . . now let's get started on the colours!'

Walters was quite a character. He was discovered by Jack Chegwyn on one of his country tours, similar to the one where John Gleeson first made his mark. A quiet, understated sense of humour made him one of the finest team men imaginable and it was a privilege to have had a hand, at Cumberland, in seeing him progress from the club side to the state team and then the Australian XI.

A captain is lucky to have in his side players of the temperament of Walters, Chappell, Marsh, Mallett, Lillee and the others. But no captain can ever be exactly certain what his players are going to say under pressure. He might know perfectly well that under pressure on the field they will be impeccable and neither the fastest bowling nor the most outlandish remarks will cause even a minute flutter in their concentration. What they say when *off-the-field* pressure creeps in though is an entirely different matter.

Dennis Lillee, for example, in 1972 had the problem of a rearranged schedule facing him when he was presented to Her Majesty the Queen. Bob Massie had picked up a little matter of 16 for 137 in his first Test match for Australia and this meant the game was over earlier than planned. It also meant the Australians had the pleasure and privilege of being invited to Buckingham Palace for afternoon tea at five o'clock instead of being presented to the Queen and Prince Philip at the ground.

It was a great moment and yet Lillee, despite all the joy of the day and the pleasure of defeating England, found himself tongue-tied threequarters of the way down the line as the Queen moved towards him. When Ian Chappell said, 'Your Majesty, Dennis Lillee,' the response was, 'G'day.' Rod Marsh was alongside Lillee and he stood as though transfixed – so did Chappell but eventually he managed to pull himself together and move off, escorting the Queen and Prince Philip to the end of the line. When it was all over and the dull flush had disappeared from the back of Chappell's neck, he found manager Ray Steele standing alongside him. 'Casta,' he said, 'you wouldn't want to know what Dennis said when I presented him to the Queen.' 'I don't need to,' Steele said tight-lipped, 'G'day – exactly the bloody same as he said to the Duke!'

Once a captain has managed to stop waking in the dark of the night, sweating at the remembrance of that kind of happening, he has other things to think about. He must avoid trying to be too clever by half or believe he is about to pull a fast one on the opposition, because it doesn't always work out.

It's so easy to be clever as a captain when sometimes it would be better to be sensible. Over the years there have been many apocryphal stories about Australian captains having tried to work into the England side players they knew to be less than Test match standard. Most of these stories though concerned pre-war cricket and I've known it to happen very rarely since the time I started playing.

There was however a day at the Sydney Cricket Ground where Alan Davidson was bowling for New South Wales against the 1960–61 West Indies batsmen Joe Solomon and Cammie Smith. Joe was as solid as they come, as we later were to find out, and he was batting well this day. Cammie was having real problems with 'Davo' and I said to Alan at the end of his second over, 'Take it a bit easy with Cammie, will you, but get stuck right into Joe. We don't want him around in the Tests.'

He bowled two great overs to Solomon but then, when Cammie eventually got the strike, he smashed Alan for two sixes and produced a variety of other brilliant strokes. 'That's terrific, Al,' I said, 'but it's enough. You can get stuck into Cammie as well now.' Through slightly clenched teeth, he said, 'I've been stuck into him right through that over but he kept picking me off. . . .'

Later in the season, on the same ground, we played the West Indies in the Third Test. When they were 329 for 5, in their first innings, we suddenly took another four wickets without any addition to the score. Then Wes Hall and Alf Valentine in a short partnership proved to be very frustrating. Wes was doing his usual thing of playing the ball on the onside and scampering five or six yards down the pitch, then beating back the throw from any fielder who wanted to have a go.

I said to Davidson, who was bowling at the Southern or Randwick end, I would quietly sidle around after one of those little pushes to leg and, wheeling in the one action, would throw down the stumps at Hall's end – at least that was the plan. What happened was, when I calmly reached across, picked up the ball and whirled, letting fly at the stumps, 'Davo' had forgotten I was going to use that ploy and he managed to get his neck between the throw and the stumps. He was laid out cold on the ground. In fact, I thought I'd done something very serious to him but I wasn't too sure whether to laugh or cry.

The rest of the team were falling about laughing – loudly and embarrassingly. As he so often did, Alan struggled back to his feet and had Hall caught behind and the West Indies were all out for 339. But 'Davo' carried the stitch marks of that little piece of captaincy planning throughout the match, which he didn't manage to finish anyway because, after taking 3 for 33 in the second innings, he tore a hamstring and was unable to play in the exciting Adelaide Test a couple of weeks later.

It is fitting that my career and Alan Davidson's should have run along similar lines because we actually started our cricket together, although in opposition, in the High Schools competition in Sydney. He went to Gosford High School and I went to Parramatta High. We played against one another not in weekly competition but in the Combined Northern and Sydney High Schools fixture. In those days he was a left-arm over-the-wrist spin bowler and it wasn't until he came down to Northern District to play in the first-grade competition he was recognised as being a future star as a swing bowler.

Our careers continued to run parallel on the 1957–58 Australian tour of South Africa. It has often been said this was the tour where my cricket really turned the corner. So it was, but the same applied to Davidson who up to that point as an opening bowler had been in the shadow of Miller and Lindwall. I took 106 wickets on the tour of South Africa at an average of 19 – Davidson took 72 at an average of 15. He took his wickets at the rate of every 48 balls bowled and it took me 56 balls for each wicket. I hit four centuries on the tour and so did he and he finished ahead of me in the batting figures with 813 runs at 54 against my 817 at 51.

It was a classic case of two young allrounders coming good at the same time and you can be certain my figures with the ball would not have been nearly as effective if Davidson had not been breaking through the top of the order almost every time he walked on to the field. I was very lucky he was there.

A fine example of good thinking came in that series from Ian Craig, our skipper, and it concerned Alan and me. In the First Test match against South Africa at Johannesburg, I made 122 against Adcock, Heine, Goddard and Tayfield and, from that moment, he kept an eye out for any opportunity to move me up the batting order. It happened in the Fourth Test match, also in Johannesburg, where we needed to *win* the game to make certain of taking the rubber.

We won the toss but it took us a laborious two and a half hours to reach

50 and, at that stage, Ian told me to put the pads on and go in and push the scoring along. It worked. I made a hundred and we were 217 for 4 at stumps and most unlikely to be beaten. As it turned out, we won the match and it was Craig's clever piece of captaincy which gave us the early chance to get the runs on the board. So too did Davidson's innings on the second afternoon where he hit brilliantly for 62 and put the South Africans in an impossible position.

'Davo' was one of my favourite cricketers and that was not only when I was captaining him but also when I was playing alongside him . . . and a great character.

In the Second Test match on that tour, in January 1958, we made 449, then bowled the South Africans out for 209 and made them follow on. Davidson dismissed Jackie McGlew straightaway, having him brilliantly caught by Colin McDonald at leg slip, then 'Davo' caught Dick Westcott off me for 18 which brought in Johnny Waite to join Trevor Goddard.

This was on the fourth day and Craig was having some trouble keeping 'Davo' going in a long spell at the pavilion end. There was no point though in giving him any respite, for if we won the game we would be one up in the series. Meckiff was injured so we were short of a strike bowler and Craig had Davidson coming in after lunch from the pavilion end, over after over. 'Just one more, Al,' he kept saying and Al was dragging his feet back to the mark and then boring in at a hundred miles an hour to move the ball off the seam or in the air and have Goddard and Waite desperately defending.

He was also bowling a very good slower ball which was cutting away from and beating the right-handed Waite and, between overs, as I passed Craig, he said to me, 'The pitch is getting slower and slower. What about coming up four or five yards at gully for that slower one? I'll tell him.' Next over, having limped back to his mark, he came racing in and bowled the slower ball well up outside off stump to Waite who square drove it with terrific power just to the right of where I was standing, now some six or seven yards from the bat.

There was a blur of red and the ball stuck in my right hand to give 'Davo' his second wicket. I was still sprawled on the turf when above the shouts of the crowd I could hear, 'It was the old trap – it was the old trap.' Every muscle ache and pain forgotten, 'Davo' was standing above me telling me the 'old combination' had done it again. I looked up at him and said, 'How are you feeling?' and the glaze faded from his eyes, 'Very sore, very sore,' he said.

It was at the end of this innings, after we had bowled them out for 99, with Lindsay Kline picking up the wickets of Fuller, Tayfield and Adcock for a hat-trick, that we made him a presentation in the dressing-room. It was a beautifully engraved copper plaque we'd had specially made, marked up as the 'A. K. Davidson Autograph Massage Table'. It was very much an 'in-joke' in the team, but at home he still has the plaque which we had tacked on to the massage table in the dressing-room. He might have spent a little time on that table and others but, as well, he gave the Springboks hell during the tour – and he gave batsmen all over the world a real going over from then until his retirement in 1963. He was one of the best cricketers ever to play for Australia; and for New South Wales, in their halcyon years, he was a giant.

He and I played our cricket together at first-class level for 14 years and he remains, for me, one of the greatest cricketers ever to walk through the gates of the Sydney Cricket Ground.

FOUR OF A KIND . . . BETTER THAN ONE ACE

Any captain with blood rather than skim milk coursing through his veins will want in his team the services of an outstanding allrounder. These days the emphasis is shifting back to the allrounder, the genuine allrounder that is rather than the imitation variety. This is partly to do with the influence of limited-overs cricket where the allrounder, able to play a total part in every match, is worth his weight in willow to the skipper.

I would prefer to have in my side, Test or limited-overs, three genuine allrounders. I still think the Australian team of 1958 to 1962 had the ideal set-up of all-round cricketers with Alan Davidson, Ken Mackay and myself in the team. All were key members of the bowling attack – Davidson and I could have held a place in the team for our bowling alone – and it made a great deal of difference to the balance of our team and to my captaincy.

I was able to write out a batting order consisting of six of the best batsmen in Australia and then add the 'tail', which read something along the lines of: Alan Davidson, Ken Mackay, Richie Benaud, Wally Grout and Graham McKenzie. It was a splendid line-up, even if we did not always score heavily, and the combination of the early free-scoring batsmen and some hitters at the end generally gave us enough time in which to bowl out the opposition, one of the most important plus marks with which a captain can be blessed.

That is the type of all-round strength Australia could do with at the moment in both limited-overs and Test cricket, not that I wish to denigrate in any way the present Australian team which is based on a completely different selection pattern. In 1982–83 the 'tail' of the Australian team consisted of, say: Rodney Marsh, Geoff Lawson, Tom Hogan or Bruce Yardley, Dennis Lillee and Rodney Hogg. That was a very strong bowling side, far too strong for England when the Ashes battle took place in Australia in 1982–83, but it was not a strong batting combination and, no matter how you try to fiddle it around, very little extra strength can be found. This selection method was certainly successful when the Australian selectors gave Ian Chappell, as skipper, Lillee, Thomson, Walker and Mallett to do the bowling in 1974–75, with Greg Chappell there if necessary for some medium-pace relief. Now, though, the Australian selectors are having problems in finding enough all-round strength for the one-day internationals and it is putting a great strain on the bottom-of-the-order batsmen.

These days the Australians could do with some players of the all-round strength of Ian Botham, Richard Hadlee, Imran Khan and Kapil Dev at their disposal. I would love to have one or preferably two of those in a team, and spectators today are fortunate they are able to see allrounders of such high quality when they pay their money at the turnstiles. Just as fortunate are the captains who lead them and the television viewers who are able to sit back and watch their every electric move.

Wouldn't it be great though to be a captain of a team nowadays and have a player like Sobers or Miller available in both Test matches and one-day internationals, and to have them promote the game on television as well. Neither Sobers nor Miller played limited-overs cricket to any extent. Miller played some one-day cricket in Australia but that was at club level and he was able to work up very little interest in proceedings. Sobers had some experience of it towards the end of his career, but neither had the chance to play one-day cricket at international level. More's the pity. Having seen them both at close quarters, I would love to be part of a season where their attacking expertise was let loose for the watching public in both types of cricket.

In discussion with other captains and players I have not been able to gain unanimous accord on that. There is a theory around that, because they were such marvellous attacking players, both Sobers and Miller might have been too expensive as bowlers when it was necessary to save runs rather than take wickets in an innings. However, I believe they were such brilliant, natural cricketers they would have adjusted instantly to whatever requirements the captain might have made of them and would have been the finest of allrounders in any era in any kind of cricket.

One of the greatest tragedies of our 'Down Under' communications world was that Miller was never really seen on television in Australia. Nowadays Imran Khan, Kapil Dev, Richard Hadlee and Ian Botham are action replays of Miller, and great entertainment they provide too for the modern-day television watcher. Magnificent cricketers, those four men are the gladiators of the present and the stars of the future.

Botham is the most experienced of the quartet, having played 63 Tests up to the end of September 1983, amassing 3548 runs and taking 277 wickets. That in itself is a wonderful performance, but when you add to it 72 catches, some of them brilliant reflex movements, 12 centuries and 14 half-centuries, as well as the best strike-rate of five wickets in an innings and ten in a match of any allrounder in the history of the game, it's not hard to see why he is and has been such an important member of the English team.

Ian Botham could never have seen Miller play but there are great similarities in their cricket, even to the problems with a bad back! English fans welcomed Botham with starry-eyed delight; here was the man to show all other countries what an allrounder should be like. Quickly they came to expect runs, wickets and catches every time he walked on to a ground and relative failure was greeted with dismay. Botham did not disappoint his fans from the time he stepped on to the field for the first time in an England cap. In those days he was a 'slip of a lad' compared with now and he made an enormous impression on the 1977 Australian team. Greg Chappell, captaining the team at that stage, was under no illusions about his ability.

'I should have known by the way he walked out that day at Trent Bridge that here was something different. Slim, but obviously immensely strong, he had a dream début against us in the Third Test of that series in a match where Mike Brearley's inspiring captaincy was at its best.

'Earlier on that tour he had given us a taste of what was to come when we played Somerset, his county and my old county when I was playing cricket in England. I made a hundred in the match which was personally gratifying, but Botham made 59 and then came in in the second innings and hit a hurricane 39 not out to give Somerset a win by seven wickets, the first time they had ever beaten Australia. It should have been a warning but when a fortnight later he fizzled in the MCC–Australia game we didn't give him a great deal of thought, other than for the fact that he was a player for the future.

'Just prior to the second Test he hit a brilliant century for Somerset against Hampshire and took eight wickets – now we sat up and took more notice. We've been doing that ever since.

'He stormed into the English team in the Trent Bridge Test taking five wickets in his first bowling stint, made 25 at a crucial time, then took 5 for 21 against us in the next Test at Headingley. He was unfit for the final Test at the Oval which must have broken his heart. There is nothing in the world he likes more than to knock over Australian batsmen or smash our bowlers around the field.'

That is the way Botham plays but it doesn't have to be against Australia. He does it the same way against India, Pakistan, Sri Lanka and New Zealand, although so far he has not managed to do it against West Indies. He has taken a burden off the shoulders of the English selectors in the past seven years but, at the same time, has had to try to live up to the almost superhuman expectations put on him by the English cricketing public. After his relatively poor performances against West Indies in 1980 and 1980–81, he re-established himself with a vengeance against the 1981 Australians. In Australia in 1982–83 he was again expected to do the job of two men. As Greg Chappell, his opposing captain in that series, says, he 'failed':

'He was reduced to being a normal human being rather than the man who could walk on water. He had to fail some time. He has been carrying English cricket on his shoulders for seven years and, at some point, something had to crack. It was our good luck it cracked over the period from October 1982 to February 1983. Ian is a very talented cricketer. No present-day Australian player has problems with him as an individual, he is respected as a player and competitor. He competes very hard. He is probably the most aggressive English player I have seen and I would take some convincing there has ever been one with a more competitive nature.'

I respect the views of the former Australian captain but I want to tell him I saw plenty of English cricketers in the 1950s who were equally as competitive as Ian. And that, I can assure you, is not the view of an old-timer but of one who was on the receiving end of the competitive thrusts at a time when the English team were thrashing us.

Botham, Miller and Sobers – how do they rate? Well, supporters of Garry Sobers tend to put him on top of the list and then start talking about the others when great allrounders are mentioned. I think he was marvellous and I can understand their line of thinking, even though it may show a tendency to live in the past. One of their arguments is that Garry played his cricket mainly against England and Australia, whereas Botham has played much of his against weaker Pakistan, India and New Zealand teams. The argument continues that Botham will have to perform in outstanding fashion against Australia and West Indies over the next 30 Tests if he is to be considered as *the* great allrounder.

Let's have a look at that for a moment. Garry Sobers played 93 Tests and Botham had played 63 at the end of the 1983 English season. Sobers played 55 of those 93 against England and Australia, 38 against the weaker countries. Botham's ratio is 32/31 so Sobers would appear to gain a few points there, but what people tend to forget is that Pakistan, India and New Zealand field much stronger sides nowadays than they did during Sobers's career. Whichever side you take, Botham's figures are quite startling and, over a period of time, it can only be statistics which provide a true guide.

A glance at his Test match figures on the accompanying table makes it clear what a match-winner he is . . . with the ball. He has won matches with the bat as well, as evidenced at Headingley in 1981, but his bowling efforts, when compared with other allrounders, are in a class of their own. Botham has been economical enough for his type of bowling but his strike-rate at a wicket every 53 balls bowled is a captain's dream. It is the same kind of rate achieved by Dennis Lillee and yet Botham has also made over 3000 runs in Test matches. He is the outstanding bowling allrounder over the past seven years, although Imran Khan is now approaching him for strike-rate.

Allrounders' Table	Tests	Aggregate	Average	100	50	Caught	Wickets	Average	5W	10W	Strike Rate	Economy Rate
Sobers	93	8032	57.78	26	30	109	235	34.03	6	–	91.91	37.03
# Botham	63	3548	36.58	12	14	72	277	24.82	20	4	53.16	46.68
Hammond	85	7249	58.45	22	24	110	83	37.83	2	–	95.98	39.41
Miller	55	2958	36.97	7	13	38	170	22.97	7	1	61.53	37.34
Benaud	63	2201	24.45	3	9	65	248	27.03	16	1	77.04	35.09
Greig	58	3599	40.43	8	20	87	141	32.20	6	2	69.51	46.33
Noble	42	1997	30.25	1	16	26	121	25.01	9	2	58.75	42.57
# Imran	49	1853	29.88	2	5	16	232	22.92	16	4	55.42	42.23
Davidson	44	1328	24.59	–	5	42	186	20.53	14	2	62.29	39.95
Mushtaq	57	3643	39.17	10	19	42	79	29.24	3	–	66.58	43.91
Lindwall	61	1502	21.15	2	5	26	228	23.02	12	–	59.85	38.48
Goddard	41	2516	34.46	1	18	48	123	26.22	5	–	95.41	27.49
Woolley	64	3283	36.07	5	23	64	83	33.91	4	1	78.25	43.34
# Kapil Dev	53	2253	32.65	3	11	19	206	29.52	13	1	56.18	52.54
Faulkner	25	1754	40.79	4	8	20	82	26.58	4	–	51.54	51.57
Mankad	44	2109	31.47	5	6	33	162	32.32	8	2	90.64	35.66
Reid	58	3431	33.31	6	22	43	85	33.37	1	–	90.81	36.75
Rhodes	58	2325	30.19	2	11	60	127	26.96	6	1	64.72	41.66
# Hadlee	44	1601	24.26	1	8	21	200	25.82	15	3	56.77	45.47
Bailey	61	2290	29.74	1	10	32	132	29.21	5	1	73.57	39.70
Armstrong	50	2863	38.68	6	8	44	87	33.59	3	–	92.55	36.30
Illingworth	61	1836	23.24	2	5	45	122	31.20	3	–	97.82	31.90

The status of Botham, Imran, Hadlee and Kapil Dev, with other allrounders of the past, is high when reference is made to their performances – and they have many years left in the game. These cricketers listed are the ones who have taken 75 Test wickets and made 1500 Test runs. Statistics can prove anything or nothing, as you please. Over a period of time however they have some bearing on a cricketer's standing as a player, but there are the imponderables of some having played in timeless Tests, others on uncovered or fully covered pitches, the early players under an lbw Law different from today.

Still playing Test cricket

In my opinion the biggest problem Botham faces is his fitness. He is big and raw-boned and definitely has a tendency to put on weight unless he watches himself. Despite his denials, and many of them have been most vehement, there is no doubt some form of back ailment has restricted his bowling action since 1980 and, unless he watches it, this could restrict his future as well.

Now ... does Botham have the dedication and the will to regain maximum fitness to hold off the challenge of the other three allrounders? Does he have the will to train hard and remain a bowling allrounder, or will he become a batting allrounder instead? This could be accomplished easily enough because there is no doubting his ability with the bat and his ability to win matches for a captain in that department. It would be easy enough to slip into that role and there is nothing to say Botham could not come back as England captain batting at, say, number six and using himself as a change bowler. It would be a pity if this happened but it is a distinct possibility, in my opinion, after watching him on the tour of Australia and against New Zealand in England in 1983 where his performances were never likely to be in keeping with his great record over the past seven years.

Seven years? Astonishing, isn't it, that a man can play 63 Test matches in seven years these days and create record after record? Miller played 55 Tests in 11 years, retiring at 36, and even in those days they were saying there was too much Test cricket.

There is, incidentally, no reason why Botham should not be bowling and taking wickets at Test level when he is 36 years of age in 1991. After all, Miller gave one of his greatest bowling exhibitions in the Lord's Test of 1956 at the same age, and that was with Ray Lindwall out of the match injured and Pat Crawford, his replacement, broken down. Miller also had back problems, even as far back as 1948 when it is said he tossed the ball back to Bradman, declining to bowl on the score of that injury. During the Australian season before the 1956 tour of England, he had broken down with a back injury and had been forced to pull out of the Sheffield Shield Centenary match against Victoria at the Sydney Cricket Ground. The effects of that back injury were to stay with him in later life so it is not something to be treated lightly. In Botham's case, I think he needs first of all to have treatment for his back and then to find some way to utilise a bowling action which gives him his best chance of taking wickets and, at the same time, protecting his back.

The two allrounder captains of the sub-continent are unlikely characters, if one is to set any store by the history of the game of cricket. India, having played their first Test match in 1932 at Lord's, had over the years a variety of allrounders, one of whom, 'Vinoo' Mankad, was outstanding as a slow left-arm bowler and opening batsman. There were others like 'Polly' Umrigar, who batted well but was an indifferent bowler, and Chandu Borde, who bowled slow legspinners and batted well, but India had never produced an allrounder who could bowl fast and consistently make runs in the middle of the order until Kapil Dev arrived on the scene.

It was much the same with Pakistan. They had Fazal Mahmood as a great bowler and Hanif, Mushtaq and Zaheer as fine batsmen, but Asif Iqbal was the only allrounder of quality and his bowling was of very gentle medium pace. No one wanted to bowl fast until Imran Khan came along with the burning ambition to be the world's finest modern-day fast bowler.

Pakistan cricket was created out of the partition of India and originally had two sections, East and West. We played in both areas in 1959, 12 years after the birth of the nation. By 1971 Bangladesh had been formed and Pakistan now have to rely for their players on what was the old West section.

Cricket for that country started with real flair. Granted Test status in 1952, Pakistan recorded a famous victory over England at the Oval in 1954 and then over Australia in Karachi on the mat in the one Test in 1956 — which also happened to be the first-ever Test between the two countries. Since then their cricket has been variable, with problems in administration, several different captains of the national team and general infighting which hardly assists the players in what they have to do in the centre of the ground.

In their teams they have had some of the best cricketers to step on to a Test field in the past 37 years, ranging through from Hanif, 'The Little Master', to the present day Prince of allrounders, Imran Khan. There have been others of the Mohammad family, Sadiq, Mushtaq and Wasir, then Zaheer Abbas and Javed Miandad, Sarfraz, Asif Iqbal, Intikhab Alam, Majid Khan and Fazal Mahmood, all of them fine cricketers. Perhaps in a way Pakistan's supporters expected too much of them, hoping those early victories over England and Australia would continue at a pleasing rate.

It has not worked out that way and, when victory was achieved over England at Lord's in 1982, there was unrestrained joy. So there was at the Sydney Cricket Ground in January 1977 when I watched Mushtaq's team defeat Australia by eight wickets. This made up in part for the loss on the same ground three years earlier when they had to make only 159 runs for victory in the final innings and could not manage it.

The 1977 match was full of excitement. Jeff Thomson was out of the Australian team, having been injured in a collision with Alan Turner at the Adelaide Oval in the First Test of the series. Australia were bowled out for 211 and then Walker and Lillee, bowling superbly, had four of the Pakistan batsmen back in the pavilion and they were still 100 in arrears. Young Haroon Rashid came in then and played a fine innings on his Test match début, adding 94 with Asif Iqbal who then stayed with Javed Miandad whilst another 115 were added. The last five wickets fell for only 40 and Australia, had they been good enough, could have pulled the game around. It was in the last innings of the match where Imran Khan produced his best effort bowling against Australia – bowling practically unchanged through the innings which lasted for just 42 overs – and the match was finished with a day to spare.

Imran Khan and Kapil Dev became leaders of their Test teams in rather unusual circumstances. When the Pakistan cricket authorities nominated Javed Miandad as captain of the 1979–80 team against the Australian visitors, the decision met with a rather cool reception from some of the more experienced players. There was no doubting his cricket ability, but what would be his reaction to the pressures of international captaincy? The fears of those senior players were realised during the tour of Australia in 1981–82 when there was certainly an indication that Javed, although a brilliant cricketer, was lacking in experience, as well as in team management. He was not assisted in his own image-making in Australia by some of the outbursts from his manager Ijaz Butt, a former Test cricketer against whom I played way back in 1959. There was a delighted buzz of anticipation in the media whenever Mr Butt had something to say and I cannot believe there was anything but additional pressure placed on Javed's shoulders throughout the tour because of this.

When the team returned to Pakistan, it was reported that Javed had complained he had not received sufficient support from his senior players during the Test series and the one-day internationals. The players then declined to play under his captaincy and eventually Imran was installed as captain. Between then and the recent series in Australia, Pakistan cricket was on a 'high', with a drawn series against England, a defeat of Australia at home and a thrashing handed out to India, again in a home series.

Imran is a hero. So he should be because his own efforts have been largely responsible for the emergence of Pakistan as a genuine force in international cricket. To look at Imran Khan is to look at a Prince. I can imagine his forefathers having plenty of action in the hills of Pakistan, seeking out the wrongdoers, rescuing maidens in distress, defeating rampaging hordes. As the modern-day Prince of Pakistan cricket, he is concentrating on lifting Pakistan to the number-one spot in world cricket and challenging Botham as the number-one allrounder.

Given freedom from injury, he would not be far away from that lofty position. The sadness is now that he has had such a disastrous tour of Australia that he may never be able to become a bowling allrounder in the future. His shin stress fracture in Australia was a mysterious business ... not nearly as mysterious though as the goings-on with his Board of Control and the Pakistan selectors. The latter resigned after their team was knocked back by the Board and then the Board members came out with several different stories of Imran and Zaheer Abbas being captain of the team touring Australia.

Then Zaheer announced he was leaving the tour half-way through and going back to England. It all made for one of the more quaint pieces of cricket administration I have seen in 35 years of cricket.

There was a time when Imran's bowling action was such that there was a grave doubt he would be able to improve a great deal. He was constantly delivering the ball from wide on the bowling crease and his back was arching more and more in the delivery stride. This must have had an effect on the muscles in his back but whether or not he changed his action because of this has never been admitted. What happened though was, in playing for Sussex, he found himself bowling at the other end from South African Garth le Roux whose delivery stride was quite different. Whereas Imran fell away and bowled almost from the return crease, le Roux stayed upright and, with a beautifully whippy action, bowled fast without putting any great strain on his body. Imran was quick to learn.

When next I saw him he was coming in closer to the stumps, had developed an outswinger and his front foot was landing much closer to the spot where the right-hand batsman would stand in his batting crease. This had another effect on his bowling and on the degree of difficulty henceforth encountered by batsmen in playing him: he managed to develop one of the most disconcerting types of delivery I have seen from a pace bowler in all the time I have been playing and watching cricket.

The closest I can come to describing it is to say, in baseball pitching parlance, it resembles an 'inshoot', a ball which starts from close to the stumps at the bowler's end and is aimed about a foot outside the striker's off stump. It then swerves in late, so late in fact that I have seen fine batsmen like Greg Chappell and Kim Hughes lose their balance in playing what started out to be an off-drive and finished up as a scrambling effort to keep the ball away from the leg stump. The most telling part about this delivery is that Imran is not restricted to bowling it with the new ball which is when the batsmen quite rightly would expect it. He bowls it with the old ball and in this sense it is a delivery better described as swerve rather than swing.

To compare any aspect of the great game with a hybrid Americanised presentation may seem sacrilege. I played baseball for many years and enjoyed it, even if I could never get the coach's signals right . . . and for me Imran's mystery ball is an 'inshoot'. Mystery it is too. I asked him on Australian television one day to show us how he bowled it. 'There is nothing special,' he said. 'Just an ordinary ball.' But at least he had the good grace to have the faintest of smiles creasing the corner of his mouth as he answered.

I was interested to see Imran installed as captain of Pakistan because I could see in his nature and temperament a leadership quality desperate for

SYDNEY SUN

KEN KELLY

Four Great Captains: Keith Miller – the best captain I played under – and Ray Illingworth, Ian Chappell and Mike Brearley, the finest captains I have observed from the commentary box.

OPPOSITE
Top left Two aspiring young
allrounders, Alan Davidson and
myself, about to board ship for
England in 1953.

Top right Happier days! Old Trafford
1982. Memories for Jim Laker of the
triumphs of 1956, and for me the
luck and determination of 1961. The
man in the centre – Bert Flack,
groundsman 1956.

Below Caught Statham, bowled
Laker 1956. An indication of the
calm assurance of Jim Laker can be
gained from this picture. Almost
six but in fact out, and he hasn't
turned a hair.

THIS PAGE
Above Brisbane, 14 December 1960:
scenes of jubilation from the West
Indies as Joe Solomon runs out Ian
Meckiff off the penultimate ball of
the First Test, thus bringing about
the only tie in Test match history. It
set the scene for a hard-fought and
enjoyable series, reflected in
Melbourne's memorable farewell
to Frank Worrell and his side at the
end of the tour *(right)*.

Above Exchanging greetings with rival captain Peter May, the best England captain against whom I played, at a reception at Australia House, London, in April 1961. *Below* Old Trafford, 1 August 1961: May bowled Benaud 0. England collapsed from 150 for 1 to 201 all out on the last afternoon. It was an astonishing turnabout and no match has ever better illustrated my theme of 'Captaincy is ninety per cent luck and ten per cent skill – but don't try it without the ten per cent.'

Sir Garfield Sobers is popularly rated as the greatest ever allrounder and with good cause.
I only played against him in two series and he was certainly a fine player. I count myself
lucky to have witnessed his complete domination of the Fourth Test at Headingley in 1966
when he led West Indies to victory by an innings and 55 runs. He hit a hundred between
lunch and tea in his innings of 174, then took 5 for 41 and 3 for 39 in a wonderful all-round
display.

OPPOSITE

OPPOSITE
Three aspects of magnificent allrounder Ian Botham, Brearley's salvation in 1981.

Top left Hooking one off his eyebrows during the Third Test at Headingley, where his contribution to England's cause was 50, 149 not out, 6 for 95, 1 for 14 and two catches. His greatest all-round performance for England? What a game of cricket it was, and the 500/1 against England winning was none too liberal at the time.

Top right With Australia requiring only 45 runs for victory, Brearley's gamble pays off as first Marsh then Bright, Lillee, Kent and Alderman fall victim to an electric spell of bowling in the Fourth Test at Edgbaston.

Below Always in the thick of it, Botham catches Yallop off Willis in the Fifth Test at Old Trafford, scene of another of his swashbuckling centuries.

THIS PAGE
Top Ian Botham is an action replay of Keith Miller, whose particular brand of genius enthralled spectators of the 1940s and 1950s. I would rate Lord's 1956 as his best all-round Test: at 36 years of age, and in a low-scoring match, he bowled his heart out (34.1-9-72-5 and 36-12-80-5) and made 28 and 30 just when runs were needed.

Middle and bottom New Zealand's recent successes have coincided with the emergence of Richard Hadlee as a top-class allrounder. Few will forget his outstanding contribution to New Zealand's victory over Australia at Auckland in 1982, and in England in 1983 he was without doubt the man of the series, taking 21 wickets and averaging 50.17 with the bat. Here he is on his way to 6 for 53 in England's first innings, followed by a stirring 84 in the First Test at the Oval.

Above From the first ball to the end, Kapil Dev was the dominant figure for India in the First Test against England at Lord's in 1982, taking 5 for 125 and 3 for 43 and scoring 41 and 89. The day will come for Kapil Dev and Indian cricket when all-round displays of this kind will bring victory, not defeat. *Below* I have seen few better all-round performances, either winning or losing, than Imran Khan's at Headingley in 1982. Despite his 67 not out, 46, 5 for 49 and 3 for 66, England won the match and Imran carried away memories of what might have been.

Above A typical 'crowd' scene at a County Championship match in England. *Below* The new generation of spectators, decried by traditionalists but fundamental to the financial survival of the game, enjoying an evening out in Sydney.

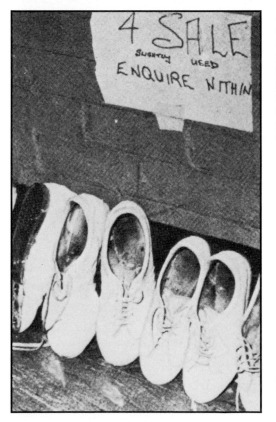

Above A controversial moment during the Lord's Test of 1956 as Peter Burge adopts a near-suicidal position off my bowling to counter Colin Cowdrey's prodding and pushing on the final day. But was it all that close a position when compared with the helmeted, padded and boxed close-in fielders of today?

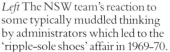

Left The NSW team's reaction to some typically muddled thinking by administrators which led to the 'ripple-sole shoes' affair in 1969–70.

Pithily captioned in *Wisden* 1981 as 'The long walk, the long wait' and 'Unbridled dissent', these two photographs demonstrate two areas where the law-makers have failed to assert their authority. Slow over-rates and players' dissent over umpiring decisions have in recent times produced a cynical disregard for the watching public.

Right Lou Benaud's two sons Richie (on strike) and John at the wicket for the Central Cumberland club in Sydney.

Below Commentating for the BBC at close of play at Trent Bridge in 1976.

release. When he took the team to England for the first time in 1982, understandably he didn't always have the right tactical appreciation for the given situation: he seemed to feel that he had to do it all himself. A case in point was the final Test at Headingley after he had led Pakistan to a great victory over England at Lord's. In the last innings of the match he had to make a choice of whether or not to bowl Abdul Qadir when a couple of lusty blows might have won the game for England but one wicket would almost certainly have won it for Pakistan. There the gambler was needed but Imran did not have the confidence in this first series to use his mystery spinner at that crucial moment. It was a lesson, painful at the time, but one I suspect he will have remembered. When the Australians went to Pakistan shortly after that series Abdul Qadir played a big part in the three Tests and Kim Hughes's team came back with harrowing tales of what a wonderful bowler he was and how it was almost impossible to 'pick' him from the hand or through the air.

Imran keeps saying, because of commitments in Pakistan, he will not play much more Test cricket – in terms of years anyway. In the space of the next two years though I suppose he could easily play 20 more Tests and could conceivably finish with well over 300 wickets and 2000 runs. His recent efforts stamp him already as one of the great allrounders since the war and he is really only just into his prime.

So too is Kapil Dev. He may have a slightly more difficult task ahead of him because India will have to go through a rebuilding programme involving both batsmen and slow bowlers. It is asking a bit much of Kapil Dev to keep carrying the side from the all-round point of view as he has done in recent times.

The batting figures of Imran and Kapil are similar but there is a difference in the bowling figures which I believe gives a true indication of the balance of the teams they lead at the moment. Kapil Dev has had to work far harder for his wickets: in order to restrict runs he has been used more as a stock bowler than a strike bowler. If the batsmen have been difficult to dislodge 'throw the ball to Kapil Dev'. If they are launching an assault on the slow bowlers 'bring on Kapil Dev'. I know the feeling because I used to do the same thing with Alan Davidson – work him harder than preferable because the batsmen were getting away from us. It will be a shame if Kapil Dev is turned into a workhorse rather than a strike force simply because there is no one there to do the extra work. It will be largely up to the Indian selectors to protect him from himself.

Kapil Dev is one of the most enthusiastic cricketers seen in the world in the past 25 years and he allies that enthusiasm to skills out of the ordinary. For a start, he is an Indian fast bowler. There just haven't been many of those over the years. Who on earth would want to bowl fast in that country where grass is at a premium and ground curators spend most of their time rolling all the life out of the pitches on which international teams are to play? When we were there on tour over 20 years ago there was not a pitch with a vestige of grass on the surface, and I'm told life is the same out there now. When England toured India in 1981–82 they lost the First Test in Bombay and in succeeding Tests the spinners and the batsmen were the only ones in the game. It was into this kind of environment Kapil Dev was born and yet his cricket has prospered: he swings the ball both ways, he cuts it both ways, moves it off the seam and has a good slower ball.

The whole cricket world is a stage. What better part of that stage than Lord's for Kapil Dev to perform the miracle for India in the 1983 World Cup and win the Final against West Indies? The match itself was dominated by the Indian bowlers and fielders after their batsmen had been restricted to 183 in their innings. Captaining is difficult when defending so small a total and I was most impressed by Kapil Dev's leadership that day. He was enthusiastic; skilful in his bowling changes and field placings; calm under pressure. The men who appointed him captain can take a bow – he is not always to be a winner, captaining is not like that, but he is a marvellous trier. Best of all, he is a thinker on the game of cricket, or so it seems from his bowling.

In fact, India's victory could not have come at a better time for world cricket. Despite some diffidence in old-timers admitting it, the players of today are very good indeed.

The West Indies, for whom I have a tremendous regard as cricketers, have been, during most of the past eight years, the outstanding cricketers on show. Their fast bowling has been their winning balance, their batting has been entertaining, their fielding electric and their over-rates, at times, appalling.

Australians have sometimes been able to congratulate themselves on having a great team, notably when Ian Chappell was given the captaincy and changed a non-winning record into one where the victories came with pleasurable regularity. With two great fast bowlers in the side, he showed once again the value of that type of attack. If the batting was at times frail at the top, it was not so in the middle where Chappell himself, his brother Greg, and utility players like Ross Edwards, prefaced the arrival of Rodney Marsh, who in those days was a splendid batsman. Their fielding was brilliant to back up Lillee, Thomson and the underrated Max Walker and their over-rates were generally acceptable, though in later years there were some ridiculously slow days.

New Zealand took a long time to win a Test against Australia (1974), then against England in Wellington in 1978, and their cricket over the years has been dogged rather than brilliant. Now led by Geoff Howarth, they are coming of age as Test and limited-overs cricketers, and there has been an extraordinary upsurge in interest in the game in the Shaky Isles.

There has been, in short, a levelling out in the standard of Test cricket the world over, always taking into account South Africa is kept out of the Test arena by politicians who insist on continuing to trade with her but will not permit the playing of sport. If South Africa were allowed to play Test cricket these days I have no doubt their standard would be in line with that of the late 1960s and early 1970s where they beat the pants off good Australian teams.

England have been weakened in recent times by the banning of players who have played in South Africa and the team under Bob Willis which lost to Australia in 1982–83 was only a shadow of the best side available had England not caved in to the sporting blackmail of other countries. The team which beat Australia in 1981 was a very good one, with Ian Botham regaining his touch and a bowling attack led by Willis able to be compared with anything England had recently put on show.

But the real improvers in the cricket world these days come from the sub-continent, where India and Pakistan have turned in some wonderful performances. They have brought on some fine young cricketers and, in Imran Khan and Kapil Dev, have two of the best allrounders ever to play the game.

In the 1983 World Cup, the premier international one-day competition, it was great to see both these teams forcing their way into the semi-finals and then India going on to the Final and eventual victory.

It was the old story I suppose of supporting the underdog and being happy to see the punters take some of the money out of the bookies' bags. Pakistan were reasonably highly thought of in the early betting charts for that event but India began at 66/1, and then dropped to 40/1 where they stayed until their marvellous first-round victory over the West Indies. Pakistan, without Imran Khan's bowling in the competition, were the equivalent of India being without Kapil Dev, but both sides should be proud of the way in which they performed. It is quite possible, as you read this page, that the celebrations are still continuing throughout India . . . certainly they were at the time of writing.

India's cricket, a legacy of the British Raj influence, has always been of the enthusiastic variety. When I first saw an Indian team in action it was at the Sydney Cricket Ground during the Second Test of the 1947–48 series. This was only nine days after India, on a rain-affected pitch, had been demolished by Australia in the opening Test match at Brisbane. Australia, winning the toss, made 382, out of which Bradman made 185, and then Ernie Toshack took 11 for 31 from 19.3 overs. India's two innings were worth just 58 and 98, 29 runs less than Bradman's contribution.

When I sat in the Sheridan Stand that day in Sydney, India had already been bowled out the previous day for a miserable 188 and the first Indian bowler I watched at Test level was Dattaray Phadkar who opened the bowling from the Northern or Paddington end. It was his Test match début and it was a beauty. On the opening day he had delighted us with a blazing 51 in India's small total and had been particularly severe on Colin McCool who eventually had him caught by Miller. It was his brisk partnership with Hari Kischenchand, where they added 70 in better than even time, which gave India the chance to achieve a semi-respectable total.

With uncovered pitches the norm in Australia in those days, Phadkar, Hazare, Amarnath and Mankad took only 46 overs to account for the Australians who, in turn, knocked over seven Indians for only 61 from 37 overs. There was no shortage of action on the three days' play, at least from the point of view of wickets falling. There was a bit of Test history created as well when Mankad ran out non-striker Brown for backing up.

This was the first time India had toured Australia and, from then on, they were generally more effective against Australian teams when playing from Bombay to Calcutta. We called in on India on the way home from the 1956 tour of England, played three Tests and then the first full-scale Australian tour was the one I captained in 1959–60.

Now, with Kapil Dev as their captain, and a shrewd blend of youth and experience in the team, they are looking good. I was very impressed by Kapil Dev's enthusiastic leadership in the World Cup because I have always been an advocate of that type of captaincy. I was never one for standing around, hands in pockets – if a wicket fell I would rather transmit pleasure at the happening to my players and to the spectators.

It was quite a task for Kapil Dev to come into the side and take over from Sunil Gavaskar after the latter had been defeated by Pakistan in the 1982 series in Pakistan. To have the assignment of leading against the West Indies as a first challenge was a daunting prospect and yet, from all acounts, he handled it well enough. Only a few months later he was a hero, with the World Cup held aloft and Gavaskar proudly holding his arm in congratulation.

Since then he has been beaten by the West Indies team and the disappointment that produced in India can be gauged by the hostile reaction from some of the spectators who had only a few months before been cheering him to the echo.

He will again be a winning captain before long and will continue to be a magnificent cricketer at the very highest level.

*   *   *

Kapil Dev and Imran Khan defy the claim of batsmen that bowlers rarely make good Test captains and fast bowlers never do so. Botham, too, has had a stint of captaincy and it would not surprise me if he were given another chance in years to come, particularly as he so clearly enjoyed his responsibilities as captain of Somerset in 1983. Of the four great allrounders of today, the odd man out is Richard Hadlee but it will come as something of a surprise to me if he is not nominated as skipper of New Zealand when Geoff Howarth retires.

Hadlee has had injury problems in recent years, notably the hamstring tear in Australia in 1983 when he and his captain clashed on whether or not he should play in the World Series Cup Finals. In the end Hadlee didn't play but the politics of the non-appearance were intriguing to an outsider. John Wright was the vice-captain of the New Zealand team in an emergency, but it would be extraordinary if Hadlee were not to be given some consideration for the position of captain of the Kiwis before long.

It is significant New Zealand's success has coincided with the emergence of Hadlee as an allrounder of class. The last top-class allrounder to play in New Zealand cricket was John Reid and I have always been of the opinion that, had Reid played in any other Test team, he would have been far more highly regarded than was the case at the conclusion of his career. Hadlee played his first Test match for New Zealand in 1972–73 against Pakistan and his early performances were no better than average. In recent times though, with his move in the off-season to Nottinghamshire, he has matured, as one would expect from a cricketer with his intelligence.

I have always found him to be a cricketer with an inquiring mind, never one necessarily to take at face value all the things these days put to sportsmen around the world. His value to the side led by Geoff Howarth is that he is an attacking cricketer in a group where attacking play is not always part of their make-up. New Zealand cricket is based far more on English cricket than Australian. Their coaches are mostly English and players' techniques are along more correct lines than the sometimes un-orthodox Australians who live only a thousand miles away. (There is no shortage of competitiveness between the two countries however, and that was *before* the underarm incident involving Greg Chappell.) To provide himself with proper competition he went to Nottinghamshire and became a much better bowler, a more sensible batsman and retained his brilliance in the field.

During the World Series Cup in Australia, when New Zealand made up the trio of teams taking part in the 1982–83 limited-overs matches, Hadlee bowled very well but off a shorter run than normal, thus incurring the wrath of some of his own supporters back home who felt anything less than a full run was selling New Zealand short. He still seemed remarkably effective and his bowling exhibition in Perth, on a lively pitch at the conclusion of the preliminary games of that series, really was something to watch.

He was no less effective in England in 1983 in the four-Test series against England. Always a handful for the England batsmen, he took 21 wickets in the series and joined that small band of bowlers who have taken 200 Test wickets. In reaching that landmark in only 44 Tests – only Grimmett, Lillee and Botham have taken fewer Tests to do so – he can justifiably rank as one of the all-time great bowlers.

I expect, in the next three years, we will see him using a short run more and more and that he will be classed as a fast-medium bowler rather than fast, and will become even more of an allrounder. In many ways this will be sad, but he may well have made the decision in the light of his experience in England where it is not necessary to bowl at express pace to have the ball move off the seam. In fact, about ninety per cent of county bowlers slow up rather than gain pace once they are astute enough to realise that to play out their career to its hoped-for length requires commonsense more than a bull-at-a-gate approach.

Of the four allrounders, Hadlee has the silkiest approach to the crease with his bowling. To me, his action is the more likely to stand the physical pressures of bowling fast and, though he may not be able to muster quite as much pace as Imran Khan, he is fast enough even off a shorter run to make any batsman hurry his stroke, and that really is the test of pace bowling.

I thoroughly enjoy watching Richard Hadlee play cricket and it is a delight to commentate on a match where he is taking part. There is only one area where I would like to see him change and that is in becoming a little less unorthodox in his batting. He is a good batsman. Not always is it reflected in his scoring and I haven't the least doubt that a slightly – and I mean slightly – more careful approach to his hitting would make the game even more enjoyable for him. There are times when there comes a slather-and-whack approach more in keeping with a village green or the town 'derby' in the Australian outback.

So saying, I saw him take part in one of the greatest limited-overs fixtures of my time in Adelaide in 1983 when England's batsmen played so magnificently they were able to set Geoff Howarth's team 297 to win in 50 overs. Hadlee was part of the New Zealand batting machine which reached the target and, with the television going live to New Zealand, it was a victory which was written into the list of great New Zealand sporting achievements. Hadlee's 79 runs off 64 balls in 73 minutes was a calculated batting assault which brought about a victory which was as close to an impossible achievement as one could find.

Hadlee's batting was seen in its full glory in England in the summer of 1983 when he headed the New Zealand Test averages at 50.17. Having scored 84 in the First Test and 75 in the historic Second Test, when New Zealand recorded their first Test victory on English soil, he rounded off an outstanding series with bat and ball by scoring an undefeated 92 on the last day of the final Test. New Zealand now stand tall in cricket and Hadlee will go down as one of the great players of the 1970s and 1980s. He is in good company with Botham, Imran and Kapil.

Those six allrounders, Sobers, Miller, Botham, Imran Khan, Kapil Dev and Hadlee were and are magnificent cricketers. They all have about them a magnetic quality for the spectators at the grounds and nowadays the latter four are the stars of the television screen. Miller strode the fields like a playboy Colossus . . . Sobers graced them like a leopard. These men making up the modern-day quartet of allrounders are images of those greats.

What a coincidence it would be if four of the national teams around the cricket world were to be captained by players who could legitimately be classed as allrounders. The interesting thing about Imran Khan is that, if anything, his form seems to have improved with the captaincy responsibility, whereas Botham's form slump coincided with his captaincy stint. This was seized on by many as an excuse that Botham should not remain as captain of England, but I wonder what they said after the tour of Australia in 1982–83 where Botham's form, when he wasn't captain, was disappointing. Nothing I suspect. It was always a convenient story that Botham was affected by the captaincy, but it would have been more accurate by far to say he was affected by losing.

That is the aspect of cricket which brings about the greatest drain of confidence in a captain and, believe me, confidence is everything in captaincy. All you can do is your best, and when the best as a captain does not bring in the victories, despite your own form, whether it be good or bad, then you are ripe for the sacking. Look at it this way. You have a captain and his own form is miserable. He has been out to some of the most remarkable catches in the history of Test cricket, he has had catches dropped from his bowling and, as well, he has not been the recipient of any of the lucky breaks of umpiring. But . . . his team is playing adequately, or even well, and they have been too good for the opposition match after match. Firstly, there will only be a *query* as to whether that man should remain as captain. The query will come in gentle fashion from the selectors, a little more strongly from the watching public and the media.

This is vastly different from a *demand* that he should not remain as captain. The latter comes when the captain is playing reasonably well but his team is losing. At that point tactics come into the argument and the media examine closely every aspect of the matches which have resulted in defeat, and argue, from several hundred yards' distance, whether the captain has been doing a good job. As a winner, the captain has a chance. As a loser, in my opinion he has none. These days the man who leads with imagination but with no success is destined for the chopping-block and that is what very quickly happens to him. Media and sports followers prefer success to failure. It is human nature!

It's difficult for any player of years gone past to appreciate the compounded problems facing captains today because of television. The pressures of the newspapers and radio commitments are very little different from those in my day; press conferences are no more awkward than they were 20 years ago. Where I have the greatest sympathy for players and captains though is with the wonderful medium of television. And it is a wonderful medium because of what it does for the stay-at-home spectator who formerly only gained his knowledge of what went on at the ground through listening to the radio and reading the newspapers that afternoon or the following morning.

In England and Australia all this has changed and every television watcher is now an expert – and why shouldn't they be? If they play cricket there is no reason why they should not know as much about the game of cricket as any other club cricketer who has become a cricket writer, a radio or television announcer or commentator. That is where captains today have their difficulties compounded. It is where the four allrounders I mentioned earlier will have their problems magnified as they move on in their captaincy careers.

5

THE MEDIA TODAY . . .
CRICKET'S GREATEST ALLY

Few cricketers, cricket administrators and followers fully appreciate the benefit to the game of cricket provided by the media. Newspapers devote a tremendous amount of space to the game, radio stations give cricket enormous play and television stations do the same, more obviously if they happen to be televising the game ball by ball. And a glance back at the sections of the media in England and Australia over past years indicates cricket should continue to give thanks to television, newspapers and radio for the amount of publicity it enjoys.

For example, in England, cricket receives far more exposure than any other sport on television – more than 300 hours of air time in all – whereas snooker, the next in line, receives around 150. There are other sports like golf, darts, athletics and tennis and, bear in mind, there are numerous sports receiving no air time at all, and probably not too happy with this state of affairs. It is worth cricket remembering that when television companies look at their ratings they are not interested so much that the sport they are showing may be a traditional one, but that the audiences for whom they are providing the viewing time are appreciative – to the extent of watching.

Cricket has no heavenly right to this; though one wouldn't necessarily gain that impression if listening to some administrators and cricket followers. Cricket has earned part of the right and must continue to fight for it and to deserve it.

* * *

I was standing outside the Channel Nine commentary box in Sydney one December evening in 1982, taking a break after a 30-minute stint at the microphone, when colleague Dick Tucker from the Sydney *Daily Mirror* walked up with some messages concerning the amount of space available for a column the following day. Whilst we were chatting half a dozen youngsters came up and asked for autographs. The first five said thanks and were away and then the last one, a fair-haired, angelic little lad of about 12, collected his book and looked up.

'Did you ever play cricket for Australia, Mr Benaud?' he said. Now what do you do? Cry or laugh? I did neither but merely said yes, I had played up to 1963, which was going to be well before he had been born. 'Oh,' he said, 'that's great. I thought you were just a television commentator on cricket.' Now it could have been his first cricket match, so I tried that as a question. 'No.' He had been to watch every match he could in the past three years and he had seen every possible match on television. Hence the question. He had never seen me in cricket gear and knew me only as the man who did the cricket on Channel Nine. He scampered away with a 'thank you' thrown over his shoulder.

It was quite logical when I sat down to think about it. At 12 years of age he had his own heroes and they were all of the modern day. His sports reading was of cricket books published about recent tours, and the more immediate problems he faced were involved in deciding which of Greg Chappell and Dennis Lillee was the greater cricketer – Benaud and Davidson were simply names. He didn't read the *New South Wales Cricket Association Yearbook*, no longer printed, or *Wisden*. Instead he read of contemporary heroes.

Since 1977 there has been an astonishing upsurge of interest in cricket in Australia. The game has held its traditional watchers but scores of thousands of new devotees have been attracted to the game by promotion, television and limited-overs cricket. Many of these new watchers are people who previously never had the slightest interest in a game which might be played over five full days without a result being achieved. They are extremely valuable to Australian cricket.

I have lost count of the number of Australian citizens, and people who have migrated there from other countries, who have told me in taxis, on sidewalks and in restaurants how much they are now enjoying a game for which previously they had no feeling whatsoever. What has happened in Australia is that, initially, the non-cricket-loving people have been attracted to the game by the one-day matches, on the basis they either are unable to go to a Test match or they do not want to go. Later, their interest heightened, they have started watching Test matches. This has applied also to their children and suddenly we have a whole new range of spectators.

Television has been the prime mover in this revolution and, far from 'the box' having a detrimental effect on attendances in *this* sport, the opposite has occurred. Parents and children who had no interest in the game have seen the night matches televised from the Sydney Cricket Ground, and day matches from other grounds, and have been instantly intrigued. When the matches come to their own state they have been keen to go to watch and, from this point of view, television and the clicking turnstiles have been complementary. There has been a conscious effort made by the promotion company, PBL Marketing, and the Australian Cricket Board to grasp the attention of youngsters throughout the country and, in turn, to have them interest their parents. And, as far as I can see, it has worked so far.

One of the most interesting aspects of the programme in Australia these days is to see what happens when the limited-overs matches are played in Melbourne prior to the school holidays and then when the Finals are played at a time when younger fans are back at school. The attendances are affected and it is not only the children who do not turn up. They are often the ones who persuade the adults to come to the ground and, with school back in session, the attendance is always down. The same applies in Sydney when there is a night match played when the kids have gone back to school after their holidays. Fewer spectators turn up, even though the match itself might be potentially more interesting.

There is a considerable difference these days in the way a youngster is attracted to cricket . . . if indeed he or she is attracted to the game. One of the problems cricket has always had is that some of its supporters believe they, and the game, have a god-given right to exist to the exclusion of all else. They label themselves as traditional cricket lovers and therefore anything not in their line of thinking on the game is regarded as, at best, heresy. Many of them are genuine, some are poseurs and some are simply a pain in the lower part of the neck. But they are determined to resist any change at all and indeed fight it with everything at their command. They detest limited-overs cricket or ideas thought of after the 1930s and would give anything, or almost anything, to have sponsorship, with its atmosphere of grubby money, thrown right out of the game they adore.

They have not the slightest interest in the fact that cricket these days really does have a struggle for survival with all the other sports challenging for a share of the spectator's dollar. They deliberately ignore the fact that the only way the game of cricket can continue at any level above club is by a shrewd combination of spectators paying their money at the gate, television fees, sponsorship fees and promotion of the game to attract the uncommitted sports follower. Cricket is a marvellous game. How it continues to exist in spite of people like this is one of the wonders of our time. How the more far-sighted administrators manage to keep their cool is quite remarkable.

The game of cricket has changed in Australia in the 35 years since I started playing, but that is hardly likely to come as a great surprise to readers. There was a set pattern for youngsters when I was a lad and it involved being interested in cricket in the summer and football in the winter, and Lord help you if you wanted to do anything else. At Parramatta High School I used to play some minor Rugby football but my main love was soccer – and that was *before* I had the chance to see some of the great soccer matches played in England at the start of the 1953 and 1956 tours. There was no scope at school though for soccer so I took it up at weekends. There was no real scope for other sports like swimming because schools in those days could not afford swimming pools and it was a long, long train ride to the nearest pool. Athletics was okay in the break between the end of the football season and the start of the cricket season, and that was the degree of importance it was accorded then before television brought the Olympic Games and the Commonwealth Games from one side of the world to the other.

In 1946, when I was in my last year at Parramatta High School, there were eight High Schools in the Sydney metropolitan area. Now there are almost three hundred. There used to be a High Schools' competition in first-grade cricket and there still is, but now it has to be divided into many sections.

There are then many more youngsters who have the chance these days to be interested in or play higher-level school cricket in Australia. They are very well off. First of all, as cricket followers, they have the pleasure of watching on television the Test and one-day international matches. That creates an enormous amount of interest among Australian schoolchildren and it is reflected in the follow-up gate attendances and the sale of cricket-oriented matters like books, cricket gear, flags, caps, jackets and badges, plus the cricket magazines which abound throughout the country.

There are a tremendous number of junior cricket teams playing the game now in Australia. In fact, as an aftermath of World Series Cricket, we had an upsurge in interest at that level, to the point where there were teams formed which were then unable to find a place in a competition, such was the lack of availability of grounds. In the past seven years there has been an unheard-of rise in the number of players taking part in matches, the number of teams registered and the amount of gear bought in order to play. And all this is taking part with the game of cricket in one way fighting against television, at the same time as television is assisting it in regard to the young player.

What happens is the youngster is attracted to cricket by the games he watches on television but then the game itself has to battle for his interest against the other programmes to be seen on television. I believe television to be a wonderful medium for the sport but there are so many other good things to be watched on the screen, or at different sporting arenas, that cricket still has to work hard to retain the interest of the youngster. There are other attractions these days too which tend to make the old-timers throw up their hands in frustration – they only knew cricket in the summer and football in the winter.

One of the most noticeable effects television has had on the game is in the way the youngsters approach their heroes. Now I wasn't worried by the remark posed to me at the Sydney Cricket Ground, 'Did you ever play cricket for Australia Mr Benaud?' but the boy's father or mother of around my own era would probably have been mortified and full of apologies. My mother and father would have been in earlier times. No apology necessary in 1984.

This is the age in which we live. Some would say a question of that kind showed a lack of respect or knowledge. Not a bit of it as far as I am concerned. What it did was show an inquiring mind, and I'm all in favour of inquiring minds in our young sportsmen. Perhaps that is because I had an inquiring mind when I came into first-class cricket but was not necessarily allowed to exercise it in the same way as young players are now.

Today young cricketers come into a Sheffield Shield team and a county team in England and they are articulate and firm. Very few of us were that way 35 years ago and it is not at all surprising when you consider the type of society in which we lived. First of all there was the stricture of never speaking until spoken to – a hang-up from the Victorian era – and you could also note that little boys should be seen and not heard.

When I came into the New South Wales team in 1948 that was very much the pattern. Because of my upbringing I was happy to sit quietly and be seen and not heard, but I would not in any way recommend it for the young players of today. And there is of course no way they would act in that manner. Life is far more democratic for the youngster and the young first-class cricketer now. The young cricket-watcher today in Australia grows up with the televising of his heroes and there is no question as well that he copies them. When Dennis Lillee and Jeff Thomson were ripping into the English batsmen in Australia in 1974–75 there was a sudden surge of young fast bowlers in the ranks of school and junior cricket. It has kept going that way because there have been more and more fast bowlers make their names in world cricket and fewer and fewer slow bowlers.

Radio was the medium which captured the imaginations of youngsters in my day. In Australia it has hardly varied from the 1940s when I used to hear ABC commentator Mel Morris broadcasting the cricket from the Melbourne Cricket Ground. The technical side of things has, of course, changed for the better, but there is not a great deal more a radio commentator can do than describe the play to the best of his ability.

Some, like cricketers, have more ability than others and at their respective peaks the best I have heard in any country have been John Arlott in England and Alan McGilvray in Australia. There have been others in various countries who did a sound job but none of them could match Arlott and McGilvray in their younger days. The odd thing was they were from such different backgrounds. Arlott, never having played the game at first-class level, was a former policeman possessing a way with words and a splendid knowledge of the English language. McGilvray was good enough to play for and captain New South Wales ahead of some very talented cricketers. He became an ABC broadcaster early in his cricket career in the days when the players were allowed to do radio and newspaper work at the same time as they were playing – they are still able to do that today but with a number of restrictions on what they are able to say.

Memory plays tricks as one ages but I seem to recall hearing in North Parramatta Arlott's voice in 1946 when cricket was re-established after the war and India toured England. The match was at the Oval and the description of play I remember hearing was that of Vijay Merchant, the Indian opening batsman, being run out by Denis Compton, who raced in and kicked the ball from mid-on on to the stumps at the bowler's end. Was it Arlott?

Two years later his voice was certainly in our living-room at Parramatta when the Australians played the first match of their tour at Worcester, Ray Lindwall bowling the opening over of the tour to Cooper and Kenyon and having Kenyon lbw with his second ball. The joy of a 16-year-old Australian cricket lover knew no bounds, even though in those days the crackling and roaring of the wireless made something of a comedy of the broadcast by modern-day standards. But it was the best we had then and we were not to know the future benefits of undersea cables and satellites beaming static free commentaries from any part of the world. Nor were we to know the benefits of television, for it was not to arrive in Australia for another eight years and then only in black and white.

Before television arrived life was much easier for newspaper men and radio broadcasters because there was no way of checking up that everything was exactly as stated. Nowadays it is no good saying the ball was played in front of square-leg if it has been played behind because people can look at the television and see instantly that it is not so. In November 1958, before television arrived in India, the Maharaj Kumar of Vizianagram was broadcasting the First Test match between India and West Indies in Bombay. Roy Gilchrist, later to be sent home because of bowling an excess of bumpers and beamers, opened the bowling and one such head-high delivery was greeted with the words to the listening millions, 'Oh . . . ohhh . . . did you see that one?'

Television's effect on cricket was not really to be seen for many years until, first of all, colour TV arrived and then cricket matches were shown to the public as entertainment rather than a closed shop for the mystics of the game. In Australia the only constant televised coverage known to the public for many years was presented by the ABC. There were times when the commercial stations provided a coverage, indeed I worked for a time with Channel Seven and then Channel Ten, the latter giving an excellent telecast in competition with and superior to the Government-funded network.

With the advent of World Series Cricket in Australia in 1977 the coverage of cricket matches was changed for ever more. And for the better. It was changed quite deliberately in order to provide as much information as possible for the viewers, on the basis that they might not be as well versed in the intricacies of the game as, say, the cricket correspondent of the Sydney *Daily Telegraph* or the London *Times*.

The TV commentary box at any ground in Australia now bears no relation to the ones of the past, where all that was needed were two monitors, a commentator and a microphone. We still have those but, as well, have a full shift of commentators who have been in the Test arena and are able to give a first-hand idea of what happens out in the centre.

Nine Network Executive Producer David Hill has introduced computers to the commentary box so viewers are able to see up-to-date statistics at any time of the day and, more important, they are able to see the score no matter when they may switch on their television set. He has come up with some brilliant ideas, notably the digital score in the top right-hand corner of the screen which ticks over as each run is made, and the box showing the batsmen running between wickets in the top left-hand corner of the screen. These two items, devised solely for viewers to add to their enjoyment of the match, have brought more favourable comment in Australia than anything I have known in years. People were stopping me in the street in 1981 to say what a difference the scoreboard in the right-hand corner made to their cricket-watching. Prior to that, they had been at the mercy of the commentator who himself was under restraint from giving the score too often.

I have been part of the media for the past 29 years and the last six have been the most enjoyable I have known. That is due in the major part to having had the opportunity to work with David Hill in Australia and with the late David Kenning and Nick Hunter of the BBC, and to be part of developing a technique to improve the enjoyment of scores of thousands of people who watch cricket on television in both countries. Hill, although not a first-class cricketer, is an outstanding producer, a man possessing real flair who originally attacked the problem of televised cricket as one who liked the game but had always been thoroughly dissatisfied and bored with the way it had been presented. There are still occasional production hiccups, as there are in any walk of life, but in Australia the telecasts have set a standard for the rest of the world.

I find correspondence from television viewers over a season generally works out about 50–50. Half of them write in to say how much they have enjoyed the telecasts and commentaries in Australia or England, the other half write in to suggest how they can be made better. Some of the suggestions are constructive, some fanciful, some would be extremely painful, but the viewers' interest is there because the letters pour in week after week.

The televising of cricket is quite different from that of other sports like football and horse racing where the action is very fast – cricket tends to meander along, although there may be some high points in the day. Usually you are required not to give a running commentary, as is the case on radio, but to provide comments at what you hope is exactly the right time. I believe you should only talk when you can add to the picture on the screen and it is possibly for that reason I have the reputation of talking less than most others working on cricket telecasts.

It is, I can assure you, very difficult to get the correct balance. You have, sitting out there, children, mothers and fathers, some of whom may not have seen a cricket telecast before or may be watching it in their first season – they want every bit of information you can give them. Then there is the person who might play club cricket, knows a lot about the game and requires a mid-way commentary – he wants some information but not nearly as much as the novice. Finally, there is the one who considers he knows everything about the game and a lot more besides, and he wants to be told nothing.

Television cricket commentaries are by far the most difficult of any, mainly because you have to try to strike a balance of conversation with the person to whom you're talking through the lens. That person needs to be a blend of everyone I have listed, requiring all the information available and, at the same time, needing none, so from that you may appreciate it is a difficult job.

It is necessary for television commentators to provide a professional opinion on the play, with an accurate assessment of the skills of the batsmen, bowlers and captains. I've always felt that humour should be kept to the throw-away line variety. Everyone has a different sense of humour and because the picture is there in front of the viewer, he can see for himself if there is something amusing. It is another matter if you are writing for a newspaper or broadcasting on radio where nothing is visible. Radio commentators and newspaper writers must paint a picture for the people who are going to digest their verbal or written essays. Television commentators would last only one day if they tried to paint a picture because the picture is already there.

One thing a television commentator must always remember is that he is sitting in a commentary box and his boss is the Executive Producer who is down in the van. There is only one boss! BBC Television have come up with some fine cricket producers since I began visiting England. We started back in the early 1960s with Phil Lewis, who has now gone on to greater things with special events and shows like 'Miss World' and 'Miss Universe'. Then there was David Kenning, who tragically passed away in early 1983 after a leg operation following a car accident. When David had moved on to handle the golf telecasts, Nick Hunter came in as Executive Producer and, over the years, the three men have done a magnificent job for a vast audience in the United Kingdom. All in their own way were brilliant and Kenning was an outstanding disciplinarian, something which may well have been a spin-off from having worked under Bryan Cowgill for so long in other avenues of BBC Television. He was always keen to emphasise to commentators that our job was to identify, illustrate and add to a picture for the benefit of viewers.

One day at Lord's there was a nasty crowd disturbance during an England–West Indies Test match and I forgot for the moment we were a camera short. Torn between keeping one eye on the monitor and describing what was occurring there, and keeping my other eye on what was happening away to my right, I committed the cardinal sin of describing the latter before the cameras arrived. By the time the camera made it the crowd disturbance magically had ceased and in my left ear I had Kenning's gentle voice saying, 'How *very* interesting, Richie – and how nice it would have been to show the millions sitting in front of their television sets the picture you were describing so beautifully.'

I never forgot it, which is one of the things the television commentator must do – he must learn from mistakes made, and Kenning was one of the finest teachers I ever had. Nick Hunter has a wonderful feel for the game and has an unerring touch for what is best editorially.

Producers work extraordinarily long hours during a Test match, beginning two days before the game gets under way when vans crammed with equipment arrive at the ground. By the time I get to the commentary box, an hour before play starts, hours of hard and frustrating work will have been successfully concluded by Hunter – or Hill – and his men, so that right on the dot of 10.55 a.m. the programme can begin. From that moment on the producer guides the commentator with all the expertise available to him. It is worth remembering a cricket telecast could actually go on without a commentator – but it could never go on without a producer.

Fewer cameras are used for a telecast in England than in Australia and in England the siting of the cameras is rather more critical. Two are generally positioned at the same end as the commentators, with a master camera as close behind a line drawn through the stumps as possible. The height of the cameras and the commentators is usually about 30 feet. The main camera provides a picture which includes bowler and batsman and it can be used to show a close-up of the batsman as he takes strike and waits for the delivery. Once the batsman has played his stroke this camera provides the producer with a picture of the batsmen running between the wickets. A second camera, its lens not so strong, is sited near the master camera and is used mainly for fielding. It is used by the producer to give viewers a picture of whichever fielder is doing the catching or chasing. For a start, the viewer needs to be able to see the whole of what is happening on this camera and the producer uses that cameraman when the batsmen are going for quick singles somewhere close to the 22 yards of the pitch itself. If a television station sends cameras to a ground, to do a proper job for their news or a special sports show they could get by with those two cameras and, indeed, for many years did so.

During the match two other cameras around ground level are used to give sidelights to the action. One of them, near extra cover, provides close-ups of the field in contrast with the more elevated camera near the commentary box. The other camera, at rightangles to the pitch, provides close-up shots of everything going on around the pitch area, or anything else the producer might desire. The positioning at the ground is dependent on the setting sun.

In England these days there is also an extra camera at the opposite end to where the main cameras are situated. This allows the producer, in the case of lbw decisions or catches at the wicket, to give a clear picture for the viewer when the action would otherwise be masked by the batsman's pads or the back of the fielder at slip as he takes a catch.

The captions come from a special caption-mixer and now, in England, there is a computer set-up as well which provides instant information on a variety of matters, ranging through the statistics of the players taking part in the match at that moment to those established by the giants of the past.

The Executive Producer in England works from the Outside Broadcasts van; in Australia he is in the commentary box and the Director is in the van. David Hill, Vice-President Sport of Channel Nine, is Executive Producer of the cricket in Australia and his preparation for a day's play always begins the previous evening.

'In a Test match I have a post mortem after the day's play with Director Brian Morelli and we look at what went wrong, how the commentators sounded, what was happening with them, ideas which worked or little production tricks we tried, the performance of the cameramen and also the state of the match. Then, next morning, the work day itself starts at about 8 a.m. when I do a weather check and arrive at the ground at 8.30. Brian Morelli and I have a discussion concerning the coming day's play and a confirmation of what went on the day before. Prior to arriving at the ground I will have checked the telex machine to see when the BBC or the NZBC will be coming to us. Then I work out the commentators' roster which varies from day to day so there is deliberately no obvious pattern with one commentator following another. I like to have someone lively at the end of a day's play – someone like Bill Lawry – as the ball-by-ball commentator so, in the event of dreary cricket, the whole thing cannot disintegrate into a boring last half-hour for television viewers.

'I've probably made a decision on the opening sequence whilst driving to the ground. I'll talk that through with Brian and the tape men who operate the three on-site tape machines we have, then if there is any fancy editing to be done they can get it under way. The opening could be, say, a music sequence – the classic example of that was when Derek Underwood was sent in as night-watchman in the Second Test at the SCG in January 1980 and he valiantly survived the final 40 minutes. What we did that night for the next morning's opening was to cut up segments of 'Deadly' facing these slings and arrows of outrageous fortune directed by Mr D. K. Lillee to a background of 'Land of Hope and Glory'. If a player has done something spectacular in the previous day's play – say David Hookes has hit fours or sixes, Viv Richards has batted brilliantly or Dennis Lillee has taken eight wickets – that is cut together and the cutter commences his job at about 8.30 a.m.

'Around nine o'clock I meet with Irving Rosenwater to find out what statistics, if any, are likely to be relevant to that particular day's play. That means I can put the details on a card and give them to Jane Prior, the operator of the Electronic Character Generator, so everything can be standing by if a statistic is needed. I also talk to Jane and the computer operator Cheryl Ammann, my Personal Assistant, about what statistics are likely to be needed and double-check liaison between Irving, the computer and the ECG to establish everything is up to date with relevant information on the players taking part.

'At 9.15 a number of things happen while I'm working in the commentary box. The floor manager goes to the teams' dressing-rooms to talk to the managers to see if there are any team changes, injuries, announced alterations in the batting order, etcetera, and when that comes through it is automatically transferred to the ECG for the opening sequence and for use during the day. Also about that time, Brian Morelli is meeting with the cameramen – nine cameras, therefore nine cameramen. He will sit down and discuss with them the previous day's tapes and either praise or constructively criticise the work. He is talking as well to the Camera Control Unit people and the technicians concerning any problems we may have found – if, say, there's been flare in one of the lenses or the mid-wicket camera might have been too high or too low, that must be adjusted to his satisfaction.

'Following our 8.30 discussion, he is also talking to particular cameramen, perhaps the two slips cameramen, regarding any "effects" we feel we might need during the day. That could be a bowler–batsman split screen, or batsman–batsman split screen. It is necessary to let them know that, when we call for it, cameraman "A", who is covering the northern end slip-cordon, has to favour one batsman left of frame, and cameraman "B", doing the south slips' cordon, has to favour right of frame, so the vision-mixer can do a straight take without complications. At that stage, there may be player-identification needed by a cameraman. Perhaps a player is new to the team or, if not to the team, it may be a player new to the cameraman.

'While many people are doing a hundred other things to make it work, at 9.30 I have a discussion with the downstream controller who is Neville Bull. I tell him what we need for the opening sequence, say the previous day's dismissals or any chosen incidents. Or, if there has been an exciting period of play – perhaps the last ball there's been some incident of note – I'll have him replay that one hundred per cent off the tapes. It all sets the scene for scores of thousands who may not have seen it the day before. Information for the viewer is of vital importance.

I will have a discussion with Neville about what we want on standby – if, for example, Wessels is batting, I may suggest Neville should assemble Kepler's dismissals from the other Tests in case a leg-stump attack is mounted by the bowlers. If that does happen, then Neville will be able to roll in Kepler's three dismissals for commentators to offer their ideas on the tactics now being employed.

'That takes us through to around 10 o'clock and we are now out recording Tony Greig's pitch report, an innovation which has proved very popular with Australian viewers. If it's a Test match, we'll prepare the graph to show what's happened to the pitch moisture over the preceding days, the standard block graph showing if moisture is leaving the pitch rapidly or slowly, and we will show temperature, humidity and wind readings. We also ask the tapes' section – who by now have finished cutting their opening sequence – to go back to the previous day or days and give us a frozen frame of the pitch so we can demonstrate how much the surface is breaking up. Viewers in Australia have been delighted with information which for years they were told about but never saw. It's another aspect of trying to involve the viewer in the mystery of the game.

'Now it's 10.15. I've talked to Ian Chappell and he is to interview a featured player for the opening, so the back-pack camera moves from the centre of the ground out to the area in front of the players' dressing-room. The interview might be with Tom Hogan if we think it's a day where the pitch is taking spin, or with Geoff Lawson if it's a fast bowler's pitch. If we're covering a one-day match, Ian will be out on the ground an hour before the start to record the toss. Also, at 10.15, while we're doing this recording and making sure our on-site tapes are checked, Brian Morelli and the mixer operator are discussing and rehearsing any special "effects" which may be used during play. Using the frames stored, they make certain we have the shot dropped in of the batsmen running between wickets while the ball is racing out towards the boundary.

'10.20 a.m. The senior commentator, Richie Benaud, has by now been in the commentary box for 20 minutes. Hopefully, that is! I'll have a discussion with him about the opening sequence and make sure anything which has to be rehearsed in the way of voice-over is organised. That takes us to 10.30. I then have a brief talk with Jane Prior and Cheryl Ammann and check again if they have any problems with the ECG or computer and that the statistics are locked in.

'10.35 is a final check downstream with Neville Bull for the stations right around Australia. I make sure also there has been no alteration to the "in-time" for BBC and NZBC and again confirm when they are coming to us. At 10.40 I try to phone QTQ Brisbane, where they do our highlights' package, and have a quick chat about the previous day's highlights. I confirm with them if they should record the first ten minutes of the telecast because there might be an interview I feel will be applicable to that day's play.

'That takes us to 10.45. Make sure the senior commentator is in position in the in-vision section of the studio and that his lapel microphone is working and his "lazy" microphone and special monitor are in good order and in the correct position. Make sure the lights are checked, make sure the commentators' lip-ribbon microphones are checked, clear the commentary box of all extraneous personnel, make sure the talk-back to Director is working, make sure the commentators' lazy microphones to the Director are working, do a final check with everyone and clear the intercom of talking. At 10.46 go through the opening sequence once more so the senior commentator hears and sees it, the Director hears it and I approve it. Relax for 60 seconds and then we're on air at 10.50. *Away we go.*'

David, seven years ago, produced ten points for Channel Nine commentators which could almost go under the heading of commandments. They are certainly commands. I would not dream of picking up a microphone without bearing them in mind, even though I still retain an individual style.

1. Keep one eye on the monitor, one eye on the field of play, and your third eye on your tongue and your fellow commentator.

2. Never talk over your fellow commentator – just as your fellow commentator shall never talk over you.

3. Remember, silence is the greatest weapon you have in your armoury.

4. Listen to your director with an ear as keen as a ferret's – just as your director will listen avidly to the commentary, thus ensuring your magic phrases are pertinent to the viewer's picture.

5. Think constantly of voice-over cassettes, animations, computers and anything which will help the viewer enjoy the telecast.

6. Make your commercial throws as tight as the proverbial fish's ear, so no ball is missed.

7. Remember this is a game of many and varied hues. As a commentator you will keep foremost in your mind that cricket contains venom and courage, drama and humour, and you will not be backward in bringing out in your commentary those aspects of the noble and ancient pastime.

8. This marvellous game has many by-ways and secret things – and you as a commentator will remember that multitudes of viewers do not understand some aspects of the art, therefore you will endeavour always to add to the picture on the screen.

9. Remember at all times that, having practised this ancient art at the highest possible level, you may occasionally dwell on the sacred mysteries to the utter confusion of the uninformed. Therefore, you will keep it simple, never talking down to a viewer by using those bastard phrases: 'of course', 'as you can see', *or* 'as my fellow commentator said'.

10. Also remember your producer and director, aged and infirm as they may be, could ask you to do things which, at the time, you feel you do not completely understand. Although your producer and director may not be properly introduced into the subtle nuances of your ancient game of cricket, they have *been introduced into the peurile art of communications, so . . . concentrate, and make it work!*

No one wants every television commentator to sound the same. But, to keep in mind the ten points D. Hill has made is to make the viewing for millions that much more enjoyable. And never, under any circumstances, talk down to a camera lens. Behind that lens are a million viewers and they know there is nothing worse than a pompous cricketer, a pompous sporting official or an overbearing cricket commentator.

All can be cut down to size at different times, and I particularly like the story of a television commentator, nice guy but not getting on too well with his producer, who, for a variety of reasons, was about to leave the programme. The scene was the very last evening the programme was going on the air with the two of them working together – or so-called working together. The frosty count-down came at 'Ten, nine . . . five, four, three, two, your fly's undone, *on air*,' and the camera caught magnificently the action of the commentator fumbling desperately at his lower groin.

No such problems over the years in working with Lewis, Kenning and Hunter in the UK and Hill and Brian Morelli in Australia. It has been a pleasure and a privilege to be part of the action.

* * *

Those 28 years I mention have seen dramatic changes in all aspects of the media. I started as a newspaperman with the Sydney *Sun* in 1956 after working as a clerk with the John Fairfax organisation for the previous three years. I had been requesting a transfer to the Editorial side during the three years and had done some freelance work for cricket magazines in that time.

My hope was to follow Keith Miller into the media world but I wanted to learn about journalism in the different areas of the newspaper, not purely in sport.

With this in mind, before I left for the 1956 tour of England, I went to see Lindsay Clinch, the Executive Editor of the *Sun*, to ask once again if I could have a transfer from the Counting House to Editorial. 'Come and see me when you get back from the tour,' he said, 'and we'll see what happens – might be able to fit you somewhere into Sport.' 'I'd rather be on News if possible,' was my reply as he waved me away.

That was in March 1956 and, after Jim Laker had taken his record haul of wickets against us in the series, the team had to back up for a short tour of Pakistan and India on the way home. Just what we felt like! The Board of Control in Australia organised that tour to last *eight months*. Can you believe that, even in those days when cricketers were regarded by adminis- trators more as chattels than sportsmen, any player could be asked to be away from home for eight months? The answer of course was the one voiced some years later by the Australian Cricket Board Secretary Alan Barnes: 'No one has to go on tour . . . there are thousands of players out there who would willingly go away for months on end and for no payment either!' That was the type of thinking pervading cricket for a long time and it has only relaxed a little since 1977 after the players were given more say in how sport should be run in a democratic society.

When the English section of the tour was finished in 1956 there was a three-week break before flying to Karachi for a Test against Pakistan on a matting surface, followed by three Tests in India. I took the chance in those three weeks to organise myself a television course with the BBC, who then ran a very good school for aspiring directors, floor managers, commentators and others. I wasn't able to have a place on the course itself but Tom Sloan, who was Head of Light Entertainment at the time, drew up a programme for me on the basis that in the three weeks available I wanted to learn as much as possible about the medium.

It was one of the best things I have ever done and although I was weary at the end of the 21 days, with a daily itinerary running from 11 a.m. to midnight, it was worth every moment. I did Outside Broadcasts watching Alec Weeks and Dennis Monger, Drama with Leslie Jackson and a host of other things I hoped one day might come in handy back in Australia.

It was the year television started in Australia and after we arrived home from India I had my first experience of Australian television technique. Immediately Keith Miller stepped off the plane he had a microphone thrust into his hand and was asked by his new employers, Channel Nine, to interview his Australian team-mates on the tarmac. It was hardly surprising he struggled a little.

I wasted no time getting back into the *Sun* newspaper office the day after arriving home, although I was feeling far from well. I had been bitten by some insect – a mosquito I suppose – in Bombay and had gone down with a raging fever the first night of the final Test match. The late Jim Burke, with whom I was rooming, said later he had never heard such frightening moans and groans on the first two nights of the match. He was unable to sleep but it didn't seem to do him a great deal of harm as he made 161 when we batted. I was almost out on my feet after bowling a lot of overs in the second innings and I hardly knew where I was by the time we boarded the plane. It turned out I had a form of dengue fever which recurred at lengthening intervals for the next 12 months. Not very pleasant because I never knew when the next attack would arrive.

At any rate, I went in to see Lindsay Clinch by appointment, anxious to know if there was any chance now of moving out of the Counting House and into Editorial. There was no better Editor in Australian newspapers then and I know of none better since that time. But he was tough. Very tough. 'Sit down,' he said. 'Want to write do you?' I gave what I hoped were the right answers to his staccato questions and then he said, 'All right, we want you to write a column for the sports department each week; they'll get someone to ghost you if necessary.'

He probably sensed my jaw had dropped a mile and he certainly sensed I was still sitting there. 'I'd like to work on Police Rounds and News,' I said. He looked at me for what seemed like minutes but was only seconds. 'Okay, go and see Jack Toohey the News Editor.' I was now beaming, said 'Thanks very much' and turned for the door. His voice came quietly from behind me, 'He's expecting you.' No wonder he had the reputation of being a 'tough little bastard'. He had known exactly what he wanted me to do but had given me the chance to accept lazing around the sports department having, on the strength of my name, a ghosted column appear once a week in the *Sun*.

When I went to see Jack Toohey he told me Mr Clinch had said I would be in and he had already spoken with Noel Bailey, the Police Roundsman, on the basis I would be working with him until further notice. Sometimes you have a lucky break in life. This for me was a *very* lucky break. Noel Bailey was one of the greatest journalists in Australia, his speciality was Police Rounds and he was highly respected in his job.

I worked under him for several years and it is a direct result of this training that I am now able to pick up a telephone at a cricket match anywhere in the world and, if necessary, dictate 40 paragraphs without referring to notes in order to catch an edition. On Police Rounds, racing for an edition, you do not always have time to make full notes if you are covering murders, assaults, accidental deaths, fires and any kind of news story which breaks close to the deadline. That training was wonderful and Bailey made certain I had a good grasp of the basics of writing for newspapers before he let me out of his sight. I had a later stint on the sub-editors' table and on Courts and Industrial Rounds, but the area I enjoyed most and where I learned most was with Noel Bailey on Police Rounds.

I also wrote a sports column for the *Sun* for 13 years until a difference of opinion on the interpretation of the wording of my contract after a journalists' strike led my wife and me to branch out in 1969 into the world of freelance media and sports consultancy work. My wife Daphne had been through two hard but most beneficial training schools, first as a television production assistant with the BBC and then as secretary to E. W. Swanton, the cricket correspondent of the London *Daily Telegraph*. No one could ask for a better grounding and the business moves along steadily today with a number of newspapers to write for in Australia, *News of the World* in England, BBC and Channel Nine Network to work for in television, and radio work to do for the Macquarie Network in Sydney plus various clients in the international sports consultancy field.

It is newspapers which remain my great love despite the fact they have changed so much in recent years. Our work pattern in Australia is that we are up every day at 6 a.m. which is the time the three morning newspapers arrive. The first edition of the *Mirror* in Sydney has a deadline around 7.30 a.m., for the Adelaide *News* it is 8 a.m. and for the *Melbourne Herald* 8.30 a.m., so whatever stories are to be filed for those newspapers must go through very quickly on the telex machine. If we are away from Sydney the one thing I make certain of each evening is to order all the morning papers. I guess old journalists cannot do without their morning fix!

One of my reasons for being so fond of newspaper work is because it was the section of the media in which I started. Another is that there is a real challenge there in beating the opposition with an exclusive story. Although the same *type* of challenge exists with television and radio, more often than not the newsreader will be presenting the story. In newspapers you are on your own and there is nothing to beat seeing your name under the headline of a scoop.

There seem to be fewer scoops in the cricket writing world these days because journalists on tour tend to keep close to one another. It was not always so. My great mate on tour was Bob Gray who, back in the 1960s, was the cricket writer for the Sydney *Daily Mirror* at the same time as I was the cricket writer for the Sydney *Sun*. When I retired from playing cricket we were in competition and we had plenty of fun as well as getting through a tremendous amount of work. We never, but never, shared stories. If you were scooped it cost you the bill for dinner at a good restaurant.

In 1964 at Lord's rain washed out play on the first two days of the Second Test, with Australia having the Ashes in hand from the previous series — well, in hand in the Long Room anyway. It rained so heavily on the opening day that, although the second day was fine enough to play, the pitch, because of poor drainage and covering, was saturated and there was no play on the Friday.

Sitting in the press box at Lord's that afternoon, Gray and I still had to file stories for the papers back in Australia and there were simply no stories around . . . just a vague rumour about an MCC meeting. We had arranged to have dinner together with friends at the then Fisherman's Wharf restaurant in Knightsbridge at 9 p.m. after all our stories had been sent from Cable and Wireless on the Embankment. Gray asked me if I were going back to the flat to work or intended to finish writing at the ground – which was our normal procedure. He said he was going back to his flat – and promptly disappeared, saying he would see me at nine o'clock.

Trying to come up with a story about two days of no play wasn't easy, looking out over the deserted ground, and there was this nagging rumour about MCC . . . what the hell was Gray up to? Going home to work was right out of character for him. He was a press box writer. Instinct took me down the press box stairs, along behind the pavilion and up to the Australian dressing-room where I asked to see Ray Steele the team manager. He had been my assistant manager in 1961 but ethical considerations meant I couldn't ask him straight out whether Gray had been to see him on any subject. Instead I took a 'flyer' and pulled out a Noel Bailey type statement.

'That's a big story about the two lost days.' 'How the hell did you get on to that?' Steele said. 'I thought Gray had it on his own.' 'No,' I said, 'I've got it, but I just need one or two of the fine details to finish it off.' 'Sure,' he said, 'so long as you've already got it' . . . and went on to tell me that MCC, on behalf of the English Board of Control, had asked for an extension of playing time over the last three days to make up for the time lost on the first two.

Steele had been surprised and had quickly declined, on the basis that Tests were played under a code of rules drawn up before the start of the series and therefore any variation merely because of rain would have set a dangerous precedent. There was also the little matter of rain having seeped under the covers and the chance of Australia being caught on a real 'turner'. He added he didn't think Australia should be put in this position merely because the covering at Lord's, the home of cricket, was inadequate and inefficient. (Nothing it seemed had changed a great deal 16 years later because for the Centenary Test the covering at Lord's, the home of cricket, was still inadequate and inefficient enough to have a day's play curtailed.)

This was a good story and was ideal for my newspapers back in Australia so I typed it up, made my way to Cable and Wireless, sent it off and then hot-footed it to the restaurant. Gray was already there. 'Beer pal?' he said. 'Thanks.' 'I think it might be your shout tonight Benaud. What angle did you go on?' 'Well,' I said, 'I didn't have anything to write so finished up with some second-rate story about MCC asking for extended hours so they could bowl Australia out.' 'You bastard,' he laughed. 'How the hell did you get that?' 'Noel Bailey got it for me,' I said. He was even less impressed when I explained.

Bob was one of the finest cricket writers Australia ever had, gifted with colourful phrases, a lover of cricket and possessed of the ability to scent a story before other journalists, including me, had even unpacked their typewriters.

One of his best stories was at the start of the 1962–63 MCC tour of Australia where Ted Dexter was the captain. Bob and I flew to Perth to meet the team and to cover the two opening games, the first against Western Australia and the second against the Combined XI. We stayed at the John Barleycorn Hotel. With a two-hour time-lag back to Sydney, our copy had to be filed by 5.30 a.m. and, on the Wednesday night, we decided to have a look at Perth's night-spots which in those days were few in number.

My, how time flies when you're having fun. We arrived back at the John Barleycorn at 5 a.m. in only reasonably good order, though I was certainly in better shape than Gray. That point was driven home to me when he went to sleep the instant his head hit the pillow and nothing I tried would wake him. I adlibbed my story to the Sydney *Sun* and then picked up the phone and called Gray's *Daily Mirror*, gave his name and adlibbed a story for him to the copy-taker. His sports editor rang him later in the morning with profuse congratulations. Great story! My sports editor telephoned me after the first edition to ask what the hell was going on. I'd made a bad start to the tour because Bob Gray had scooped me in the *Mirror* with a good story about Graham McKenzie likely to be Australia's outstanding player in the coming series. There wasn't much I could say other than in future I would try harder. Gray, when he awoke, thought it very amusing.

As a captain and a full-time journalist I was in a unique position when I played for Australia from 1958 to 1963. It was the first time any captain had been in that position and it gave me a great chance to publicise the game and, at the same time, make any point I wished on the team's behalf to fellow journalists. Whether they would accept the point, and often they didn't, was quite another matter, but at least one could try.

When we went to England in 1961 the game had just gone through the traumas of the Geoff Griffin throwing inquests as well as the 1960 Throwing Conference at Lord's. There were widespread statements that the side I was leading was one of the weakest, if not *the* weakest, ever to leave Australian shores. I'm not sure why this was the favoured feeling because we had thrashed England in 1958–59, had then gone on to defeat Pakistan and India in 1959–60 in their own countries and had defeated West Indies – no mean feat for a bowling side claimed to be weak.

As it turned out, my own bowling was to fall away in England because of a shoulder injury, but at the close of the tour more bowlers than ever before in the history of Australian visits to England took 50 first-class wickets – eight of us. No one took 100 wickets but eight passed the half-century in what was a magnificent team effort. When Crawford White had a go at me about the weakness of the bowling attack I could only point out that, first of all, we had beaten England and, second, we had established this record. Did that in fact make us the greatest bowling side ever to leave Australian shores? His reply was unprintable!

When we were on our way over on the ship on that tour we had plenty of team meetings where I was able to stress the importance of good relations with every area of the media. That's one aspect of modern-day cricket where I think the players these days lose out. The newspaper writers and television and radio men now are no different from my playing time, in the sense of needing to get a story and at times going to great lengths to do so. It would do no harm if players and captains had a better appreciation of the problems facing the media . . . some of which can be of their own making.

You certainly do have to be careful when you are writing, broadcasting on radio, or commentating on television, that you do not offend, either by accident or design. The splendid writer Alan Ross managed one day to get into his copy the fact that Bob Cunis had spent part of the previous day purveying bowling much like his name . . . 'neither one thing nor the other'.

John Arlott has managed, straight-faced, to slip one or two little gems in occasionally and, in 1973–74, a television commentator in New Zealand had the task of trying to avoid too much mention of a streaker racing across the ground followed by police. The players and spectators were watching the chase and the commentator unfortunately for a moment took his attention away from that and looked at the scoreboard on the left of the ground where it showed the 85th over was being bowled. With perfect timing the producer cut to a shot of the streaker caught on top of the fence at the very instant the commentator, keen to keep the watching audience appraised of the situation in the game, said, 'And, as you can see, there's a new ball due . . .'

Journalists, like players, come in all shapes, sizes and temperaments. There was no tougher journalist in Australia in my time than Jim Mathers with whose two sons I went to Parramatta High School. The elder son, also Jim, was my First XI cricket captain at the school and the younger son, Mick, had a son who played Rugby Union for Australia. Jim was tough, but he was good. There were plenty in England who had come up in a hard journalistic school and were not inclined to let you forget it. They were also fine writers.

There was some television then, but radio and newspapers were the best avenues for cricket watchers to keep up with life. It was a hard game! In Australia there was an inherent distrust of the press in those days and when the Australian Cricket Board made me captain, very much against their earlier intentions, it must have been with great misgivings about the role I might play. I managed to justify all those misgivings in the first 24 hours I was captaining the team in Brisbane in the First Test. I invited any journalist who wished to do so to come down to the dressing-room at the close of play when I would be happy to pour him a drink and have a chat. Journalists all knew the players were bound by the player/writer rule – which meant that they were not allowed to be quoted in the press – but I would be happy to help if possible. This was regarded with deep initial suspicion by the writers. For years they had been kept away even from the door of the dressing-room – now they were being invited past it. What was the trap?

Well, they soon learned there was no trap: it allowed our Australian team to see that, contrary to the views of some people, the press were not all ogres; and it allowed the writers to gain valuable background for articles they might have to write at a later stage – providing always the players were not quoted. There were very few times this was abused and on almost every occasion it was because of lack of thought rather than any malice.

Players are quoted in the media far more than back in the 1940s and 1950s when, in Australia anyway, there was a player–writer rule which almost debarred the player from breathing let alone opening his mouth to make a statement. It was not always so in England. Cecil Parkin once rushed into print after Arthur Gilligan wouldn't give him a bowl against the South Africans in a Test match at Edgbaston and announced he had no wish ever again to play for England. Looking back on the records of that game, it seems rather an odd thing for him to have said – he finished with 0 for 38 from 16 overs and England won the match by an innings and 18 runs. His captain and the selectors took his statement at face value and into the England side came Richard Tyldesley. In the Second Test match at Lord's, without his presence, England turned in an astonishing performance to make 500 runs in a day, the only occasion it has happened in Test cricket. Tyldesley recorded match figures of 6 for 102 and England went on to win by the same margin as before, an innings and 18 runs!

It is not always easy in 1984 to find common ground between players and the media on how much the respective camps know about the job and the needs of each other. For example, the media tend to think players are likely to flounder when faced with the task of writing an account of a day's play or talking about it on radio or television. Most times this does less than justice to the players' intelligence, because when they are interviewed on television it is often a real eye-opener to listen to some of the constructive matters they put forward concerning the game of cricket. Then there is the other side of the coin, with the players wondering how a newspaperman, who has never actually played in a first-class cricket match, can possibly know what goes on out in the centre. Over the years I have found this just about the most contentious question of all, and of course the answer is he can't. But if he has played club cricket he will have a good idea of what is happening, even though it is impossible for him to know at first hand the pressures of playing in front of fifty or sixty thousand spectators.

There is too the problem that newspapers today have changed their style and have found it necessary to report not only the play but also, because of television providing an instant coverage of the cricket, the background to the game and players. This may account for the fact that players of all Test teams tend to lock themselves away rather than make themselves available to the media these days.

In England in 1981 Mike Brearley said he felt today's press were more demanding and inquisitive. 'They expect answers, quotes and co-operation.' Brearley went on to say he found, when he took over the captaincy at Headingley, an England team more embittered by the press than he had ever known. He said Ian Botham refused to speak to them after his century at Leeds and Willis was outspoken on television immediately after the same match. Brearley added that the style of writing fostered by the modern craving for excitement and sensation puts today's public figures under pressure unknown to their pre-war predecessors. That may be so, but some of the problems are fuelled by the leading players themselves.

Many of them these days write for newspapers or magazines. Some write their own copy, but others rely on a 'ghost' writer. Many of the problems associated with 'ghosting' come from the fact the player himself has been too busy to talk fully to the journalist before the piece is written, and then, in the haste of going for a deadline, it hasn't been possible to get back to the player with the finished article. In order to avoid such problems, I believe there should be a sequence along these lines: player talks to the journalist; journalist writes the copy; journalist shows the finished copy to the player *who signs it*; copy goes to the newspaper or magazine. By adopting this procedure, the journalist knows the copy has been signed by the player and the player knows he has signed a true copy which has gone to the newspaper. If anything different appears, it can only be because it has been changed on the sub-editors' table.

I am not saying every player has to sit down and write by longhand or type his own copy, although that would be the ideal. Some players talk better into a tape recorder than they do when given the task of writing by hand and they are much better able to express themselves. I think the system set out above would work perfectly and would take a lot of the steam out of the controversy we have now.

In 1983 Chris Old was fined £1000 by his new county, Warwickshire, for comments made about Yorkshire, his former county. He was then hit with a £2000 fine by the TCCB (subsequently lifted). In Australia, players have been fined for commenting on selection and other matters but, if the guidelines noted here were adhered to, there would be far fewer problems. It would be better than the system of 'take the money and run'.

Because of my long association with the media I have a clear understanding of the problems of both players and journalists and I understand writers must find stories. The editor is never likely to be overpleased if he has to put a picture of a rose on the back page because his cricket writer has not been able to come up with the goods. Lack of cooperation with the media sometimes reaches ludicrous extremes, as happened when Kim Hughes, as Australian captain, was fined by the Australian Cricket Board in 1983 for having made comments about Dennis Lillee's return to the team after injury. There was nothing wrong with the comments, it was just that no one, not even the skipper, is permitted to comment on the selection of players.

It is a quite extraordinary situation. To whom else but the captain of the team would the media direct their questions concerning the fitness of players or their possible return to the side? If the captain has a press conference and the questions come at him, is he to say, 'Sorry, but I can't answer questions of that kind about my team.' It becomes even stranger when you think that on tour he *must* answer questions about the likely make-up of his side or be branded as ungracious and unhelpful.

The whole thing comes back now to two points. First, the ACB need to sit down and work out a sensible method of having the players able to say what they think about various aspects of the game, providing they do not bring it into disrepute. Second, the captain must be in charge of all aspects of liaison with the media. The difficulty, as we have seen, is that when he was a selector he was bound by the same code of silence as the rest of the committee.

When the players were pressing so hard for representation on that selection committee, I went on record as saying it was a move detrimental to their long-term benefit. Nothing I have seen in the meantime has changed my view one little bit. There are now five selectors instead of the old number of three. Soon there will be seven, with Victoria and Tasmania wanting to know why on earth they should not have representation. Who could blame them? They might as well all have a go, on the strength that, if they have a representative, then at least there will be one voice to push the claims of local players who might otherwise have been unseen by the committee.

If the players had perceived the commonsense of setting up a Players' Committee instead of worrying so much about having the captain as a selector, then their cause would have been far better served. As it is, they will have to make the best of it, but they must get together with the Board to sort out the problem. To have the captain of the national team fined for answering a media question on the make-up of the team is extraordinary.

* * *

The two best writers on sport I have ever had the pleasure of reading are Ian Wooldridge from England and Dan Jenkins from America. Both are writers of features and columns and both have flair and a delightful sense of humour. Jenkins has written some very funny books as well, in particular one on the television industry and one on grid-iron football.

Wooldridge has been with the *Daily Mail* for more years than he possibly cares to remember, but we first met in 1962 when he was sent to Australia to cover the MCC tour, of which Ted Dexter was captain and the 16th Duke of Norfolk was manager. Wooldridge was sent in place of Alex Bannister, the *Mail*'s cricket writer, an appointment only moderately popular with some of the other English writers. I hadn't met Wooldridge at the time.

The tour was going along satisfactorily though even in the early stages there was disquieting news about some of MCC's defensive on-field tactics in the southern states. Perhaps it was only an experiment. Then Neil Harvey captained an Australian XI in Melbourne and came back most unhappy at what he saw as a tactical trend: five on the legside to the faster bowlers operating at middle or leg stump. It happened again in the next match when I captained New South Wales against MCC at Sydney and, after the day's play, I made a decision to try to do something about it.

When asked by a Melbourne journalist, John Priestley, if I had any comment to make on the tactical ploys I had seen, I remarked, 'I might have to change a few of my ideas on the game.' With no play on the Sunday, I was telephoned at home by one English journalist, on behalf of all the others, for some extended quotes on what I had said the previous evening in the dressing-room. I gave them and asked if he would pass them on to all the other English writers. 'Of course.'

A little later in the day a sixth sense made me phone Wooldridge, who was an odd man out, to check he had received the quotes. No he hadn't, but he would be most grateful to have them because otherwise his sports editor, a Mr James Manning, might do something very painful to him which could preclude his chances of fatherhood. It would have been the classic 'miss' of the tour, with every other morning paper in Britain headlining the Australian captain's critical quotes and the *Mail* having nothing.

We have been firm friends ever since. Perhaps there are things on which we think alike. He cannot stand humbug, pretentiousness from those who have nothing about which to be pretentious, *poseur* sports figures who take themselves too seriously, and he doesn't mind laughing at himself. The latter trait becomes more and more necessary in these serious days.

Over the years Wooldridge had been named Sports Writer of the Year and Journalist of the Year and no doubt it will happen again, providing he manages to keep his seat-belt fastened when dashing up and down the motorways. He has been in a TR-7 when it became a TR-3½ and was lucky to escape a crash in a BMW last year – neither of them his fault but, even so, a trifle disturbing. Given just one wish in life? To be able to write like Wooldridge would be very high on the list.

The classic writer on cricket in England was Sir Neville Cardus and, of English writers, I prefer his work to any other. His essays were not always completely factual but they were beautifully descriptive. I first met him in 1956 at a magnificent party given on the rest day of the Lord's Test by John Arlott where, for the first time, I saw a whole cheese which had been soaked in some splendid port – I think over a period of several months.

Keen to become a sports writer for a newspaper, I was overawed by Cardus's presence. The next morning he was kind enough to write in his newspaper something pleasant about my prospects for the day, even going so far as to say that, before I was much older, I might do something to demonstrate my natural ability. That was the day I made 97 in two hours and 20 minutes and Australia won the Test match by a good margin.

Of all Cardus's books, *Australian Summer* – a delightful record of the Test matches of 1936–37 – is closest to my heart. No team had ever before lost the first two Test matches then won the last three, and it couldn't have been more opportune that Cardus was on hand to chronicle for us events which still make fascinating reading almost 50 years later.

It is a delight to read again the story of those matches because, once we moved to Parramatta from the country, it was those Tests I replayed time and again on the back verandah. Select two teams, toss, play a Test match. It was always based on the 1936–37 series because I had a copy of the *New South Wales Cricket Association Year Book* covering that series. The game was with a tennis ball and a cut-down bat and it was, more than anything, the reason I had a flourish at the top of my backswing when batting in early years. Well . . . you try holding a bat in your left hand, bowling right hand against a brick wall and then putting your right hand on to the bat to play the required stroke!

You finish with a flourish.

6

ONE-DAY CRICKET, SPONSORSHIP AND THE PAYING SPECTATOR

Cricket was originally played over only one day so it is no real surprise the wheel has turned full circle and these days spectators throughout the world again enjoy the original form of the game. It could hardly be said that one-day cricket or limited-overs cricket enjoys the backing of all administrators and all cricket followers. Many hate it and would do anything to find some way to keep the three-, four- and five-day game financially viable without having to bother about 'the rubbish of the sport'.

War-time cricket in both England and Australia had an accent on one-day cricket, for the very good reason that those who were in the army, navy or air force, or were engaged in civil defence activities, could not always manage to get successive Saturdays as part of their leave. R. C. Robertson-Glasgow was one of many who advocated, in the 1940 edition of *Wisden*, 'the improvising of one-day matches whenever and wherever possible. . . . There will be plenty to play and enough to watch such games. Many would delight to see again a few early-Edwardian drives and a late-Victorian pull or two.' Administrators in both England and Australia decided one-day cricket was a good idea and I was one of many who benefited from such a move.

In Sydney in those days the one-day game was played on a time basis rather than on overs which allowed, say, two and a half hours for each side to bat with no limit or minimum on the number of overs to be bowled. There was of course no time-wasting because it was the participants' only chance of sport and exercise during the week in what were anxious and often depressing times. They were days of tremendous excitement for me aged 11 because I was able to go with my father to all the matches and see some of the great players in action, names I had only read about in my copy of the 1936–37 *New South Wales Cricket Association Year Book*. This book I carried everywhere, along with my little *Unrivalled Pocket Scoring Book* in which I scored all the matches and faithfully recorded my father's deeds.

The first year of one-day cricket in Sydney in the 1941–42 season was a mixture of one- and two-day matches. It made no difference to the very strong St George team which had already won the competition in 1939–40 and 1940–41 and then went on to win it again in 1941–42, 1942–43 and were runners-up in 1943–44. The great Bill O'Reilly led them and I can still see him pounding in at Cumberland Oval against the team for which my father played. O'Reilly and New South Wales's legspinner, Hughie Chilvers, and another allrounder and legspinner, Ken Gulliver, took most wickets in those years – damning indictment of some who were inclined to say the leg-break bowler would disappear because of one-day cricket.

In 1941 Arthur Morris made most runs in Sydney grade cricket and then three other interstate players, Les Fallowfield, Sid Barnes and Bill Alley, had most runs in the three years of one-day cricket. O'Reilly had an astonishing record in grade cricket then, heading the bowling averages in 12 out of 14 seasons from 1931 through to 1945, and only just being nudged out on the two other occasions – first by Vince Collins in 1936–37 when 'Gubby' Allen's side was in Australia and O'Reilly played very little grade cricket; and then when Alan McGilvray, later to become the ABC broadcaster, was on top of the Sydney figures. I never saw Alan play but he must have been a useful cricketer because the following season he headed the batting averages for Sydney grade cricket against some great names, and it was around this time he was given the privilege of captaining New South Wales.

Towards the end of the war, the Advisory County Cricket Committee met at Lord's to discuss the eventual resumption of first-class cricket. Despite its obvious success in a time of crisis, the committee members saw no place in the scheme of things for the continuation of one-day cricket, concluding that 'any departure from the existing method of three-day matches would be detrimental to first-class county cricket'. By this time, Robertson-Glasgow had changed his tune and, writing in *Wisden* in 1942, he stated that those who urged most strongly for the retention of a form of one-day cricket would be the earliest to tire of the experiment. He added that it was a false analogy that all spectators are in a hurry and therefore players should be in a hurry too (and that was 40 years ago!).

Limited-overs cricket was much slower to return to Australia than it was to be taken up by England's cricket authorities as the financial saviour of the game. There was in fact no real reason for an earlier introduction to Australia because cricket at grade level out there, even with very small crowds, was quite buoyant and exciting right through the late 1940s and 1950s up to the time when English authorities were becoming extremely nervous about the way their game was being played and attended.

Cricket administrators had not been prepared to pay attention to what had been happening since the end of the war when understandable euphoria, and the chance to watch again great players in action, had increased county attendances to almost 2,500,000. On the 1956 tour of England the weather had been poor but, even allowing for that, there had been a sharp fall in public support. By 1959 the attendance figures for county matches were down to 1,370,000 and in 1960, when I went across to England to cover the South African tour, attendances plummeted to just over a million. Part of this was to do with the throwing controversy and spectators' fear of injury at the hands of demonstrators, part of it due to bad weather, but a lot of it was due to the structure of the game not being appreciated by spectators who did not have enough time to go to the three-day matches. With the finances of the counties at rock-bottom, the counties asked MCC to set up a committee to examine the whole structure and funding of cricket at first-class level.

Although there were many who urged caution in the adoption of anything to do with one-day cricket as part of the cricket scene in England, thoughts went back to those wartime matches where there had been such good entertainment at a time when not a great deal had been expected of the players other than that they should enjoy themselves. The advocates of one-day cricket had further evidence to lay before the committee: around the end of the 1950s and the early 1960s there were televised matches played under the sponsorship of the Rothmans' company and they were a resounding success.

Eventually the advocates of one-day cricket got through to England's cricket authorities who came up with the idea for a knockout competition which, in 1963, became the Gillette Cup. Traditionalists were not amused when it was suggested that there could be a place in the structure of the game for the one-day match and many people were suspicious about bringing in as a standard feature of the English cricket season something which had only been shown on television and, depending on your point of view, had produced all that was best and worst in a style of cricket last played in wartime. The overriding thing though was that administrators were now knuckling down to the task of providing matches, and therefore entertainment, for spectators when they were able to come to the grounds rather than at times when they were working.

When the Gillette Cup arrived in 1963 it was pronounced, as far as the public were concerned, an instant success, although there were still many who queried the advisability of bastardising the game of cricket and going away from the traditional three-day match. By the late 1960s the Gillette Cup was established as a premier competition in England. It had provided a great deal of excitement for county supporters and, above all, it had provided competitive cricket from first-class players at a time when the spectators were able to go along and watch.

After six years of successful Gillette Cup cricket there followed the John Player League, played on Sundays over less time, fewer overs and with shortened run-ups. *Wisden* commented: 'The one-day Gillette Cup has done much over the past six years to shake up the slothful performers and now we have a new Players' county league each Sunday. The public have already shown their appreciation for clear-cut single-day contests and one wonders whether the Championship itself and even Test matches will retain their appeal without change in some form to the maximum number of overs permitted.' The tremors from this were felt around the cricketing world.

There was no question one-day matches had revitalised the game in England where many batsmen had revealed unknown talents and, from the spectators' point of view, the John Player League turned out to be an immediate success. Of it *Wisden* said: 'Every ball counts in limited-overs cricket. It is a vital part of today's sport. The batsmen have to sharpen up their strokes, go for the risky single and the fielders have to be on their toes. The majority of these games produced wonderful fielding in the way runs were saved, as well as superb catching. There was a feverish tempo and something no one could expect in three-day Championship matches, let alone a five-day Test. Nevertheless this instant one-day cricket must never be regarded as a substitute for genuine first-class cricket. That it proved to be so popular was partly due to its being played by first-class cricketers brought up on the three-day basis.'

So by 1969 England had two limited-overs competitions: the straight knockout competition of the Gillette Cup, with the final played at Lord's at the end of the summer and bringing down the curtain on the year; then the John Player League of 40-overs-a-side duration with a restricted run-up for bowlers. In 1972 came the third of the limited-overs ventures, Benson and Hedges inaugurating a League Cup played with preliminary rounds and counties divided into zones, quarter-finals, semi-finals and a final three parts of the way through the season, also at Lord's.

There was now even more disquiet from those who detested the thought of one-day cricket. They were at last reluctantly prepared to acknowledge the spectator was being looked after, but what about the game itself?

Various theories came out of the early spawning of these limited-overs games, notably that you must always send in the opposition on winning the toss and spinners were of very little use. Both were quickly shown to be fallacies and what has come through in one-day cricket in both England and Australia is that a captain makes decisions in exactly the same way as he would in a three-day match. You bat or field according to the pitch conditions, weather conditions and, in some cases, the time of year which would have influence on the quality of light later in the day. The captaincy decisions must be made quickly and purposefully. And your better players will be your stars in about 90 per cent of cases in a one-day match, as indeed they are over a long season of three-day matches.

If I were captain of a team of young players these days I would be intent on making certain they know all about the tactics of both first-class and one-day cricket. One-day cricket has done a lot for the young cricketers throughout the world. It has shown them that to play cricket successfully at top level you must be fit, far fitter than were the majority of players around my time. It has shown them they must be able to think about all aspects of the game, not just the part of it played in leisurely fashion over four or five days. It has shown them that to be an allrounder is likely to be an advantage when they move on to being a grade cricketer and then a first-class cricketer. It has also shown them that some of the strokes and techniques used in batting in one-day cricket can be dangerous when applied to Test cricket. The fact is, though, the genuinely good players will not have their technique damaged by one-day style cricket – the good player will be good in any circumstances.

There is a misconception about one-day cricket that it has been responsible for the demise of the legspin bowler in cricket at first-class level and also the holding back of the left-arm orthodox spinner. Nothing could be further from the truth. In England the legspinner was on the way out well before one-day cricket became the financial salvation of the first-class game. Youngsters now see very few legspinners at Test level whom they can copy. Sadly this is also the case in Australia these days where the emphasis on the faster bowler has come about because of a combination of their skill and the pitches made to suit them.

Recently I read an article on that particular line about legspinners, setting out to denigrate one-day cricket. The real story of the loss of the wrist-spinner is that they disappeared fast from English county cricket as far back as the time I made my last tour of England in 1961. That year I can recall seeing only four, Robin Hobbs, Colin Atkinson, Ian Bedford and Bob Barber. Of those, Hobbs and Barber played for England, Barber's selection being based more on his skills as an opening batsman than a leg-break bowler. Ten years later, when Ian Chappell's team toured England, Hobbs was the only English legspinner left in the country, although there were four foreign over-the-wrist-spinners, Mushtaq, Intikhab, Latchman and O'Keeffe. Ten years after that there were none.

Legspinners disappeared partly because of the widespread belief that on rain-affected pitches they were ineffective when compared with finger-spinners. That belief is correct as legspinners only really flourish on firm, dry surfaces. I am simply not going to have it though that the demise of the legspinner in England is the result of one-day cricket which, conveniently, is the whipping boy for all the ills of cricket. When someone says to you it was different a few years ago and every county had one over-the-wrist-spinner, you can bet your life they are talking about 1946 or earlier when none of today's great Test match cricketers were even born.

I am never against change in the game of cricket, even though it horrifies some people that anything in the great game should be altered from the time several hundred years ago when it first became part of England's heritage. I am very lucky to have been able to see at first hand all the changes and innovations which have come to cricket over the past 36 years, many of which were a result of World Series Cricket.

Few things in my lifetime have been more exciting than the first night match at the Sydney Cricket Ground. People in Sydney had already seen floodlit cricket beamed from Melbourne's VFL Park and they thronged to the Moore Park area that evening. Instead of closing the gates when the ground was full, the gates were thrown open and all those wanting to come in could do so, something I had never experienced at a cricket match before.

The atmosphere when night cricket is being played is quite breathtaking, even though the games do not always produce unending excitement. In some areas there was a fight against the white ball and coloured clothing being used for night matches, but if you have a white ball you need coloured gear to provide the contrast, otherwise the ball will disappear into the white-clothing background. And why should there not be coloured gear? After all, coloured shirts were in vogue up to 1880 and they became common as a uniform, as did various patterns of checks, stripes and spots – and you can't have anything more traditional than Oxford and Cambridge, who for many years wore dark and light blue shirts. We are told the Harlequins originally wore blue trousers and at Rugby School in England the coloured shirt survives. It all looks very effective under lights at the Sydney Cricket Ground where this aspect of World Series Cricket now produces entertainment for those unable to go to daytime matches but still keen to watch cricket.

Quite the best innovation brought into one-day cricket by World Series Cricket was the fielding circle, within which a minimum number of fielders must be at the moment the bowler delivers the ball. When World Series Cricket began in 1977, and the matches were divided between Supertests over five days and one-day games between the World side, the West Indies and the Australians, we had already determined on the Governing Committee that the boring front-foot Law would be adjusted to the one Australia played under in England in 1961. Experience showed that to be a great move appreciated by umpires, bowlers and batsmen in the World Series matches, and it was Tony Greig who put up the idea of the fielding circles, which he had seen in operation in South Africa, at our Governing Committee meeting. We used two circles, one at either end with a 30-yard radius from the stumps. Later those two circles were to come into other one-day matches in Australia and then they became two semi-circles at either end of the pitch joined with a straight line, which is what is now used in all limited-overs matches in England and Australia.

Fielding circles have the effect of denying the fielding captain the chance to put every man on the boundary, keeping the interest up for the spectators the whole way through the innings and, above all, making the captain and the players think a little more rather than allowing them to fall back on defensive ploys which frustrate everyone. In a way it is a method of manufacturing attacking cricket but I see nothing wrong with that – one-day cricket is something fine-honed from 1963 onwards, and anything which is going to maintain the interest of the spectators and still keep the game a great battle between bat and ball can only be beneficial.

Back in 1942 it was said in England, 'There will always be found those who understand no batting except that which keeps the balls far, high and often.' It was not appreciated that 25, 35 and 40 years later those tactics, in an entirely modern type of cricket, would be drawing spectators to grounds rather than sending them away. The additional phrase was, '. . . such spectators [who enjoyed this sort of game] frankly are not wanted at county cricket.' Well, they don't go to county cricket now, nor do they go to Sheffield Shield cricket in Australia, for a variety of reasons, including for potential spectators a great deal more leisure time, the use of the motor car and pastimes and sports available for people who, many years ago, would only have been watchers.

No one should ever lose sight of the fact that spectators in 1984 are rightly concerned with receiving value for money. This is an aspect of the sport far too often forgotten in the endeavour to change nothing of a game which was great in the 1800s and remains great today. That changed line of thinking for spectators has come about, I believe, for two reasons.

First, spectators have a very real appreciation these days of what *is* value for money and what is not. Even though there may be a good deal of aesthetic pleasure in sitting quietly watching a three-day county game or Sheffield Shield game, when it comes to putting down their money and reserving a seat somewhere they will want to make sure it is a Test match or something along the lines of the modern one-day internationals. Tied in with this is the fact there is so much more Test cricket played nowadays. The 100th Test match was played in 1908, a span of almost 40 years from the time the first one had been played in Australia. Between the wars the number of Tests doubled and it doubled again between 1946 and 1962. At the end of the 1982–83 season in Australia, more than 900 Test matches had been played, 600 of them in the time I have been playing, captaining and watching cricket at first-class level from 1948 onwards. This means something over 600 Test matches in 35 years, compared with slightly more than 300 in 71 years. So it can be readily seen there is far more emphasis on Test match cricket now than was the case up to the start of the Second World War.

The youngster of today in Australia lives in an instant age. He has colour television and a transistor radio so he really has three avenues of leisure available to him: he can go to the beach or on a picnic with his radio and listen to the cricket (he may even take a battery television with him); he can stay at home and watch television; or he can go to the match. The young man is very fortunate. These days he has an unrivalled coverage of the sport in every part of the media and I often think the cricket authorities the world over do not realise how lucky they are. There are many other sports played by youngsters and adults nowadays, far more than in those far-off days at Parramatta High School. At that time cricket was given a moderate coverage at Test, first-class and grade level. The Tests had the best exposure but it was nothing like today's extensive coverage.

Now if there is a Test match in Melbourne the coverage of that Test for a keen youngster living in Sydney goes along these lines. There are three newspapers in the morning, all of which devote columns to the game and its sidelights. There are two afternoon newspapers doing the same and then the match is on radio, ball by ball. It is also telecast ball by ball for six hours by the Channel Nine Network and by the ABC to all country areas. In the capital city of origin it is telecast only for the last two hours. It has been shown clearly in recent years that the television coverage does not adversely affect the attendance at the Tests, though it is equally clear people will not be bothered going along to watch a sports event at lower than top level.

Who can blame them? Well there are, as it happens, many people who blame them who are unable to come to terms with the fact that very few people are willing to spend their hard-earned money on anything but the best in sport. For that reason the Sheffield Shield and the County Championship attract very few people, resulting in anguished cries for less Test cricket. It is stated that if there is less Test cricket there will be a consequent increase in gates at matches involving first-class players at a lower level.

One has only to look back at the rapid decline in attendances after the initial euphoria at the end of the Second World War to know that that wouldn't work. It's not that Sheffield Shield and county cricket is not good. Some of the games are magnificent matches with all the ingredients one associates with what is best in the game of cricket. But cricket followers in Australia and in England prefer to watch Test cricket at the ground or on television and to read about Sheffield Shield and county cricket. Those who bewail this state of affairs are simply banging their heads against that impenetrable barrier – the consumer's choice. Not only will crowds no longer go to those matches, despite them being the nursery of Test match cricket, but they will never again go to them.

What must be done is to continue in Australia and England with the successful blend of Test cricket and international and domestic one-day cricket so the financial viability of the game as a whole may be continued.

In 1981–82, when Pakistan and West Indies toured and played three Tests each, Test matches with 30 playing days, against 19 Benson and Hedges World Series Cup days, had slightly more spectators. So it was in 1982–83, with England playing five Tests over 25 days and New Zealand joining in on the World Series Cup. The figures were:

1981–82	Tests	WSC
	446,903	445,703
Approximate		
average per day	15,000	23,000

1982–83	Tests	WSC
	556,601	553,922
Approximate		
average per day	22,000	32,500

Cricket needs every one of those spectators, every dollar they put into the game, and it needs every television watcher, radio listener and newspaper reader. Competition is tough and players and administrators face a never-ending battle to keep the game on a sound financial basis. They will only do this with a modern outlook and by living with the changing times.

It was interesting to hear the reaction of some English cricket followers in Australia for the 1982–83 summer when Australia regained the Ashes and many English supporters then stayed over for the first of the one-day matches at the Sydney Cricket Ground played under lights. They were ecstatic the Test series had been so well attended and were able to boast with complete justification Test cricket was the established way; but it was instructive then to hear them make the usual derogatory remarks about international one-day cricket. They liked it – but hated it – because it wasn't Test cricket. It was the same old error. There is, other than the names of the participants, no connection between Test cricket and one-day cricket. Test cricket has as its nursery four-day Sheffield Shield cricket and three-day county cricket: sometimes it will be great, sometimes it will be boring, but it will always be played that way.

On the racecourses of the world I have seen horses wearing blinkers but possessing more vision than some of the people who want cricket to be played as it was before the Second World War. They are the same people who either decry sponsorship of cricket or who hope vehemently the sponsor will merely provide the money and keep his nose out of anything else connected with the game.

Behind-the-scenes sponsorship is, with spectators' attendance money, the financial lifeblood of sport everywhere these days. The growth of sponsorship has been rapid from 1977 onwards as regards cricket and it is very necessary for the continued survival of the game. I am always delighted when sponsoring companies have a hand in the way the game is presented, rather than merely sitting back and not having the slightest idea whether or not they are getting value for their money.

I heard one of the most astonishing statements in my time in cricket some years ago when an English administrator said of one of the sponsoring companies – Schweppes – that they were a marvellous sponsor because they paid their money and didn't bother administrators from then on. That attitude is typical of some administrators who believe sponsoring companies should hand over the cash and then it should be used by the sport without any further reference to the sponsor himself. I wouldn't have liked to have been the marketing manager of that company on the Monday morning when the chairman had to ask him to explain whether or not they *were* in fact getting value for their money. After all, a company enters into a sponsorship commitment not because it has too much money and wants to give some away, but because there is likely to be a commercial advantage obtained by that sponsorship. We have come a long way since rich patrons organised their cricket teams without regard to cost.

In England, the cricket sponsors are more varied than in Australia and include Cornhill, who handle all the Test matches; the National Westminster Bank, who took over the premier one-day competition when Gillette moved out of cricket; and the two tobacco companies, John Player and Benson and Hedges. The Benson and Hedges Company sponsors all major cricket in Australia and a chill wind ran through the corridors of cricket administration when, in 1982, it seemed clear that sponsorship of sport by tobacco companies was likely to come under increasing fire from, first of all, the state governments and then the Federal Government.

If legislation preventing sponsorship by tobacco companies were to go through the State and Federal Parliaments, then the financial lifeblood of Test and first-class cricket would quickly drain away. Politicians are very keen on their own lobbies for every subject under the sun, so I know, out of fairness, they won't mind if I and a few others conduct a campaign against a government banning tobacco-company sponsorship of cricket. There are many of us who believe not only in freedom of choice of how to vote, but also in freedom of choice for a responsible sports organisation to choose or retain a sponsor. Cricket authorities in Australia are well aware that it would be impossible to find another sponsor as enthusiastic and beneficial to the game as the Benson and Hedges Company.

An outstanding sports sponsorship from another tobacco company in Australia is the Rothmans' National Sport Foundation which concentrates on producing coaches in various sports. I had the pleasure of setting up the original plan of the Foundation coaching scheme with Brian Taber, the former Australian wicket-keeper who is now Australian Director of Coaching. It is an imaginative scheme whereby coaches at various levels are produced – in the case of cricket, there are four levels and coaches sit for exams. The enormous benefit for children's cricket shows through every year in Australia, with fathers and even mothers passing their lower coaching certificate so they can be of some assistance to the little lads' teams in their Saturday morning competition. The same type of coaching scheme is in force in other countries and interest in cricket has been heightened by the number of new coaches produced each year.

If we lived in a society so affluent money was unlikely to be a factor in any business venture, then I would suggest that would be the time to ask sponsors to spend their money without any regard to obtaining value. In the meantime, all cricket administrators should be courting the sponsors because, if they are not looked after, there are plenty of other sports itching to get their hands on available money and expertise.

The structure of the game before the war and the low cost of tours meant sponsors were not needed, providing the players' payments could be kept as meagre as possible. Those were the days when cricketers in England were divided into the very distinct camps of amateur and professional. It is hard to believe that right through to 1962, when the distinction was dropped, cricketers had to change in different dressing-rooms and enter the field through different gates according to whether they were amateurs or professionals, 'gentlemen' or 'players'. Players' payments stayed at an unrealistically low level throughout the cricketing world although, in Australia, Cricket Associations could afford to buy buildings – the excuse being it was prudent business to have one's own building if you were in the business of cricket administration.

When sponsorship arrived, even in a small way, and when the players began to murmur about sharing in the financial structure of the game with superannuation funds being mentioned, then the portents were that the players intended to become more militant. The spectators were not really bothered by all this, wanting only to be entertained and to receive value for their admittance money and, preferably, to be housed in reasonable conditions at the ground.

Those spectators who pay their money to come through the turnstiles are very important to cricket. They are the lifeblood of the game in that they provide finance and atmosphere and they are only marginally less important than the competitors themselves. Cricket does not always have the best of amenities for them.

I know it is not easy for ground authorities to produce something akin to one of the decks on the QE2 as regards bar facilities, food, luncheon-rooms and cloakroom arrangements, but the contrast between some of the new grandstands and those which have been there for many, many years is quite appalling.

The best cricket stand in the world is the Brewongle at the Sydney Cricket Ground which was built at considerable cost by the Sydney Cricket Ground

Trust. Quite rightly, it is the most popular area as far as cricket fans in Sydney are concerned and, although it is not behind the bowler's arm, it is the place I reserve for any of our friends who want to go to see the cricket. The facilities are magnificent but they are no more than the spectators deserve.

One of the problems cricket faces is that, in many cases, it can do nothing to upgrade amenities for spectators because it does not own the grounds concerned. Administrators and ground authorities of the future however will live to regret the failure continually to upgrade facilities and make certain the patrons are happy. Sponsorship is great and so too the money derived from television fees. But if administrators continue to use that as a back-stop to their problems in cricket, rather than being one hundred per cent concerned with the well-being of the spectator, then they are in for a great shock in the future.

Entrance fees will rise for spectators in line with inflation so the game may remain financially viable. Sponsorship grants will rise so the game may remain financially viable. But, will inflation also see a rise in spectator comfort and amenities, or is it only a one-way ticket as far as the administrators and ground authorities are concerned?

Even though in Australia the crowds have flocked back to the game, I am still worried about the comfort of the spectators and I believe there should be a new comfort attendance figure set by police and ground authorities for every major ground. In the past few years, where the facilities of some of the grounds have been sorely taxed, the authorities have moved swiftly, but I believe they must come up with new figures. My favourite ground is the Sydney Cricket Ground yet I feel for the spectators there. The ground capacity of the SCG is approximately:

Members' Stand	2,400		
Ladies' Stand	2,250		
M. A. Noble	5,000	9,650	
Bradman	5,000		
Brewongle	6,500		
Sheridan	3,850	15,350	
Hill	25,000	25,000	(20,000)
Total	50,000	50,000	(45,000)

The figure has been reduced from 50,000 to 45,000, but that is still not good enough. In January 1983 we had one experience in Sydney of the gates being closed after the police and ground authorities had been very careful to publicise the manner in which that would take place but, to me, the ground was overcrowded and the spectators uncomfortable. I would bring it back even further to 40,000 or lower by selling only 15,000 or 10,000 Hill tickets and, at that point, closing the gates.

I believe the SCG Trust should make up the deficit by:

1. Adding on $2.00 to the price of the Hill tickets on sale.
2. Adding on $1.00 to each of the seats in the Bradman, Brewongle and Sheridan stands.
3. Adding on $33.00 to each member's subscription for the year.

You would then guarantee spectators some degree of comfort, which should be their right, not a privilege. The same system, in my opinion, should apply to each ground in Australia, other than Melbourne where I doubt if we shall ever again fill the ground to capacity, although in 1983 84,000 spectators watched a limited-overs game.

Grounds are so small in the West Indies crowd comfort is non-existent. They are packed in like Caribbean sardines and any trouble which occurs on their grounds is generally because of overcrowding. There is, I'm afraid, no solution. No one in the West Indies is likely to build a grand stadium in each of the major islands where the Tests are played, but a quite different situation exists in Pakistan and India where crowds are vast. Their stadiums are more like Melbourne than Barbados in seating capacity and, as in the Caribbean, no one seems too worried about the comfort level. There crowds are enormous and what will they be like I wonder if India defend the World Cup at home in 1987?

England have their well-policed crowd levels, so it is Australia where I believe the major problem exists. Having got them back to the game, it may seem strange now to suggest cutting crowds but, for the spectators' comfort, I would do just that. And, for heaven's sake, make certain that, once comfortable, spectators stay beyond the boundary fence, rather than be allowed to rush the field. Already players have been injured; one of these days there will be a serious incident and administrators will have only themselves to blame.

Cricket is cheap for the spectator from the point of view of value for money. Six hours' entertainment for $7 for an adult is splendid value but, for that, there should be a comfortable seat and excellent facilities. But as the players' place is on the ground, so is the spectators' place in the spectator areas.

One of the things administrators must do is try to keep a fine balance between the admission prices charged for first-class matches and Test matches and the ability of the public to pay. Also implicit in anything to do with turnstile prices is inflation and, as that rises, so too must the cost to the paying public. It would be bad administration if inflation were to escalate by ten per cent a year and admission prices remain stable – there would be no quicker way for any business to go broke and it would be asking for trouble not to keep up with the financial times.

This, in turn, brings criticism from county members and those in Australia who go to Sheffield Shield and Test matches, because they always have the feeling, if they should not get in for nothing, then at least they should get in for the absolute minimum price. Since PBL Marketing and the Australian Cricket Board started working together in Australia, there has been an enormous improvement in the general marketing aspect of cricket in that country and, in particular, in the availability of concession seats and reserved seats at the different major grounds.

It has been shown clearly in Australia, against what administrators previously thought, that the cricket public will definitely book in advance for matches they wish particularly to see and, when England and New Zealand were scheduled to play the triangular Benson and Hedges World Series Cup games in 1982–83, the reserved sections were sold out weeks ahead of the actual matches. This is one of the reasons for the improved financial set-up in Australia as regards cricket, in that these days the Australian Cricket Board is able sensibly to budget ahead.

At the moment there are interminable arguments about the type of programme which should be undertaken by touring sides in Australia. Related to this is the question of tour guarantees.

Although the guarantee system seems to be working reasonably well in Test match cricket these days, I am a firm believer in tour guarantees being geared to the amount of cricket played in the summer in a particular country. The touring programmes in Australia have had to be changed over the years to meet the requirements of the public. For example, it would be silly now to continue playing return matches between the touring side and the states, other than to make absolutely certain the touring side has enough practice. The games have ceased to be crowd-pullers.

What I believe should be done, as regards guarantees in Australia, is to take a basis of five Test matches and 20 one-day games for each team and calculate those matches will bring in a gate figure of, say, one million spectators. I would nominate this figure in clear understanding that the only time it has ever been reached in Australia was in the 1982–83 season and it is possible for the figure to fluctuate.

However, I would take this as a starting point and, allowing for ten per cent inflation each year, work back from that to decide how much gross income is likely to be gained from the full summer. There should be an easy pattern evolve which will very quickly give the two countries concerned a monetary figure to be used as a starting point.

If the administrators of the touring team decide they do not want to play the number of matches set out on the pattern, then the tour guarantee would be reduced accordingly. If, for example, they decided they wanted to play only 12 one-day games in the World Series Cup and the best-of-three Finals instead of best-of-five, as well as the five Tests, then the guarantee would be reduced from, say, $600,000 to $400,000. This, in effect, sets a monetary value on each match on the tour so far as the visiting team is concerned.

In this way it would be entirely a matter for the touring side to work out if they wanted to play the full programme desired by the Australian Cricket Board and cricket followers in Australia, or if they wanted to play their own programme – and no one could object to their decision. I believe this method would make the negotiating simple and straightforward. It would also be sensible business.

In 1983 counties were warned that if they fielded sub-standard sides against touring teams they would be in danger of losing their fixtures against future visiting teams. Quite right too. England were the first ones to start the business of leaving out their best players and playing a scratch side against a touring team. It only needs this kind of eroding for county members not to bother going to those matches and then they will stop going to county games.

There was a time when it was a sought-after privilege to be chosen to play against the tourists. No longer, and to me it is a sad aspect of the game today. It's not as though counties can really afford to miss out on the finance which could be gained from spectators attending an interesting fixture. Counties, in fact, seem to me to be in the position of needing every pound available.

7

THEY DON'T ENJOY THE GAME AS MUCH AS WE DID . . . DON'T YOU BELIEVE IT

One of the favourite games of the older cricket watcher and follower is to wander over and say 'Bet you wish you were out there, Richie?' The answer, in fact, is that I do not wish I were out there because if I were, at the age of 53, some smart, young fast bowler would be trying to knock my head off and some smart, young batsman *would* be doing so. Time has caught up! No, I have no wish at all to be out there. What I am very happy doing is watching and following the game around the world with all its changes of tempo and style. Some days are good, some days bad, just as in any other walk of life.

The next thing they say is, 'Of course, they don't enjoy the game as much these days as you fellows used to . . .' And I look at them and think, 'Now, why on earth would anyone say that?'

I would love to be playing cricket now, given a return of my youth and skill. That, of course, cannot happen but my impression is not that the players of today do not enjoy themselves. On the contrary, with better accommodation and travel and more money to make, I'm certain they enjoy their cricket every bit as much as we did.

I was in the era when ship travel was the norm for a tour of England. Nowadays there is no ship travel because it would take too long and the administrators would have to pay the players for the three or four weeks they were doing nothing on the ship, as indeed they had to pay us. But, as we were paid 'peanuts' – or, as they say in the United States, in their own vegetarian way, 'small potatoes' – in those days, it didn't amount to a great deal of money. I was, in fact, the last of the Australian shipboard cricket captains way back in 1961 and every minute on board the ship was a pleasure. I hasten to add you must like shipboard life for that to be so: there are many passengers who cannot handle the seasickness, which can be a real problem, and there are many who find shipboard life boring and cannot wait to get back on land and do something constructive.

A typical day on board ship for me was to rise at 7.00 a.m. and go for a half-hour training run or, if that were impossible, because of the roll of the ship, do 100 sit-ups or whatever might have been the set exercises for that day. Training was an elementary affair yet there weren't many fitter cricketers in the 1950s and 1960s than me. There were definitely no fitter cricketers than Australian Frank Misson who was on that 1961 tour . . .

Frank was the kind of cricketer for whom I always had a very high regard. He was a great trier, a good fast-medium bowler, a useful batsman and a brilliant fielder. He made his début in Adelaide in 1961 against West Indies, when Alan Davidson was unfit, and he did a fine job in searing heat. It was his fitness which helped him through . . . and possibly his sense of humour on those five trying and very exciting days. He became great mates with Bill Lawry and, as both are practical jokers, they had a good deal of fun in England in 1961 with some gentle leg-pulling of the captain, the manager, assistant-manager, and any of the players they were able to snare at a given time.

The following season in Australia, 1961–62, was a magnificent one for cricket, with sometimes crowds of 6000 to 7000 people turning up to the Sheffield Shield games. In one memorable match early in the New Year, we had over 12,000 people in on the second day of the game against South Australia. They had made 250 in their first innings, with Ian McLachlan hitting a glorious century. Then, on the second day, there was the confrontation between the new spin-bowling sensation in Australia, David Sincock, and the New South Wales top batting order. It brought a flurry of excitement when Simpson and Harvey fell to the youngster for 18 runs but Booth made a century and New South Wales got a handy lead, and then bowled South Australia out cheaply a second time.

It was in this euphoric mood we started battle in Sydney against Lawry's Victorian side on 26 January, the Australia Day weekend, and Frank Misson was our opening bowler with Alan Davidson. Although the on-the-field activities were very serious and Ian Meckiff turned in a dangerous spell of fast bowling, matters were in much lighter vein in the dressing-room at the end of each day's play. Victoria made 321 and Davidson, scoring a brilliant century, then gave us a first-innings lead after he had shared a last-wicket partnership of 59 with Doug Ford. Davidson made 58 of the runs and the remaining single was a leg-bye, Ford facing only three balls. It was astonishing stuff.

That evening the two teams were to go to a reception at Government House and, as often happened, I was running a little late. I didn't know it at the time but I had developed a habit, in the course of getting dressed, of making certain the last thing I put on were my shoes – those were the slip-on type and I always stepped into them, moved off and made haste to make up any time lost. Lawry and Misson must have been studying this closely throughout the 1961 tour. At any rate, they had laid their plans very carefully because, with everyone in the team watching intently, I said, 'Come on, we're late – let's get cracking,' stepped into my shoes . . . and tried to take off. All would have been well other than for the fact that I remained vertical because someone had nailed my shoes to the floor. It was no good asking Lawry or Misson who had done it – they were helpless with laughter, supporting themselves on the door frame!

On that 1961 boat trip with Misson as my trainer and having recovered from a tonsilectomy, I was ready for the sports' deck where I would play, with Neil Harvey, our own version of deck tennis. Although there were lines painted on the court similar to the lines on a tennis court, we would try to catch everything and play as though on a court double the size. Highly competitive, it was a great method of training and by the end of the three weeks on the ship we would be the fittest we had been right through the summer. Legs would be thinner and trimmer and firmer, excess weight would have disappeared and, by the time we arrived in England, we were suntanned and in good shape.

That was marvellous but it really was a holiday more than anything else and there was no way you could have cricket practice on board the ship. In many ways it was a waste of time and money. I often hear people saying these days what a pity it is teams no longer travel this way and I'm inclined to agree with the sentiments – providing someone else pays. Nostalgia for this kind of thing often comes from my media colleagues who had a taste of it when they were writing about the game and I was playing. They would like their newspapers to send them by ship and pay for their holiday and they would like the ACB and the TCCB to send the Australian and English teams by ship. Well, much as I liked the shipboard life with its dressing for dinner in first class and its other luxuries, these days I would prefer to get to London or to Sydney as quickly as possible and get on with my work.

I am certain the Test players of today feel the same way. For one thing, they have not really been brought up with anything other than jet travel and they have their own fun when they arrive at the next overseas city. Often they have wives and children and girlfriends travelling ahead or just behind them and they will be settling them in, as well as the most important aspect of mixing with the team and readying themselves for the arduous tour ahead.

If some of the players today want to sample shipboard life, there is nothing in the wide world to stop them going on a ship cruise of their own once their tour is over and taking wife, girlfriend or family with them. After all, they have something like 11 weeks more time in reserve than I had, if you compare the round trips by sea and jet. The time for the Sydney–London–Sydney jaunt in 1961 was four weeks over and, because of ship breakdowns, seven weeks and one day back. Tremendous!

Where else could there be a legitimate reason for saying the players of my day had more fun than those representing their countries today? Accommodation? All the modern-day accommodation I stay in is better than the equivalent of 25 years ago. That is certainly so in Australia and it also applies as far as I am concerned to England, although there were one or two places like the Raven at Droitwich where we enjoyed the rural atmosphere. The teams today stay in the cities. Sometimes I am told by others this is one of the reasons they don't enjoy themselves as much and to that I say 'nonsense'. The players stay in the cities because that is exactly what the players wish to do. Their accommodation is carefully worked out (or most of the time is carefully worked out) at meetings between the cricket authorities, the travel agents and the players' representatives. They stay in the cities because that is where the entertainment is; the cinemas, the theatres and the best restaurants. They do not wish to be travelling 20 miles to those spots and then have to travel back again to their hotel or motel. No, from the point of view of accommodation on tour cricketers these days have a life considerably more enjoyable than the one I had 20 years ago.

Most aspects of a cricket tour haven't changed a great deal, with travel, accommodation, entertainment and cricket as the four basic ingredients. The modern-day player is also luckier in that there are fewer official functions. Although one misses the brilliance of speakers like Lord Birkett and others, there were some who rose to their feet at functions in my nine-year span from 1953 to 1961 whose verbage was based on quantity rather than quality, even though the quantity was well meaning and from the heart. A plus then for the modern-day player.

What about cricket? Do they mean, the querulous ones, when they say cricketers don't enjoy themselves as much now, that they don't enjoy their *cricket* as much? In what way I wonder?

Let me tell you about how I enjoyed my cricket and then try to relate it to what happens on the field nowadays. I was a raw youngster when I came into the New South Wales Sheffield Shield team under Arthur Morris's captaincy in 1948. I made only two runs and didn't take a catch, nor did I bowl because the administrators were then in the process of one of their 'think-tank' operations and were trying to wipe the spin bowling fraternity off the face of the cricketing earth. There were many rumblings about the batsmen having things too much their own way and they managed to bring in that Law which said a new ball could be taken every 55 overs in England and every 40 overs in Australia. Administrators have done some strange things over the years but that one stands as a monument to them for ever more.

It is true though I enjoyed my cricket, and it was a tremendous thrill to play for New South Wales. At the time I was two years out of school and was working in the office of a chartered accountant, having started at a pound a week and graduating to two pounds a week in the second year. In the third year I moved on to three pounds a week and then, when I was in my second season of cricket in the state side, I found myself out of a job because the chartered accountant couldn't afford to pay me the six pounds a week which should have been my lot. I moved on to the *Sun* newspaper in Sydney where the man in charge of the counting-house, Bert Scotford, gave me the job formerly belonging to Graeme Hole who was later to play for Australia. Graeme had moved down to South Australia in 1950 because it seemed there was a better chance of a place in the state side and was later followed there by Les Favell — indeed the only reason I was in the New South Wales side in 1949 was that the Australian team were on tour in South Africa and some of the challengers had moved interstate.

I had my first tour to England in 1953 and enjoyed it — then went back to Australia to try to find some way to make a down payment on a house from what had been saved out of the small tour allowance. Impossible! I went to West Indies in 1955 and England again in 1956, South Africa in 1957 and India and Pakistan in 1959–60, followed by England in 1961.

I enjoyed it all but I would be less than honest if I were to say I believe I enjoyed it more than the modern-day player enjoys his tours and his way of life. A dinner jacket may not be required baggage now but the cricketers still have to hit that little piece of leather with the carefully shaped stick of willow in the same way as thirty years ago.

Then there is one-day cricket, the giant-sized difference between cricket in my day and cricket now. First of all I am desperately sorry I never had the chance to play one-day cricket. I reckon it would have been one of the great challenges of our time to have to switch from Test matches to one-day matches and find a technique to adjust to both. It may be I would not have been successful because there is often a feeling these days that spin bowlers cannot play a part in the matches we see. But, would it have been out of the question for the Australian teams of 1948, 1953, 1956 and 1961 to hold their own with some of the one-day teams of the modern day?

From that point of view I believe we had it less good in my day, though I know many players of my era who simply do not like one-day cricket. Perhaps it is because I have been a part of the cricket scene at first hand since the Gillette Cup began in England in 1963 that I have no qualms at all about one-day cricket, and I so much enjoy watching and commentating on this part of the game. The modern-day player enjoys it too in my opinion, though they all, with one or two exceptions, still regard Test cricket as the ultimate. Glenn Turner of New Zealand nowadays is one who doesn't like Test cricket and prefers the one-day variety, but it appears he is in the minority.

One of the reasons the majority of modern-day players enjoy their Test and one-day cricket is they know their future is tied up in the combination of both methods of playing the game. In the past 20 years cricket has sometimes suffered from moderate-standard administration and sometimes moderate-standard play, but the introduction of limited-overs cricket by the administrators is a great big shining plus mark.

The modern-day player has something else going for him – *television*. This is the medium which has made the greatest advance as far as sport is concerned, and it has been the single most important influence on cricket in Australia since I started my career. The quality of television at present taking cricket to the cricket followers is quite astonishing and it is reflected in Australia in the tremendous enthusiasm for the game now engendered among children. The modern-day player is well aware of this and, as far as I can see, it is part of the fact that he enjoys the game as much as he does.

Is their work-load too great compared with ours? There has been a trend in Australia over the past couple of years for players once again to wonder if they are being adequately recompensed for the amount of work they do.

There was a discussion between Greg Chappell, Dennis Lillee and myself in the press in 1982 as to whether the Australians were being badly done by in view of the programme the Australian Cricket Board had agreed with overseas touring teams after consultation with the players' committee. I do not believe the programmes shown below for dual tours and a single touring team bear out the players' contention. Certainly for single Test tours in Australia, with one-day internationals, the work-load seems reasonable.

Readers can judge for themselves if, in view of the financial rewards, they consider what is asked of the players in these modern times to be too much, just about right, or even a little on the light side. When you look at the programme opposite bear in mind the players, in addition to those matches, have commitments to practice; travel by jet plane; and *are also engaged in team or personal endorsing, advertising and promotional activities which may be additionally tiring but are beneficial to them financially.*

There has also been a definite trend for English cricket authorities, and my fellow mediamen in England, to criticise the amount of cricket played in Australia and the amount of work done by the media. It is the old syndrome of wouldn't it be lovely to get back to the days of leisurely cricket tours where travel was by boat, there were days and days of golf and beaches and, one assumes, the whole thing would take eight months. I agree it would be delightful – if someone else were paying for it.

In the meantime, a comparison of the cricket seasons of England and Australia (*page 152*) makes interesting reading. My work-load is just about the same in each country and it is difficult to see whence comes the claim regarding too much televised cricket in Australia.

Incidentally, could there ever have been a more thorough justification for the type of programme used in Australia than when Pakistan toured last summer? With interest in the five-Test series at a minimum after the opening two Tests where Pakistan were outclassed, the public knew they had the chance to see the World Series Cup matches in the new year. Had that system not been operating, there would have been a whopping great loss for the Australian Cricket Board.

Players' work-load in Australia with a season of a dual tour and Benson and Hedges World Series Cup matches.

	Australian Players
15 October to 7 February — 116 days	
Test playing days	30
McDonald's Cup	3
Benson and Hedges World Series Cup – maximum	13
Sheffield Shield – maximum	20
Playing days out of 116	66

	Touring Team 'A'
23 October to 16 January – 86 days	
Test playing days	15
Benson and Hedges World Series Cup – maximum	13
Other matches	27
Playing days out of 86	55

	Touring Team 'B'
13 November to 6 February – 86 days	
Test playing days	15
Benson and Hedges World Series Cup – maximum	13
Other matches	22
Playing days out of 86	50

Or if only one team is touring and the second team arrives to play in the Benson and Hedges World Series Cup, as was the case with England and New Zealand in 1982–83.

	England
Tests – five	25
Benson and Hedges World Series Cup – maximum	13
One-day matches	1
Two-day matches	4
Four-day matches	20
Playing days	63

	New Zealand
Benson and Hedges World Series Cup – maximum	13
One-day matches	2
Four-day matches	12
	27

	Australia
Playing days	66

Comparative Cricket Season, Australia/England

	Australia	England
	22 Oct–20 March	20 April–11 Sept
Season	150 days	145 days
Matches	80	440
Tests	6 or 5 matches	6 or 5 matches
	30 or 25 days	30 or 25 days
Touring teams	Two/one	Two/one
One-day matches	30	225
Other matches – Two-, Three- and Four-day	18	45
Number of states/counties	6	17
Sheffield Shield/ County Championship	30	200
Television coverage	Channel Nine	BBC
	50 days	45 days

The ones who have it that the players are not enjoying their cricket as we did are the same ones who criticise them for being overenthusiastic when a wicket falls and for showing their pleasure. I'd rather have that than the player who sticks his hands in his pockets and slouches around the infield when a wicket falls. When I look at some of the old-time movies and stills of the cricket played before the war I see very few players smiling and laughing. On the contrary, there seems to be a sombre touch about it all, yet I know that to be incorrect because of the many stories which come out of the various early eras.

There were plenty of characters around in those days but it must have been they just didn't make it clear they were enjoying themselves. Old-timers like to call the modern-day player 'a show pony' – the latter thinks of the old-timers as obviously possessing a sense of humour, but unable publicly to show that aspect of their character. The old-timers were lucky they had the writers to build them up as characters. Cardus, Robertson-Glasgow and the others may have been, in turn, lucky they wrote in pre-television times.

It is possible we old-timers can score a few points on the dressing-room scene. At the end of the day we would sit around wrapped in towels, have a few beers and then wander off home. What do they do these days? Well, I'm led to believe, because of the reluctance to drive home with more than .05 under their belts, they take a taxi or they go home earlier than we might have done. Less dressing-room camaraderie today perhaps?

We had plenty of characters in our dressing-rooms in the 1950s and I'm sure those like Bill Tallon livened up the 1930s no end. Playing for Queensland in those days may have needed a sense of humour if you were to come up against Bradman twice a year.

Bill, who had a slight stutter, was to make his début against Bradman, a nice Yuletide present from the selectors . . . but perhaps all was not lost. That Queensland team, skippered by Bill Brown, had taken some hammerings in Adelaide over the years but they always came back smiling, and now they had come up with a special plan to take care of the South Australian batting strength in their match in Adelaide over Christmas in 1938. With a bowling attack of Jack Ellis, Geoff Cook, 'Chilla' Christ and Bill Tallon, the idea was they were going to frustrate Bradman by keeping the ball well outside his off stump and allow him to take singles to a deep-set offside field. Tallon takes up the story:

'He had just made a slightly subdued 143 against New South Wales and the New South Wales boys told us they thought he had become a little frustrated with this plan of campaign. At any rate, on Christmas Eve, we were out for 131. Disastrous it was, Grimmett got 6 for 33 and then Jack Ellis and Geoff Cook opened the b-b-bowling for us. Big Jack Ellis got Ken Ridings to edge one and b-b-brother Don did the rest. The little bloke, Bradman, was next in and he got off the mark straight away of course. And then, in the next over, Dick Whitington played forward and b-b-brother Don stumped him brilliantly down the legside off Geoff Cook. Badcock had to come in then and the shine was still on the ball and we got stuck right into him and allowed the l-l-little bloke, Bradman, to take the occasional single to this deep-set field.

'Suddenly, there I am at mid-on with the s-s-sun beating down on me and "Braddles" goes for a pull, gets a top edge and Glen Baker races around from mid-wicket towards me. I say, "For C-C-Christ's sake Glen boy, c-c-catch it" . . . and he does. Three for 351.'

On the slightly less humorous side, there was the England tour of Australia in 1954–55, captained by Len Hutton who is alleged to have suggested to his team they were to fraternise as little as possible with the opposition. How would I rate that tour in the enjoyment stakes? Very low. Not only because of that supposed edict which had some of the English players looking over their shoulders, but because we were smashed out of sight by Frank Tyson, Brian Statham and the other English fast bowlers.

That always makes for a less enjoyable series . . . or almost always. I think the West Indians in Australia in 1960–61 actually enjoyed their tour even though they were beaten.

Try as I might, I am unable to come up with any valid reason to say the modern-day cricketer enjoys his cricket any less than I did. I would *like* to find a reason, rather than merely make the statement, because it would be pleasant to think we were happier, of sunnier disposition and made a better all-round impression on the world. That would be nice, but I will need to search around for a long time before I am able to come up with the evidence because there are not many unhappy cricketers around.

There are players today who need a quick surge to get them motivated, just as there were some of us in the past who at times needed a quick kick up the backside. Whether you were at the receiving end or giving the orders, one's enjoyment of the game was not affected. The same applies today. Cricketers now are almost clones of the cricketers of yesteryear, providing you take into account the way lifestyles have changed through the years.

There is one area where we are all alike. We like to win. That is the case with players and it is, I can assure you, the case with captains. The worst cricket series I played in at Test level were the 1953 and 1956 series in England and the 1954–55 series in Australia against England. We lost all of them. The best ones I played in were the 1955 series against West Indies in the Caribbean and the Tied Test series in Australia in 1960–61, as well as the 1957–58 series in South Africa, the 1959–60 series in India and Pakistan and the 1961 series in England. We won every one of those. The intermediate one was 1962–63 which was drawn and I enjoyed it as much as was possible without winning.

I have a belief that cricketers and all sportsmen enjoy their chosen vocation more if they come out on top. Because cricket's traditions have been handed down like no other sport, there has been a popular misconception that winning doesn't matter. The theme has always been, at the very least, that winning isn't everything and I suppose an argument of sorts can be made out for this. But although it may not be everything, it sure does beat the hell out of what's next best. The Test series I mentioned above – 1958–59, 1959–60, 1960–61 and 1961 – were to me most enjoyable experiences because the Australian team came out on top, and because I was a member of those teams. This was vastly different from the previous years where the Australian team spent much of their time being beaten after the well-oiled machine of 1948 began to run down. There was enjoyment in playing then but I can assure you there was no enjoyment whatsoever in losing. I would be astonished if the same feelings did not prevail these days and in the 50 years prior to my first-class début.

A modern-day cricketer can tell you in all sincerity and honesty that he has enjoyed a tour, but no one in his right mind can tell you he has enjoyed being beaten. In my opinion it is sheer nonsense to say losing doesn't matter, and therein lies one of the problems many cricket followers have in evaluating the enjoyment or otherwise gained by the modern-day player when compared with his earlier counterpart.

You only have to look at the last few years of Test match cricket for that to be made quite apparent. For example, take the 1981 Australian tour of England. Kim Hughes was skipper of the Australian side and one day at Headingley in the course of that series he looked like being a hero. Australia had won at Trent Bridge in the First Test and had drawn at Lord's. Now at Headingley, after making England follow on, they were within a touch of going to a 2–0 lead in the series. Ian Botham had been stripped of the English captaincy and Mike Brearley was in the hot seat and on the verge of losing. The English selectors who had made the captaincy change for this match were gloomy, and so they should have been. Then came Botham's magnificent innings and the hero touch deserted Hughes then and for the rest of the series.

After being beaten at Edgbaston and Old Trafford as well, every Australian in that team was as desperately unhappy as we were in 1956 when Jim Laker destroyed us on the turning pitches at Headingley and Old Trafford. That doesn't make them any more susceptible to the claim that they enjoyed their cricket less than we did. When England were beaten so comprehensively in Australia in 1982–83, the fact they had long faces didn't mean they enjoyed their tour less than Peter May's team of 1958–59 which went down 4–0.

On the sub-continent India recently suffered a humiliating reversal against Pakistan in Pakistan and there were cries for the heads of some of their players. Gavaskar, in fact, lost the captaincy and the selectors turned to Kapil Dev as one of the youngest-ever captains of a national cricket team. This came not long after England had been beaten by India in India and the delight on the faces of the Indian players in *that* series showed only too clearly what they thought about winning and losing. Those Indian players were the perfect example of what is meant by players enjoying their cricket. Not so in defeat after they toured the West Indies a year later and were given a hammering.

Invariably those claiming the modern-day cricketer does not enjoy the game as much as the players of 20 or 30 years ago are of the latter era . . . which is my era. It is a little like claiming the modern-day player is not as good as those of 20 or 30 years ago. It is a natural thought for we 'older-timers' but it has about it little factual basis. Bradman is the only player I would except from that line of thinking – from what I have been told he was in a class of his own, and he remains the only man for whom a whole new concept of the game was devised. The despicable nature of 'Bodyline' would not have become part of cricket had it been Ponsford, Woodfull or Jackson making so many runs against England. In every other cricket team over the years there have been fine cricketers and ordinary ones, and the standard of the game hardly changes, even if the method of playing it does.

No, I would not have one regret if I had to play my cricket in the modern era instead of having finished 20 years ago. I would be able to play some club cricket, together with first-class and Test cricket, and I would have the added challenge of playing limited-overs matches at domestic and international level. I would have the benefit of being in a much higher income bracket because of new sponsorships and the change in thinking forced on administrators by World Series Cricket, and I would be able to play Test matches against the same countries, other than South Africa, I played against over a 15-year span. I would travel in modern cars, trains and Jumbo jets and stay at modern hotels far better than much of the accommodation I enjoyed from 1948 to 1964. I would be very happy doing this and I haven't the slightest doubt the modern-day player is very happy doing it. He is happier still if his team is winning, for the simple reason this will, in theory anyway and subject to the whim of the selectors, allow him to stay in the team and continue to reap the benefits of the modern-day game.

When next you hear someone moaning that the modern-day cricketer doesn't enjoy himself as much as Richie Benaud, or as much as the others did from earlier times, ask yourself: 'Is that really true? Or is it just wishful thinking on the part of we golden oldies living in the past?'

It is important though to be able to bridge the gap and appreciate modern cricket as well as that of yesteryear, and to remember all the time the game is being played by human beings not machines. One of the worst things about having not played first-class cricket for almost 20 years in Australia is suddenly you begin to realise you are an 'old-timer'. You read about them in the newspapers and in magazine articles, and you hear about them when you talk to the players, but a non-playing span of 20 years certainly qualifies you for that august company. The phrase is no compliment however when allied to the belief of many of the modern-day players that 'old-timers' see only the good things which happened in the past and nothing happening in the modern era.

One big advantage I have had is being able to cover every cricket season since 1963 for the media, first of all in newspapers, then in radio and, after that, in television, starting with BBC in England then moving on to commercial channels in Australia. I have a rule when listening to fellow old-timers that, no matter what they tell me about the astonishing times we had when they and I played together or against one another, I will try to think of something which happened on the field that wasn't brilliant, exciting, magnificent and unique. It is, in a sense, an endeavour to try to keep one's perspective and not slip into the trap of believing if anything is modern it can't possibly be good.

There aren't too many of my time for example who believe any of the modern-day fast bowlers like Lillee or Thomson, or Willis or Holding or Roberts, could be as fast or as good as Lindwall, Miller, Tyson, Trueman or Hall. It's the same with the batsmen. I regarded Neil Harvey as a magnificent

Australian player and no one of my era would countenance he was not a better player than Greg Chappell or Ian Chappell, Vivian Richards or David Gower. Nothing in anyone's modern era is as good or artistic as in the days of the past and the main reason for that is one can remember only the good things. The great Yorkshire bowler George Hirst was quoted, looking back on matches between Lancashire and Yorkshire, that he didn't think modern-day spectators – in the 1920s – got the same excitement out of the games as was the case in the 1890s. It was ever thus.

We old-timers say today the bowling of our day was more astute and the batting more dynamic, the fielding better and the captains far more brilliant with their field-placings and bowling changes. Seventy-five years ago Lord Harris slammed English batting. He claimed to have seen more bad batting than in any other season. Gave it a real 'blast' he did, and yet nowadays we are assured that was one of the great periods of cricket. So it was – they all are. And those who look at the modern-day player and think he is not as good as the players of, say, 1955 to 1960 only need to wait a few years!

There is one area however where I do feel sorry for him. Because of the glare of publicity from newspapers and television, he cannot get away with anything. Newspapers have a different role today, in that they must search for background material rather than describe the play and those background incidents often make delightful headlines.

An incident in which a modern-day player is involved leads to him being called a larrikin. Years ago he was a personality. Bad language today means you are a loud-mouthed 'yobbo'. Years ago you were a character, adding to the charm of the game. You were among the real humourists of the world and, as the tales grew over the years, you became part of the great history of the game. It's all in the eye of the beholder and the era in which we live. Today an exposé of something happening at a ground, in an hotel or at a private home, provides an account of someone regarded as an insensitive boor without the rudiments of manners.

I was very lucky in that my first captain at Test match level was Lindsay Hassett. He had taken the Australian team to South Africa in 1949–50 and the tour had been a wonderful success because he was a fine captain and ambassador, the team was a good one and it was managed by the astute and generous 'Chappie' Dwyer. No one was better at breaking the ice at a party than Lindsay, though he had no liking for overbearing stuffiness and was quick to put it down.

On that tour, when some of the team were invited to an evening cocktail party at the luxury home of all luxury homes, Lindsay and a few others went to play golf in the afternoon. They arrived a little late at the party and were rather nonplussed to find the other guests in black tie, in sharp contrast with the sports jackets and slacks of the team.

The hostess rather flamboyantly continued to remind Lindsay the party had been for 6.30 not 7.30 until he gave her a puckish look, finished his drink and tossed the very expensive glass over his shoulder into the fireplace. 'Old Australian custom,' he said calmly to the wide-eyed lady. 'We always do it when we're late for a function.' From that moment she never left his side, keeping one hand and a nervous eye on his throwing arm and, with everyone else relaxed, the party was a magnificent success. I'm not too sure Rodney Marsh would have got away with the same touch of humour these days and, in any case, it would have been on the front page of every newspaper in the land.

Three years later we arrived at the Park Lane Hotel, London, after the boat trip to England and, having unpacked, went downstairs for lunch in the grill room. I was sitting at the table next to Lindsay and when the waiter came to serve the ice-cream there was an accident. He dropped the ice-cream – all of it – on to Lindsay's trousers. There was a long, or what seemed a long, silence in the room, and we waited to see how the mess was to be removed. The waiter knew. Already perspiring slightly, he grabbed for a napkin and was about to mop up Hassett when the latter rose to his feet . . . and took off his trousers . . . in the grill room.

He handed them to the bulging-eyed waiter, saying, 'Just have these sponged and dried for me please,' and sat down again. 'Oh and I'll have another ice-cream thanks.' When the trousers were returned he stood up, put them on and went on drinking his coffee.

Perhaps no modern-day player would have the panache to try it, but could anyone get away with it these days? It was one of the funniest poker-faced acts I have ever seen. He was a great character but I don't recommend Ian Botham try it at the Savoy.

Then there was the little matter of the team tossing the bottle of Bollinger champagne at the clock in the dressing-room at the conclusion of the final Test in 1953 – direct hit too. It was then a boyish prank and typical of the character of those in the Australian side.

What would now be the classification I ask myself? Those of us who recall it with pleasure, if, that is, there is anything pleasurable about a day of defeat, know it was light-hearted and the financial damage was made good.

I shudder to think what would happen today if an English player at the Sydney Cricket Ground or an Australian at the Oval did the same thing. The modern-day player is watched much more closely than years ago when we were regarded as the delightful flannelled fools of the game.

8

UMPIRING, INTIMIDATION AND THE ODD RIOT OR TWO

For years in England there has been a theory that because English umpires have played county cricket they are consequently the best umpires in the world. That no longer holds water. There is no reason why English umpires *shouldn't* be the best (some of the best umpires I've seen in cricket come from England) but to make a blanket claim like that these days is going a little too far. The theory is that if umpires have taken part in county cricket for many years they will appreciate what goes on out in the centre and will therefore make better umpires, more likely to withstand pressure. This might make them better umpires in county cricket, compared with their counterparts in Sheffield Shield cricket in Australia or in Shell Shield in West Indies – although I am not even completely convinced of that. But there is one point which is not noted strongly enough by those who make the claim for England's umpires: cricket has changed so much in England on the county scene that there is no connection between playing in a county match and a Test match, and there is definitely no connection between umpiring a county match and a Test match.

Years ago county games would pull in big crowds. The Roses matches were played in front of capacity houses and played with all the fervour of an England–Australia clash, as indeed were the matches between New South Wales and Victoria in the Sheffield Shield in Australia. The pressure would be tremendous for the umpires in those matches. Now though, county cricket and Sheffield Shield cricket is often played with crowds little larger than three men and a dog plus the relatives of those taking part in the match. The pressures on the umpires which used to be so evident in first-class matches with big crowds is no longer there. England, just like all the other countries, now finds itself short of umpires who have had experience of controlling a match in front of a very big crowd. Add to this the fact that crowds nowadays are much more noisy than was the case 20 or 30 years ago, and any umpire coming from the county grind into a Test with 20,000 people present at Lord's has problems. And what of the player who used to take part in county matches, but was renowned for not being able to stand the pressure of a tight finish? If he had difficulties as a player in this regard, might he not also have them as an umpire?

There is not one country in recent times where there has been no trouble with regard to umpires, and it has always been in connection with the side visiting that country. They think they are badly done by, which has been the case since I played and, I'm certain, well before that. Visiting team criticises, home team defends. Nowadays, though, television replays highlight the umpires' mistakes – real or imaginary – and it is fair to say they are put under much more pressure than in my playing days.

The two areas where technology usually has the advantage over umpires are run-outs and, to a lesser extent, stumpings. Run-outs are the most difficult matter on which an umpire has to give a decision. The batsman is hurtling for the crease, there is a flurry of dust, sliding of the bat and everything is going *across* the umpire's vision. When the action is run at normal speed on television it is almost impossible for anyone watching to give a decision. Nonetheless, the television slow motion replay shows perfectly whether or not the batsman made his ground before the stumps were broken.

Television can also be reasonably sure about a stumping, although there is sometimes a problem in making a decision if the video tape is between frames. But no one watching a TV set can make a decision on lbws and catches. For a start, the cameras are on different angles from and much higher than the umpire's eyes, and I defy anyone to give any kind of an 'out' decision on television about an lbw. I don't believe you can say a batsman who is given out was not out and I certainly don't make a practice of doing that. The best you can do is say it was close. It's the same with catches, particularly bat-pad catches. No one I know is able to look at a television screen and say, 'Yes, that ball came from the inside edge of the bat on to the pad.'

However, recent controversial dismissals have, as ever, led to a call for neutral umpires, whatever that may mean, but I remain in favour of the umpires in the home country standing in international matches. The phrase 'neutral umpires' doesn't appeal to me at all because I've never in my time as a player, captain or commentator, seen an umpire who is not neutral. I've seen some better than others or, if you like to take the negative point of view, I've seen some worse than others, but I've never seen any who were not neutral.

Does anyone seriously contend the umpires who supposedly have made mistakes in New Zealand and India and Australia and England will now stop making them, just because they are independent umpires standing in another country? What those in favour of this move are saying is, 'Okay, all the same mistakes may be made but there will be no argument now because neither of the umpires has any form of home-country affiliation.' First of all, a remark like that is an insult to umpires. Secondly, if you are to take it to its hypothetical conclusion and say, 'Okay, some umpires may have home-country affiliations,' is it not reasonable to assume this lack of ethics would continue even though they are now supposedly independent umpires?

I think it is a regrettable decision we may be about to make with independent umpires. That is when the *real* problems with umpires will start and I hope it can be delayed for as long as possible.

In a misguided attempt by the administrators to make the lot of an umpire easier, in recent times there has been a call from some quarters to outlaw appealing by any fielder other than the wicket-keeper and bowler. Fortunately, in 1983, the county captains and the Cricketers' Association in England realised that was simply an over-reaction and one which had been made without any thought to the possible after-effects. This is so often the case with administrative suggestions or deliberations: they just don't think the whole thing through.

How on earth could you bring in a law along those lines where only the wicket-keeper, say Bob Taylor, and the bowler, say Bob Willis, would be permitted to appeal for an lbw or catch at the wicket? Take the catch at the wicket for example. Willis finds the outside edge of Hughes's bat and Taylor dives to take a marvellous tumbling catch. Do you really mean to tell me the only people permitted to appeal for that are to be Taylor, the man who took the catch, and Willis, the man who is still in his follow-through? Am I to believe the slips, gully and everyone else around the field have to stand there, hands on hips, and do absolutely nothing?

Appealing has been part and parcel of the game ever since I can remember and the types of appeal have varied from year to year, and so they do these days. I have seen English fielders in Australia appeal from short square-leg for lbw, and yet I can't see the harm in it. The umpire is there to give a decision and I don't know of any umpire who would stand up and say his decision is going to be influenced by the number of people appealing or the loudness of the appeal.

Some bowlers and wicket-keepers, and others for that matter, are better at appealing than their mates. Jim Laker was always an apologetic appealer, Tony Lock a demander, Peter Heine and Neil Adcock did it from a yard or two away from the batsman's nose, Bill O'Reilly they tell me was terrifying. Cec Pepper, however, was in a class of his own.

Cec became an umpire which, in the light of his great bowling and appealing, was an interesting exercise – as a cricketer, he was the ideal type of allrounder for a captain. He was a marvellous hitter and a brilliant leg-break bowler who made his career in the Lancashire League but never went on to play in county cricket like others of his ilk such as George Tribe and Bruce Dooland. Cec had a magnificent 'flipper'. When I was taught the 'flipper' by Bruce Dooland it was along the lines of the one Clarrie Grimmett used to bowl where the ball comes out from underneath the bowling wrist. Pepper's was different – he used to hit it off the bulky part of the hand and it came back from outside the off stump with the speed of a striking snake. It was often too much for Lancashire League batsmen and sometimes it was even too much for Lancashire League umpires.

This little chap standing at Pepper's end one day was plainly unable to come to terms with the wording of the lbw Law, or so Cec thought, because time after time he was hitting the batsmen on the pads and getting no result. All he was getting was a sombre shake of the head. Cec, in addition to being a splendid cricketer, also had a splendid vocabulary. After three overs he had almost exhausted that vocabulary, having explained to the little umpire, and to anyone else who might care to be listening or interested, every facet of the umpire's life, his wife's life and the miniscule influence the umpire's own parents may have had on his birth.

He got nowhere.

Thinking there may be another way round the impasse, he walked out at the end of the over with the little umpire to square-leg and talked quietly and earnestly to him, explaining that Australians were very down to earth people and they often said things they didn't mean. In fact, there were a lot of phrases used in Australia which really were terms of endearment and what he was saying to the little umpire meant he liked him very much, he was a nice chap and, contrary to what he may have thought, Cec believed he knew everything about the Laws of cricket, particularly the lbw Law. 'And above all,' he said, 'you must always remember Australians say exactly what they think and they like everyone else in the world to say what they think as well. That's the kind of people we are.'

The little umpire said nothing.

Cec walked in with him to bowl the next over from the southern end and, as he walked back past him, he said, 'You won't forget, will you, Australians like people to say exactly what they think?' The little umpire said nothing. Cec ran in, bowled his 'flipper', the batsman played back to it and, for the fourteenth time, was hit shin-high right in front of middle stump. Cec whipped around, leapt in the air and screamed at his new-found friend, 'How was THAT?' The little umpire looked at him: 'Not out ... you "scungey" Australian bastard!'

Is everything as light-hearted on the field these days? Despite this example, the authorities should set out completely to eliminate players' *dissent* from umpire's decisions. Now there would be something worthwhile. I am all for players appealing because it is a spectacle which adds to the excitement of a game of cricket, but I'm dead against the players showing dissent because I think it's a lousy thing to do.

Because the authorities didn't think the thing through, their idea on appealing fell apart in 1983 and yet, if they had come out and announced players would be permitted to appeal as much as they liked but that under no circumstances would any player be permitted to show dissent from the umpire's decision, otherwise he would be fined $5000 and left out of the next match, then they would be getting somewhere. Thinking that through, I can guarantee you would immediately stop dissent from umpiring decisions in any country in the cricket world.

It is said frivolous appeals disturb the concentration of the batsmen. No – any batsman worth his salt will not have his concentration disturbed in the slightest, no matter what kind of appealing occurs, and those who consider that to be the case can have little appreciation of the type of concentration which goes on in the centre of a cricket ground in a Test match or a tough first-class game. I can only think they have never been in the centre of a ground where there is heavy pressure.

Under the heading of dissent with umpires also comes the question of walking, which has been one of the most contentious aspects of the game of cricket for many years. In my days it was a widely held belief – a fallacious one in most cases – that county batsmen in England walked on appeal if they knew they were out caught at the wicket or close in from a bat-pad catch. This was at odds with our thinking in Australia where we were brought up – or at least I was – to wait for the umpire's decision. If he said you were not out when you looked up, then you stayed there and didn't make a fool of him. Likewise, if he gave you out lbw to a ball which you knew had come off the bat you made haste to get off the field as quickly as possible.

Now on the 1961 tour of England we had to make a decision about whether our batsmen should follow the English 'tradition' to walk on appeal and, although in the end we left it up to the batsmen to judge for themselves, I went on record as captain as stating that I would indeed walk if I knew I had hit the ball. As it turned out, I walked on a 'pair' and every time I see Alan Oakman he still laughs at the circumstances.

We had a marvellous match against Sussex at Hove early in June in which my shoulder had come through a reasonable test in good shape and I'd taken 5 for 83 in the first innings and picked up 1 for 36 in the second. Although Peter Burge made a magnificent 158 out of 281 in our first innings, we were still 55 behind on the first innings and Sussex, by the time we bowled them out, had set us 245 to make in three and a half hours at a rate of something like three and a half runs an over.

In the first innings Ian Thomson had bowled me for nought and when I went out in the second innings, on a 'pair', we were 184 for 4 and were moving along smoothly to what we thought might be a very satisfactory victory. I was facing Ronnie Bell, a left-arm spinner who was bowling around the wicket, and Oakman was fielding at slip. I tried to drive Bell, missed, and the ball spun from the footmarks outside my off stump past the wicket-keeper and Oakman dived and caught it at the same time as every Sussex man shouted for the catch.

My brain flashed 'walk' to me because of the appeal and I had taken two steps towards the pavilion before I half stopped and thought, 'Hell, I didn't hit it.' I couldn't stop then though and after the game, where we finished nine runs short of victory with one wicket to fall, all the Sussex boys at the bar were falling about and wanting to know why on earth I'd walked. 'Why did you appeal?' I countered. 'Well,' they laughed, 'it was the excitement of seeing the ball fly to "Oakie" but we knew you hadn't hit it!' My 'pair' is still in the score-book and it added another string to my contention that it's better to leave the whole thing to the umpire.

That incident at Hove might rank as gamesmanship, but there has always been gamesmanship in cricket, even though there are many who would put their hands on their hearts and say that is not so. It has always happened at village level, first-class and Test-match level, but these days it comes under much closer scrutiny because of television and, in many ways, that is a very good thing. I do not believe though, in general terms, that players' behaviour is any worse today than in my time, taking into account the change in lifestyle of the world.

One of the things about which we can be quite sure is that youngsters watching the game at home on the television set are inclined to copy what they see from their idols, or those who may not necessarily be idols but are actually playing at top level. Captains must realise that it is up to them to set the correct standards of behaviour on the field and nowhere is this more important than in the attitude to umpiring decisions. If they themselves show dissent, there is bound to be trouble. . . .

Sunil Gavaskar had been captain of the Indian side from December 1978 and he brought the team to Australia in 1980–81. They won the final Test match against Australia in Melbourne by 59 runs after one of the most sensational incidents I have witnessed on a cricket field involving a captain. Gavaskar was given out lbw to Dennis Lillee at the MCG and, in a flurry of temper, tried to take his opening partner, Chetan Chauhan, off the field with him to forfeit the match to Australia. By the time he arrived at the gate the team manager was waiting for him, ordered Chauhan back on to the field and told them to get on with the game. Gavaskar says he nicked the ball on to his pad. The Australian players say he did not touch it and, providing the other aspects of the lbw Law were satisfied, he was out. Gavaskar says it was a bad decision and he 'snapped'.

Well, I'm afraid captains are not allowed to snap. Captains need to keep their wits about them and they need to keep their players on their toes, happy and playing as a cohesive unit. At the same time, they need to tell their players – either by action, innuendo or lecture – that they cannot get away with abusing umpires and walking off the field just because they receive a decision which might not at the time be to their liking. Gavaskar is a fine batsman and his run-getting and his batting technique are to be enjoyed by everyone, but I was not at all surprised to see him step down from the captaincy for the tour of West Indies immediately after the defeat by Pakistan – anyone who tries to stage a walk-off from a Test match because of an umpiring decision deserves a very short tenure of the leadership.

It is amusing to contemplate what would have happened to an Australian captain in India had he attempted to take his team from the field after receiving a 'bad' decision. Incarceration? Decapitation? Diplomatic excommunication? A day in the stocks or a day in the office of the Australian High Commissioner would have been, respectively, a possibility and a certainty. But the one thing of which I can assure you is that I, or Bill Lawry, or Bob Simpson, or Kim Hughes would not have been at all popular. Appalling though Gavaskar's action was, it was not, in my opinion, nearly as appalling as the lack of reaction he gained from it. In fact, he got away with it, with apologists for modern-day player behaviour murmuring that he was obviously under a lot of pressure.

Times have changed. When we toured India in 1959–60 the umpiring was of a very ordinary but very honest standard. No one suggested we should fly in two Pakistan umpires or a couple from the West Indies because in those days you got on with the game, despite what had been the supposedly good or bad thing done to you by the man in the white jacket. When we were playing the Madras Test on that tour, the bulk of the bowling was done by Alan Davidson and myself, with Lindsay Kline as the second spinner. Just before lunch on what was to be the final day of the Test, I had Buddy Kunderam caught by Wally Grout off an attempted square cut. He had been batting in marvellous attacking fashion and it was, to say the least, a disappointment to see the umpire shake his head.

Wally, after an incredulous look at the umpire, threw the ball back to me and I stood and watched it go past me at shoulder height to mid-off where Colin McDonald was fielding. He tossed it back to me, I finished the over and it was lunch. When we were walking off the field, Colin chipped me for not having caught the ball, thereby letting it be seen I wasn't happy about the decision.

As we arrived back in the dressing-room, Colin's brother Ian, who was our team doctor, had something to say about the same thing. This brought a quick response from, of all people, gentle Ken Mackay, and when I announced I was off to have a curry lunch to cool me down, they were still at it. I stopped at the door and said they could argue all they liked, but bloody well finish by the time I got back . . . which they had.

What do you think would have been the reaction if I had led, or tried to lead, the team from the field because the umpire had made an honest mistake? I certainly would not have been given a very sympathetic hearing from the Indian spectators, administrators or the media.

Later that tour, in Calcutta, I was watching through one of the small windows in the dressing-room when Colin McDonald was given out lbw to

Chandu Borde. I was side-on to the play but, even so, it seemed a very odd decision, in the sense that the ball never seemed to reach his pad. I gathered this to be so when bat, and then owner, returned to the dressing-room – he had played forward and the ball had snicked the outside edge of his bat and flown past slip for four runs. The umpire had raised his finger in response to the shout of disappointment from Borde who thought he had had a catch missed off his bowling. He hadn't even appealed! It was only half funny I suppose, and I could have finished up with a bat wrapped around my skull, but I did take the risk between laughter to point out to Col that now he had some idea of how I felt in Madras.

On a harsher note, to my mind one of the prime requirements of modern-day cricket is that administrators should act if anyone makes a nonsense of the game of cricket. Just as they should have read the riot act to Gavaskar, so too should they have done to Dennis Lillee and Javed Miandad after the incident at the WACA Ground, Perth, on the fourth day of the opening Test match of the 1981–82 series in Australia.

At 3 p.m. on that day, 16 November, Lillee was bowling the final ball of his ninth over during Pakistan's second innings. Pakistan were 78 for 2 and Javed Miandad (28) was taking strike and he pushed a single off the relevant ball in front of square-leg. Lillee had finished his follow-through, had turned and was walking towards the stumps at the bowler's end as Javed came through for his single. Lillee, with his back to Javed, moved to his right at the same moment as the Pakistan skipper was moving to his left. Javed was looking towards the fielder, who by now had the ball in his hands at mid-wicket, and the two players collided, Javed pushing Lillee away with both hands holding his bat as he continued to try and make his ground to the crease.

In my opinion Lillee moved off a straight line and that was the cause of Miandad colliding with him. Then followed a heated exchange between the two, Lillee kicking Javed's left pad and Javed raising his bat in an endeavour to strike Lillee, who quickly backed away. As the two moved towards one another again, umpire Tony Crafter came between them and he and umpire Mel Johnson took over. That is the incident as I saw it. The matter then was under the control of the umpires and ultimately under the control of the Australian Cricket Board.

That season there was a code-of-behaviour system operating whereby the Australian players were able to sit in judgement on their own team members, at Sheffield Shield and international level, if an incident took place. The code did not, unfortunately, apply to the touring side and therefore Javed Miandad was not the subject of an Australian Cricket Board investigation.

The umpires lodged a complaint against Lillee under Rule 1 of the code and they also sent to Ijaz Butt, the Pakistan manager, a letter setting out a complaint they had made about Javed Miandad's behaviour which was forwarded to the Australian Cricket Board. The umpires' complaint on Lillee was handed to Greg Chappell, as Australian captain; also called into the adjudication of it was the vice-captain Kim Hughes and the general manager of the Western Australian Cricket Association, Mr John Rogers.

The upshot of all this was that Lillee was fined $200 by the players. The two umpires, as they have the right to do in Australia, protested against the decision and the matter was taken up by the Australian Cricket Board for final adjudication. At this stage Mr Butt was having plenty to say about the possibility of taking his team home — in fact Mr Butt had plenty to say throughout the tour on almost every subject known to the cricket-following world. After the umpires lodged their protest, Mr Bob Merriman was announced as the ACB adjudicator and, at the end of a hearing in Melbourne attended by the main participants in the incident, Mr Merriman decided the $200 fine was too lenient and he suspended Lillee for two matches, the two games in question to be in the Benson and Hedges World Series Cup.

The Australian team defended Lillee, claiming the fast bowler had been judged through television replays of the incident before people had time to consider it. The team also felt the impression given was that Lillee was the only one involved whereas they were convinced from replays Javed Miandad had played an even part in what happened on the field. Javed denied that at the time, a denial which took an added interest after he gave an interview to Mudar Patherya in an Indian sports magazine in 1983.

Javed was asked about his views on the abusive language and poor behaviour of players, and also his reaction to criticism of himself for kicking a ball at Edgbaston, knocking out a stump during a tour of India after he had been given out lbw and picking a fight with Lillee during a Test match. His reply was as follows:

'It happens on the spur of the moment on many occasions. Afterwards of course you apologise and regret that it should have happened so. When you lose your temper on the field you lose your power to think. In a way you become mad. And the most you can do afterwards is repent for it. Most of us after doing it feel very sorry and admit to having done wrong. Sometimes, of course, what one does is misinterpreted. For example, during the infamous incident with Dennis Lillee I was not to blame. I was merely going for a run fast — there was a second to be got — and looking at the other end. I was unsighted and Lillee came towards me muttering something intentionally. Suddenly I saw him in front of me so I tried to push him away as I had to make it to my crease. He stumbled and when I was returning for my second run he kicked me from behind. After that I lost my temper. The opinion of many was that the team should have been taken off the field. But let me tell you there were people who said I should have proceeded to hit him on the head! Personally speaking, I thought I had done the right thing in picking up my bat but not hitting him. Lillee was later punished by the Australian Board.

'On the question of knocking out the stumps, unfortunately the stumps were just there and they came in the way. I had certainly not done it as say Rodney Hogg had against us in Australia. About kicking the ball, let me say nobody creates a hue and cry when we try to run a batsman out in that manner. I see it as a way of passing the ball to the bowler and in that situation it was done with that intention. At Edgbaston an appeal for a catch had been turned down. Just because I had returned the ball to the bowler by kicking it, it should not have meant that I was showing my displeasure. If the authorities view it in a different sense then all I can say is, "Sorry".'

The Rodney Hogg incident mentioned occurred on 11 March 1979 when Pakistan were playing Australia in Melbourne and Hogg was run out by Javed Miandad after he had played a ball defensively and had stepped from his crease to pat down the pitch. Hogg turned and knocked over all three stumps with his bat and although Mushtaq Mohammad, the Pakistan captain, tried to recall him, umpire 'Mick' Harvey refused to permit a reversal of the decision after the appeal had been made by Javed. There were two other incidents in that two-match Test series, with Sikander Bakht run out backing-up at the bowler's end by Alan Hurst in the second innings in Perth; and then Andrew Hilditch, after he had picked up the ball when 29 not out and tossed it to one of the Pakistani fielders, was given out 'handled ball' on an appeal.

It must have been a pleasant series!

I thought the Lillee/Javed Miandad incident and its aftermath were badly handled. It was a matter for the Pakistan authorities, if they wished, to deal with Javed Miandad who had been having a verbal exchange with Lillee that day. They had in previous years been far too keen on chatting to one another. But the penalty imposed on Lillee was far too light. It should have been $2000 and a two Test match suspension, and a statement should have been issued that future transgressions by *any* Australian player would mean automatic doubling of the fine. Thus the penalty for the second offence would be $4000 and four Tests; and for the third offence $8000 and eight Tests.

You would put a stop to that kind of nonsense inside one season. This incidentally is not written with hindsight – it is what I wrote and said at the time in Australia.

It seems in modern times there is too much chatter on the field, although I remember in my own day there was always a bit of talk out in the centre. It has always been part of the game and I particularly like the story, related to me by Ian Peebles many years ago, of that character Walter Robins making his way back to the pavilion at Lord's after coming off second best in the battle against J. C. 'Farmer' White in a May match in 1935. 'Robbie' had given White the charge, missed and kept walking from the Nursery end straight for the dressing-room. The fielder at silly-point, possessed of a nice sense of humour, looked straight ahead and said, 'He's missed it.' Without turning to look, Robins hurled himself backwards, stretching out to try and make his ground, only to look up to the astonished gaze of wicket-keeper and first slip who by now were having a little chat to one another as the umpire moved in to replace the bails.

That's the sort of conversation on the field I prefer, rather than what goes under the name of 'sledging' in the 1980s.

* * *

Umpires, with the video screen behind them and the players in front of them, face many difficult situations these days. Slow bowlers like Abdul Qadir appealing for lbw sometimes inflame the crowd, but generally the faster bowlers, with the pain and sweat and tears driving them, are in there somewhere and have been so in Australia over the years. In recent times it has been Lillee and Thomson and the other fast bowlers who have since joined them, and there is no question fast bowlers seem to have a lower flash point than their slower counterparts.

There are times when it is better for players to say nothing at all when the fast men are bowling at them. Way back in the 1951–52 season, when I made my Test match début, it was alongside two Victorian opening batsmen, Colin McDonald and George Thoms, both of whom had such good seasons for the southern state they too forced their way into the final Test against the West Indies. They did it I might say with considerably better performances than I had to my credit that summer, even though I had made a century against South Australia in Adelaide and taken a few wickets as well. McDonald and Thoms had each made over 500 runs at an average of better than 50 and it was on George Thoms's first sighting of Ray Lindwall that he assured himself of a permanent niche in the lore of Australian cricket.

New South Wales in the December 1951 match had made 533, 412 for 2 coming on the first day. For George Thoms, as he walked out with Colin McDonald to open the Victorian batting, this was his first sight of Ray Lindwall and, with that vast total ahead of them, he was understandably a trifle nervous. He said nothing for a time until Lindwall had him play and miss at two in one over and then found the outside edge with another, the ball flying wide of gully. Lindwall was standing, hands on hips, looking at him as he ran past and it could only have been sheer nervousness in the confrontation with the great man which caused George to say, 'Gee whizz, you must have been fast a few years ago.'

Down the other end in the slips we didn't know what had happened but we knew it must have been something interesting because the next two overs from Lindwall were as quick as anything he had bowled in the whole of the season, and that was the year when he gave the West Indian batsmen a tremendous going-over in the Test matches. I think George realised very quickly that, if he were to try conversation in the future, it should not be along the lines of suggesting anyone might possibly be over the hill at 30 years of age.

Lindwall and Miller, when they'd played together for New South Wales, were always difficult for opposition teams and in the 1956–57 season I found myself facing Lindwall, now playing for Queensland, and understanding what it must have been like for them over the years. At the time, Queensland were making a determined bid for the Sheffield Shield and in the end missed out by only one point on what would have been their greatest-ever achievement. We won the toss and batted on the first day when Lindwall, coming in from the Southern or Randwick end, bowled superbly with a gale at his back.

He wasn't given full support by his fielders and, additionally, the Queenslanders considered themselves hard done by with some umpiring decisions, notably when Johnny Martin, who was batting with me at the time, square drove Wally Walmsley very hard and fast to Jim Bratchford at point. Bratchford dived forward and claimed the catch – the umpire said 'no'. Lindwall was one of the most easy-going cricketers ever to play the game, but he was extremely angry and upset at this and next over came steaming in at me and bowled me one of the fastest overs, or part thereof, it had ever been my displeasure to face.

I played defensively at the fifth ball and it flew off the shoulder of the bat straight to Peter Burge at gully who took a comfortable catch at waist height. As I turned to leave for the pavilion, Lindwall was storming down the pitch at me, gesticulating and saying 'Blooing New South Wales cheats. Why don't you stay there? Don't go, don't go – wait for him to say, "not out".' (Lindwall never swore. The strongest he ever used was 'Blooin' – which was a cross between blooming and bloody.) It sounds comical now, and it was out of character for Ray, but I whipped round at him and we had a short, sharp exchange along the lines of if he couldn't find anything better to say then shut up. He kept on with his sarcastic invitation for me to stay there and we finished up wagging fingers at one another in the middle of the SCG. No television for that match of course, so it's imprinted on the memories of few people, compared with these days if the same thing happened.

Aggro from fast bowlers often has its origins in the type of pitch provided. If a good pitch with even bounce is produced there tends to be much less aggro than if it is a green-top where the fast bowler is able to punish the batsman by digging the ball in just short of a length and making life very uncomfortable for him. At the Sydney Cricket Ground in the 'fifties, when Bill Watt was curator and we had Miller and Lindwall, there was often likely to be a lot of grass left on the pitch and there is no doubt this made life decidedly uncomfortable for many of the batsmen coming from interstate to play at the SCG.

Even a past chairman of the Australian Cricket Board was not immune from aggro in those days, particularly in one match in the 1951–52 season when South Australia came up to Sydney. We had a bowling attack then of Lindwall, Walker, Brooks and Alan Davidson, though Davidson for this game against South Australia unfortunately was injured, and that at a time when he was having a magnificent season. Alan Walker, who had played for Australia and later played with Nottinghamshire, had a whippy bowling action and could be very, very fast when the mood took him. The mood took him this day in Sydney and the quicker bowlers accounted for South Australia for only 159, with Bruce Bowley retired hurt early in the innings after he ducked low into a bouncer from Walker. We made 428 in reply – the match was the one in which Ian Craig made his first-class début and he and I shared a 150-run partnership.

When South Australia had to bat again they got themselves into all sorts of trouble, were bowled out for 259 and the game finished with a day to spare – not however before Phil Ridings, who made 103 out of the 259, was part of an incident which, had it happened today, would have been flashed across every television station in the land and on the front page of every newspaper. Walker, who finished with 1 for 69 from 11 overs in the second innings, was bowling his tenth over when he let loose a spate of bouncers against Ridings and Bowley who, in a desperate bid, had come in to try and prop up the innings. Walker was warned for intimidatory bowling by Herb Elphinston and he was also warned by Ridings that, if by chance or design he hit him, it would be most unfortunate for Walker because Ridings would chase him around the ground and flatten him with the bat which he was now brandishing under his nose. Phil's 103 might not have saved the side but it accelerated moves in that season, some 30 years ago, to have fewer bumpers bowled.

Not long before that match in Sydney, on the same ground, the Victorian batsmen had also taken a lot of bouncers from Walker, Miller and, to a lesser extent, Alan Davidson, and complaints had gone in to the authorities. Extraordinary isn't it? Here we are in 1984 talking about too many bumpers being bowled, yet I can assure you in those days bowlers bowled half as many bumpers again as they do now and got away with it. They got away with it because, although isolated instances such as this might have come to the administrators' attention, there was no television to accent the fact there was perhaps a surfeit of short-pitched bowling.

Two comparatively recent incidents, both seen on television, spread waves of alarm through the cricket world. The first occurred when Bob Willis hit night-watchman Iqbal Qasim with a bumper during the Edgbaston Test on the 1979 Pakistan tour of England. What the frustrated Willis had done was merely get sick and tired of having the night-watchman place his front foot down the pitch and play with a dead bat, knowing full well Willis wouldn't drop anything short at him. Iqbal Qasim, in fact, wasn't a tailender this day, he was a number-three batsman having come in late the previous evening after Mudassar had been bowled by Phil Edmonds for 30. The first wicket had fallen at 94 and Iqbal Qasim was sent in to play out time and then resume on the Monday. This he did and added 29 runs with Sadiq before the incident occurred.

Both Willis and his skipper Mike Brearley came under fire for the injury sustained by Iqbal Qasim, but I felt there was a much too rigid interpretation of the playing conditions which stated, 'Captains must instruct their players that the fast, short-pitched balls should at no time be directed at non-recognised batsmen.' I agree with the sentiment, but what do you do about a non-recognised batsman who is deliberately put in to avoid the loss of the wicket of a recognised batsman and then deliberately sets out to take advantage of that playing condition? If you *are* going to have playing conditions of this kind, the next logical step would be to ban night-watchmen. As soon as you let a night-watchman come in to face up to fast bowlers, try to take the shine off the ball and deliberately take advantage of a law, then you have real problems, as was shown that day at Edgbaston.

The second incident to spark off a storm of controversy occurred in New Zealand when Ewen Chatfield was badly injured by a bouncer from Peter Lever. This was the classic case of a tailender frustrating a fast bowler, with Chatfield and Geoff Howarth, the present New Zealand captain, sharing in a last-wicket partnership of 44. Lever bowled a bouncer, Chatfield played defensively, the ball flew from his glove on to the side of his forehead and it turned out later he had sustained a hairline fracture of the skull. Those who rush in these days wanting the bouncer to be banned, or penalised in some extreme way, tend to use this incident in the mainstream of their argument.

What they say is Ewen Chatfield was almost killed by a bouncer from Peter Lever. That is absolute nonsense. The people making such statements know it is nonsense but they go ahead anyway and make it for their own purposes. The hairline fracture of his skull posed no more problems than is normal with an injury of that kind and it was healed in plenty of time for Chatfield to take his place in domestic cricket the following year, and later again to play for New Zealand.

What actually happened though was Chatfield swallowed his tongue. This sometimes occurs on the football field but it was the first time I'd known it to happen on the cricket field and I can tell you, watching from the press box, it was a most distressing sight. Fortunately, Bernard Thomas, the England team's physiotherapist, rushed to the centre of the ground, quickly diagnosed the problem, pulled Chatfield's tongue out of his throat and gave him mouth-to-mouth resuscitation which saved his life. Thomas said later it was the worst case of tongue-swallowing he had seen and he wouldn't want to witness another. I don't blame him.

Being carried from the cricket field is no fun I can tell you. It happened to me back in 1949 when I went down to Melbourne with a New South Wales Second XI shortly after I had been chosen also for the New South Wales Sheffield Shield team. We played the Shield match one week and then travelled to Melbourne where, as a Shield player, I was asked by skipper Brian Dwyer to go in as night-watchman. The basis of the request was that I was already in the state side and had far less to lose than some of the other batsmen. I was quite happy to do that. In fact, I was not out overnight and the next morning faced two fairly quick bowlers – Jack 'Dasher' Daniel and Bernie Considine. Jack Daniel let me have a bouncer which I tried to hook. I missed and it hit me above the right eye, fracturing my skull badly.

I was taken off the field moaning, with blood running out of my nose and pins and needles in my arms and legs, and I wasn't sure exactly what was happening to me, but I knew it wasn't very good. Astonishingly, the hospital could find no sign of the fracture because you could have jammed a cricket ball in the hole in my forehead. It wasn't until I got back to Sydney that they found on other X-rays there was a very large dent in my skull and I had to have a lengthy operation and was hospitalised for a fortnight. I didn't play any more that year so I had plenty of free time on my hands to ruminate about short-pitched bowling. Once I recovered though and was able to get back on the field, I hadn't lost any of my confidence and I think I can say, right up to the time I finished playing in Test matches in 1964, I was still able to hook with the best of them – or perhaps I should say the worst of them!

I firmly believe the bumper is a legitimate weapon for the fast bowler and on many occasions it is 'money for jam' for the batsman. Too many bumpers bore me to tears as a watcher and commentator, not because of the intimidation aspect but because I think it's such a waste of time. Cricket is a contest between bat and ball and too many bouncers devalue that contest: the fast bowler ploughs the ball into the turf about the middle of the pitch and the batsman nods his head at it as it goes past. The whole process is then repeated. What poor reward for the spectator who has paid his money at the gate!

These days we have all kinds of suggestions for remedying the amount of short-pitched bowling. They range from having a line drawn in mid-pitch, with a no-ball to be called if anything lands shorter than that, to adding ten runs to the score every time a ball passes a batsman at hip height. The latter is one of the strangest things I've ever heard – anything passing that height past the batsman should be four runs every time, and what happens if the ball does get up shoulder height and the batsman smites it for four? Does he have another ten runs added to the total because he has thrashed his opposition bowler? That would be a classic case of administration going berserk and not paying any attention to the after-effects of some new law introduced: the after-effects would in the end make a nonsense of the law.

* * *

The same day Willis hit Iqbal Qasim, a Rugby Union footballer in South Wales was convicted of causing grievous bodily harm for punching an opponent. The conviction was the first of its kind for violence on the Rugby field and made me wonder if there might be a spate of incidents with batsmen sueing bowlers if they're hit by bouncers, or even fielders sueing captains if they're injured on the field having been put in too dangerous a position by their skipper.

I used to field as close as anyone for Australia's bowlers and have had my share of injuries over the years in an era when helmets were not even thought of. There was also an occasion where I was instrumental in placing a team-mate in rather a dangerous position, but that was for a quite deliberate purpose. It happened during the Lord's Test of 1956.

The First Test at Nottingham had been drawn, with rain making a result impossible. I had had a moderate match in the first game, making 17 in a total of 148 and not taking a wicket in 18 overs, and, as well, had the mortification of seeing my mate Alan Davidson badly injured when his ankle twisted in a foot-hole while he was bowling from the pavilion end. He chipped a bone in the accident and, on the same day, we lost Ray Lindwall with a torn thigh muscle. Consequently we went into that Lord's Test match with Pat Crawford to open the bowling alongside Miller, the remainder of the attack consisting of Archer, Mackay, Ian Johnson and myself.

Crawford tore a muscle after bowling five overs which left the attack rather depleted, although in the end it turned out not to matter because of the tremendous effort put up by Miller and the other paceman, Ron Archer, the latter turning in a magnificent performance to keep the English batsmen playing and missing during most of his 54 overs. I made only 5 in the first innings of that game and then, with a first-innings lead of 114, shared a sixth-wicket partnership of 117 with Ken Mackay in the second innings. Eventually we were able to set England 372 to win with eight hours and 40 minutes to bat.

It was on the final day there came the close-in field-setting and Colin

Cowdrey was the batsman. He had opened with Peter Richardson and, after Richardson and Graveney had fallen to Archer and Miller respectively, Cowdrey and May came together in a dangerous partnership. Cowdrey was allowing all the scoring to be done by Peter May, who was in splendid form, while he was simply pushing his pad right out at everything I bowled him and holding his bat alongside and just behind it. I was shouting for lbw without any result even to topspinners fizzing off and going, as it seemed to me, straight for middle stump three parts of the way up.

I got sick of this after a while and spoke to Ian Johnson. I told him I wanted Peter Burge to go in very close to the bat at short mid-on – the closest fielding position I had ever asked for. Quite rightly, Johnson wanted to know why. I told him I was tired of having Cowdrey prod forward, not bothering to play a stroke, and I'd decided, if Johnson were in agreement, I would crowd him and try to force him on the back foot. My reasoning was that he might not want to play forward with a man that close in because of the possibility of the ball coming from his pad, on to his bat and then flying up in the air. Peter May indicated to Ian Johnson that any responsibility for injury to Burge would be on Johnson's head and I was very grateful to the skipper for backing me to the extent of saying, 'Yes okay, I'll accept that.' All he did was move Burge a couple of inches squarer.

It worked out exactly as I'd hoped and soon after Cowdrey, having been pushed back on to the back foot to play some slower leg-breaks, was plumb in front to a quicker topspinner. We took some stick in the press the following day – Colin was such a nice chap it didn't seem proper to attack him in this way – but I would have none of it and Johnson was strong enough to back me up. If Cowdrey were going to push forward without bothering to play any shots, in an innings of over three hours in which he compiled 27, then it was up to us to find some way to trap him, which is exactly what happened.

In 1948 Sid Barnes, the Australian opening batsman, received a severe injury fielding close in at Old Trafford when Dick Pollard was batting. Barnes, after he collapsed when going out to bat in the Australian second innings at Old Trafford, was unable to play in the following Test match at Leeds. There have, of course, been many other injuries to players fielding close to the bat. In recent times there have been several occasions when umpires have been asked to intervene to try to persuade captains to have their fielders stand back. Now incorporated in the Laws is a precise definition of exactly where the fielder is not permitted to be when the ball is delivered: 'No one may stand on or have any part of his person extended over the pitch measuring 22 yards by 10 feet.'

That is one thing, but it is an entirely different matter with some of the close-in fielders these days who have the luxury of wearing helmets and who also seem to find it impossible to stand still when batsmen are playing their strokes. Whether from the cricket and legal angle a fielder should be allowed or even forced to wear a helmet is a different matter. Philip Russell of Derbyshire was struck in the face at short-leg by a shot from Malcolm Nash of Glamorgan at Chesterfield in June 1978, the ball lodging in the visor of his helmet. He suffered a fractured cheekbone but might have been killed without the helmet.

The TCCB have ruled that the wearing of a helmet gives the fielder an unfair advantage. A batsman can be out however if he snicks the ball on to his own helmet. I couldn't possibly wear a helmet because it would be too uncomfortable. I have tried and know it wouldn't work, but I am in favour of other people wearing them if it is to save them being injured. The older cricket follower hates them and will proudly tell you of the times he has seen players get up and soldier on after being laid out whilst batting or fielding. Helmets worn by close-in fielders bring a shudder and when Mike Brearley first wore his helmet at Lord's people laughed. Why anyone should laugh at the fact that a sportsman might prefer not to be seriously injured or killed is a matter for some conjecture.

*   *   *

The first riot I saw where players were in danger of physical injury occurred during the final Test match in Sydney in 1971 when Ray Illingworth took his men off the field to allow a cooling-down period. Illingworth came under a great deal of criticism for this from some areas in England but I thought he handled things extremely well in that 1971 fracas.

I was watching the game from the press box as well as doing a ball-by-ball radio broadcast with Bill Lawry. The circumstances were that Terry Jenner, batting at number ten for Australia and facing John Snow, had ducked into a short-pitched ball which he thought was going to fly and, in fact, kept low. At this stage umpire Lou Rowan warned Snow for bowling persistent bumpers and Illingworth protested against the decision. When Snow went down to the fence alongside the Paddington Hill a drunk grabbed him and cans were thrown on to the field at both ends of the ground.

I had every sympathy for Illingworth, who took his team off the field to allow the ground to be cleaned up and also to enable the crowd to simmer down – it was the ugliest demonstration I had ever seen in Australian cricket, although I wasn't around watching the game when the Bodyline series was played.

A typical piece of heavy-handed Australian administration then came into the game, with the administrators and umpires warning Illingworth that if he didn't go back on the field (I assume irrespective of the circumstances and whether or not the surface was covered with cans) the match would be awarded to Australia – not *could* be mind you but *would* be. Some people said that that was a strong piece of administration, but I regarded it as being extremely weak. I would have thought the administrators would have wanted to make absolutely certain everything was in order back on the field before making such a high-handed demand on an English captain. What in any case would they have done if Illingworth had said he felt he needed further assurances that his side would be physically safe if they went back on the field? Would they have awarded the match to Australia? Of course not. It was simply a piece of bluff, with not very much commonsense attached to it either.

England had over the years been involved in other riot scenes at different times, mostly involving matches in the West Indies. When Len Hutton took his team there in 1953–54 there was tension on the tour even before the first match got under way. Umpires were threatened with physical violence and, having talked with some of the English players who toured, I can imagine it must have been one of the least enjoyable experiences of their lives. Threats were made against one of the umpires, Perry Burke, and his family to the effect that their house would be burnt down after he gave J. K. Holt out lbw to Brian Statham when Holt needed six more to make a century in his début Test.

In the Third Test of the series at Georgetown there were some disgraceful crowd scenes when Cliffie McWatt was given run out trying for a second run – the fielder was P. B. H. May. The decision by umpire Badge Menzies brought the crowd to their feet, hurling bottles and packing-cases on to the ground in what was a mixture of anger at the dismissal, annoyance at the loss of wagers and a deliberate bid to have the game held up.

At this stage West Indies were trying desperately to save the follow-on, England having made 435 in their first innings. Len Hutton however refused to leave the field and eventually the ground was cleared and the game continued. On the fifth day England managed to enforce the follow-on and win the game. They drew the next match in Port-of-Spain, this game being played on the mat, and then won the Fifth Test in Jamaica by nine wickets and so squared the series – a series full of incident, still remembered as much for the rioting as for whatever landmarks were reached in the cricket itself.

Then, during the 1959–60 MCC tour of West Indies, in the January Test match at Port-of-Spain, England won by 256 runs after play had to be abandoned on one of the days. This was a match which at the time created attendance and gate-taking records for a game in the West Indies. The trouble began on the third day, 30 January 1960, when Singh was run out to make the West Indies' score 98 for 8, a disastrous reply to England's first-innings total of 382. The crowd of almost 30,000 began throwing bottles on to the field and then the spectators themselves raced on the ground and the English players had to be escorted from the arena. No further play was possible that day but, when the game did get under way again, May didn't bother enforcing the follow-on and eventually declared at 230 for 9, setting the West Indies over 500 to win – a task which was beyond them and they were bowled out with an hour and 50 minutes to spare for England.

In February 1968, when Colin Cowdrey was captain, there was another bottle-throwing incident in mid-afternoon of the third day in Jamaica and, on this occasion, it involved Jim Parks diving away to his left behind the wicket to catch Basil Butcher. The bottle-throwing and tear-gas held up play until late in the day and England, after holding an enormous advantage on the first innings, barely managed to scramble out of the game with a draw, being 68 for 8 in their second innings – almost a victory for crowd violence.

There have been other crowd problems over the years and the worst instance recently was during the Indian tour of Pakistan in 1982–83. This riot was organised by the Jameeat e Tulba e Islam, a student organisation at Karachi University. Their members had been involved in student election violence 12 months earlier and some had been jailed. This riot at Karachi was because the organisation was trying to publicise its cause by creating attention at international occasions. It was said the Test match, with its political overtones, should never have been held there at that time. Imran Khan was quoted later as saying, 'Well, there were these maniacs running on to the pitch and shouting – Naara e Takbeer – and one of them raised a stump and rushed towards me.' The pitch was dug up, petrol bombs were thrown and exploded and it was a miserable occasion as far as sport was concerned.

Back in 1969 in Karachi, the game was abandoned on the third day when Alan Knott needed only four more runs for a début Test century. Students and citizens were rioting all over Pakistan at that stage and it must have been one of the most ill-conceived tours ever. Politicians were insisting the tour go on, irrespective of players' safety, and, even though rioting broke out during the First Test match at Lahore in February 1969, the players were forced to remain in Pakistan and go through the motions of Test cricket.

The behaviour of students in this type of riot is purely political, whereas the behaviour of the West Indians in those earlier days was occasioned more by disappointment, rum, betting on various happenings on the field and a belief that umpiring decisions were going against the side on which they had their money.

More recently in Pakistan, crowd violence has again been a problem. When the Australians toured in 1982 fielders were pelted with rocks and fruit and they were not only fed up with the crowds but, as well, were in real danger of injury.

In England in 1975 there was the affair of the Test match at Leeds where the pitch was dug up as a protest against the jailing of George Davis. This was the four-Test series played after the Prudential Cup was won by West

Indies and Australia had won the first of the Tests at Birmingham by an innings and 85 runs, the last time Mike Denness captained an England side. When the Australians got to Lord's for the Second Test, Tony Greig was made skipper and scored a dashing 96 out of England's total of 315 in a drawn game, with Australia 329 for 3 in their second innings.

It was the Third Test at Leeds which was abandoned, Peter Chappell being jailed for 18 months and three others who admitted to damaging the walls and the pitch at Headingley being given suspended prison sentences. The man they were attempting to have freed was a London East-ender serving 17 years in jail for armed robbery. The final match of the series at the Oval was drawn but featured a tremendous fightback by England who, after Australia had scored 532 for 9, replied with 191 and, in their second innings, 538.

Even the Centenary Test at Lord's in 1980 was the subject of a crowd disturbance, and not in the outer ground either! Play had been held up because of inadequate covering of the pitches at the Tavern side of the ground – almost unbelievable. The scuffle in which the umpires, one or two members and the captains were involved took place on the steps of the pavilion. As a result, the umpires were physically abused, the reputation of MCC members shaken and the match status damaged. Two and a half months later, after a thorough enquiry where some of our BBC film was used, Peter May, President of MCC, announced appropriate disciplinary action had been taken. It was stated to be no more fitting for members of a club publicly to question the decision of the umpires, let alone abuse them, than for players to do so on the field. One result might have been that better covering would be provided so the same kind of incident will be avoided in the future.

*　　*　　*

Not all the riots have been at the cricket grounds around the world, though it is fair to say this is where the majority of the trouble has been. Administrators have had their problems too, and I suppose selectors have often given way to temper when they have not been able to get their own way.

The biggest bust-up in the early days of Australian cricket was the battle in 1912, before the team was chosen for England, between the players and the Board over whether the players or the Board would nominate the manager. Frank Laver had been manager of the 1909 tour, when players were able to nominate their own man, and as his treasurer he had Peter McAlister who had been, and was at the time, a useful state cricketer who played eight times for Australia with little success. McAlister made his début in 1904 with 'Tibby' Cotter and later became a Test selector, which he was when the problems with the Board were looming in 1912.

Apparently the Board decided Laver was not their man for the Triangular series in 1912 and, as a consequence, Armstrong, Cotter, Ransford, Hill, Trumper and Carter declined to tour. Clem Hill was captain of Australia at the time and was well known as an advocate of the virtues of Frank Laver's bowling. As Hill was likely to be captain of the team to go to England, there was every chance he would be remembering that, in 1909, in the previous series in England, when Laver managed the team as well as played, he had bowling figures of 3/75 and 1/24, 1/15 and 0/6, 8/31 and 1/25, and 0/13. He must have wanted Laver to be considered. Monty Noble was captain of this team and Hill had succeeded him.

The three selectors of the Test matches in Australia in 1911–12 were Hill, McAlister and Frank Iredale who played his cricket with New South Wales and with my old club Central Cumberland. At the selection meeting prior to the Fourth Test, Hill complained bitterly that Laver was not even playing in the Victorian team, although he was good enough in his opinion to play for Australia. I find it difficult to believe the Board/player split was not influenced by the fact that Laver was not to be considered as a player.

At this time Australia were taking a hammering from England and, as is always the case in situations of this kind, tempers can become a little short. The story goes Hill and McAlister had words about first of all the fact Laver could not get a game in Victoria, then over the allegation that Charlie Kelleway and Roy Minnett were not being used by Hill in the right manner. Hill, with eight-wicket and seven-wicket margins against him in the previous two Tests, after winning the first by 146 runs, was not amused. He was even less amused when McAlister, in the course of a continuing heated argument, stated he was a better captain than Hill and, in fact, Hill was the worst captain he had ever seen.

Not a great start to the selection committee meeting you may think, for they had not at this stage got down to putting on paper the first name for the Fourth Test.

Nor were they to do so.

Hill was so incensed over McAlister's remark he reached across the table and punched him flush on the nose. With blood everywhere and both of them grappling at one another in front of the window 40 feet above the pavement, things could have been really nasty but for the intervention of Iredale who dragged them apart.

This then was the delightful preface to the Fourth Test match which was won by England by an innings and 125 runs – the Fifth went the same way by 70 runs. It was hardly surprising. There must have been enormous dissention in the camp at that time and the Board were already preparing their plans for the nomination of the manager of the touring team. It was certainly not to be Laver for he could not get in the State side, but that selection meeting may well be where everything came to a head.

Hill was only 34 years of age then and he never again played for Australia. Syd Gregory was recalled to captain the Board's team to England and then Warwick Armstrong, one of the original rebels, took over the Australian team immediately after the war.

Syd Smith was secretary of the Board at the time of that fracas and would, I suppose, have been present to take notes of the selections, or rather the non-selections, and to say a few words. Sixty-one years later he was responsible for a longer speech and a great riposte!

There are some great speech-makers in this world. Many of them are connected with cricket and fortunately, over the years, some with a command of English and a sense of humour have been chosen to speak at functions tendered to a touring team. There are other occasions though where the going can be a bit rough. Not least of those times was in 1952 when the South Africans came to Australia led by Jack Cheetham, with Ken Viljoen as manager.

Mr Smith was the President of the New South Wales Cricket Association at that time. He was a good talker and he made the welcoming speech – at least I think it was a welcoming speech. He spoke at some length on the fact poor old South Africa had only ever won one Test match in their history of contests against Australia. In fact, they were pretty lucky to have done that because the 1910–11 team, skippered by Percy Sherwell, should not actually have been in Australia. It was only on the condition that the South Africans agreed to come to Australia that the Australians would play in the Triangular tournament in England in 1912. It was emphasised Australia won the series 4–1. Also brought out was that on the previous two occasions when the sides had met, when Lindsay Hassett and Vic Richardson skippered teams to South Africa, both had resulted in 4–0 victories to Australia – and quite possibly this 1952–53 series in Australia would go the same way.

The delicate silence with which the start of the speech had been received was by now changed to the sound of eyebrows being raised. The *pièce de résistance* came when he said that the last time a South African team had played in Australia they'd made 36 and 45 and been beaten by an innings and 72 runs at the Melbourne Cricket Ground, and Australia had only needed to make 153 first-innings runs to achieve victory. Smith noted also that South Africa's present cricket was at an all-time low, and on this tour there was a possibility of them suffering some appalling defeats which could do long-term damage to the game.

Jack Cheetham was by now gripping his glass quite firmly and looking slightly over the top of the President's head. A gentle and urbane man, he thanked the President for his hospitality and good wishes and also thanked the New South Wales Cricket Association for the words of welcome. There was an embarrassed hush. He pointed out that, to date, his side hadn't been beaten and they had headed Western Australia on the first innings. Then, although having been led on the first innings by South Australia, they had fought back well enough to force a draw and the most recent match of their tour had also finished in a draw when rain had washed out play in Melbourne.

He added, with a glance at the ceiling, that his country, either in cricket or business, didn't set itself up to be of the same standard as Australia, and this was partly to do with the energetic manner in which Australians approached those aspects of life. For example, he continued, it was well known that the wool, sheep and cattle industries in Australia were far in advance of anything South Africa could hope to achieve. This applied in particular to the area of exporting stud bulls where Australia were light years ahead of South Africa. In fact, he said, after listening to tonight's speeches, he could go back to South Africa and tell his business partners that Australia, without doubt, had some of the best bull-shippers in the trade. . . .

Brought the house down he did and without even cracking a smile as he was doing it . . . or did I see a tiny little quirk at the corner of his lips?

9

SOUTH AFRICA: A CASE OF DOUBLE STANDARDS

There are two essential ingredients of the South African question in international cricket, genuiness and hypocrisy. There are many genuine people who wish to have nothing at all to do with a country where no coloured cricketer has yet reached Test status. There are just as many hypocrites who see the situation as a marvellous political exercise and a great chance for protest and demonstration.

This of course is not news. It has been the case since South Africa's Prime Minister in 1968 rejected an MCC touring team in which Basil D'Oliveira, a Cape coloured, had been chosen. The English cricket authorities quite rightly called off the tour. No one should be permitted to tell another country what should be the composition of their team, as West Indies were to discover in 1983. South Africa had every right to refuse a group of people from England, Australia or any country, but it was being naive and ridiculous in the extreme to expect anything but the reply they received.

In retrospect, one wonders how England managed to cancel the tour with such courtesy. My inclination, looking back on the events, is to think it was one of the most diplomatic cancellations of its time – or any other time for that matter. It was a decision forced on England by a piece of boorish behaviour, in keeping with a belief of invincibility on the part of South Africa's politicians.

Normally politicians as a whole are uninteresting. They have a job to do in the running of the country, they are appallingly underpaid, they are expected to work hours which would have union officials screaming blue murder, they are asked to lead private lives that are on the whiter than white side of impeccable and, with few exceptions, they are not outstanding in personality. They are a little like a cricket team in some ways: possibly a great player or two in an era, some good, some ordinary. Occasionally in Australia we have had outstanding people like Menzies and Evatt and, more recently, Fraser and Hawke, but, brilliant or ordinary, talented or run-of-the-mill, intellectual or otherwise, they all have one thing in common. Whether pro or anti, they go berserk when South Africa is mentioned.

South Africa will never play another official Test match. They will play plenty of unofficial games – such as the ones between West Indies and the

Springboks in 1983 during that tour which caused so much controversy – but they will never play against another *country* unless there is a split in the cricket world with West Indies, Pakistan, India and Sri Lanka playing against one another and England, Australia, New Zealand and South Africa making up the other four. The chances of this happening are remote to say the very least. South Africa's problems accelerated when Basil D'Oliveira was named in the English touring team as the replacement for Tom Cartwright at the end of the 1968 Australian tour of England. 'Dolly' had come into the England team for the Oval as a last-minute substitute for Roger Prideaux and, after being dropped by Barry Jarman at 31 and then three more times after reaching his century, went on to make a brilliant 158. When the team for South Africa was announced D'Oliveira was not included but Cartwright, as expected, then failed to pass a fitness test and D'Oliveira came in as his replacement. It was at that point John Vorster came on to the scene and announced the England team would not be welcome as chosen. Having met the late Mr Vorster once in 1976, I am not surprised that eight years earlier he was an inflexible spokesman on sporting matters, though I doubt he knew a great deal about the delicate aspects of cricket. Rugby football was far more likely to be his métier.

If some country turned around tomorrow and said a player in an Australian sports team would not be welcome, then I would do everything possible to make certain that team did not make the trip. The exception would be of course where there was a valid objection such as a criminal record or a history of something clearly against the laws of the land. Other than that, dictating to Australia who should be chosen cuts no ice at all with me. It would be the same if I lived in any other country. At the same time it must be recognised that any country at its borders has the right to refuse entry to an individual. When they expect however that the rest of the team or a new team will be nominated it all becomes impossible.

D'Oliveira was rejected by South Africa in a move they will never have ceased to regret and England's Cricket Council gave the most civilised reply along the lines of in that case there would be no tour. The gist of their statement was that if he were not acceptable then neither was the team and England and South Africa would not meet again until England could choose and have welcome the team nominated.

Then, in 1970, the South African tour of England was called off and in its place Rest of the World matches against England were substituted. The same happened in Australia in 1971–72 and a Rest of the World team captained by Garry Sobers played Ian Chappell's side in what turned out to be a great build-up for the tour of England in 1972. The calling off of the South African tour of Australia was close to inevitable once the same thing had happened in England. In 1970 there were genuine fears there could be bloodshed, with anti-apartheid demonstrators clashing with those who wished to see the South Africans play. When the South African rugby side played in Australia in 1971 it was hard enough for the police to keep control in a sports fixture lasting only 90 minutes. Over a full six hours it would have been impossible.

There are many aspects of the South African question which can be argued from the two points of view but in any discussion one always goes back to the high-level Vorster declaration of 1967 where he made it quite clear on behalf of his Government there would be no mixed-race sports events. He was of course wrong, but the damage done to the modern-thinking South African sports administrator was immense and it is something from which they still have not completely recovered. Mr Vorster said there would be no compromise on the matter and when he followed up this House of Assembly statement 17 months later with his refusal to accept the English team or, more to the point, D'Oliveira, it was little wonder that when the English cricket programme for 1970 was announced in September 1969 the demonstrators began painting their banners and rehearsing their violent anti-police tactics. The politicians began rehearsing their speeches after a House of Commons emergency debate and there was a statement from the Cricket Council that they believed it was the wish of the majority that the tour should take place. The Home Secretary, Mr Callaghan, stepped in and, on behalf of the Government, requested the invitation to the South Africans be withdrawn. This was done and at that point there came to an end another of those most controversial aspects of cricket which have been part of the game since it was first played.

South Africa were given a list of matters to attend to in the normalising of cricket in their own country. It was an imposing list and those who drew it up in the context of South African society at the time thought it would be difficult if not impossible to achieve. But achieve it they must, so they thought, if they were to be considered as cricket opponents at Test match level in the future. There were many of South Africa's detractors who quietly rubbed their hands together at the reading of the conditions. At a conservative estimate it was likely to take 20 years to fulfil.

In fact they did it easily, so easily there was widespread disquiet that, having been given the task and having achieved it, South Africa might logically be admitted back into the Test arena. It was then there was a sudden move of panic proportions to have South Africa debarred from the international sports field until everyone in the country had a vote. 'One man, one vote' became the catch-cry, though at times it was couched differently as 'no normal sport in an abnormal society'.

In 1975 I was approached, at the conclusion of the World Cup and the four Tests between England and Australia in England, to see if I would be prepared to play in or take part in a private tour of South Africa. Playing was out of the question because of a bad back and a determination to retire completely from that side of the game. I had always sworn, having been a player and seen what troubles they cause managers, I would never under any circumstances become a manager, so I declined the offer. Then, with two distinct areas of pressure being applied, I began to have second thoughts. One pressure group was constantly telling me South Africa were doing *all* the right things; the other group was telling me *only* critical things about the country. I decided to have a look for myself and make up my own mind.

Frank Twiselton was the assistant manager of the tour and he took a lot of the work off my shoulders and allowed me to get out and meet with cricket officials throughout the country once we had arrived. I liaised with Joe Pamensky, whom I have known since the first time I toured South Africa in 1957, and in the course of correspondence I listed a number of requirements for the tour before I would finally agree to participate as manager. I stipulated that, except in members' stands at the various grounds, audiences must be allowed to mix freely and bars, other than in the members' stand, must be open to all. I insisted on complete freedom to meet any non-white cricket officials I wished whilst in the country and told the organisers of the tour I would be the sole selector of the International Wanderers team. I added a little rider as well: every time a South African opposition team walked on to the field there were to be three non-white players included. The latter proviso could easily have been a problem, not for the obvious reason but because everyone at the time was talking about selection on merit. The difference was that, even though on the surface there were no Basil D'Oliveiras hidden away ready to be selected on merit, I was interested to see if we might unearth one or two.

It was, I can tell you, a tour with a difference. The first thing about it was that all those matters listed for the South African cricket authorities to attend to had certainly been completed. They had gone much further in fact in connection with club cricket being integrated and I was very surprised at the advance which had been made.

We played our opening match, a one-day affair, in Soweto and the opposition captain asked if we would do his team a favour. He said he knew the game could easily be prolonged by fiddling about when his team batted on the matting pitch but they would like to find out what it was like to face top-class Test match bowling in match conditions. They would, he said, never improve without having some idea of what standard they eventually had to reach. Though bowled out cheaply, they were suitably impressed by what they were given and it was refreshing that their attitude was not one of 'please take it easy on us and let us make a few'.

There were one or two hiccups during the tour, as one would expect in what was, in some ways, a first. Derrick Robins had previously taken four teams to South Africa and had done a splendid job in fostering the game there. Here now we were on a slightly different tack and we were not always certain in which direction the tour was taking us.

Eddie Barlow was the captain of the South African side and it was his task to handle the assimilation of the non-white players into the team. Those players go down as some of the bravest people I have met on a sporting field. They played their matches in the face of threats of physical violence to them and their families and other equally frightening threats of destruction of their property. Through it all they gritted their teeth and refused to be intimidated by those of their own race who were trying to stop them playing in the South African team. It was quite an education for me. I could have believed it if some wild Afrikaaner were to try to stop them playing in an international fixture. For their own to try to disrupt the tour was something else and it made me much more determined, if possible, to see the tour went smoothly to the end. Give or take a couple of midnight dashes by officials to promise someone his house would still be there in the morning, it did go relatively smoothly.

There were two occasions when I had to make it clear that my conditions would be invoked unless certain matters were attended to. They both took place in Port Elizabeth but were of completely different character. The first was on the morning of a one-day match where one of the local black administrators came to see me to say he had been refused service at the bar at the back of the stand. I had an agreement with those running the tour that if anyone had trouble of this kind they would find me and let me have the details. I went to look for the local officials in charge of the match and then together we went to find the chief of police who had created the problem. His opening remark was that he would continue in the same vein because the required papers had not been signed saying the whole world could drink in any of the bars other than the members'. He was, to say the least, a very determined-looking character. He also looked as though he would have been a formidable opponent in the front row of any rugby team, but he agreed after a short discussion that he would after all be able to make the necessary arrangements. This instantly reduced to zero the chance of all my players catching the following day's plane out of Johannesburg for points east or west. It was gently put to him that he could be either amenable or famous and he chose to be amenable.

That night one of the more prominent South African officials, smarting under the defeat of the day, said to me that it was the last bloody time they would allow themselves to be forced into choosing three non-white players. In future it was going to be a test of strength. When the teams got to Johannesburg, South Africa would have their best possible team in the field and they would carve up bloody Lillee and the rest of them. It only took moments to sort that out, along the same lines as the earlier misunderstanding, but I waited until the right moment in Jo'burg to let Dennis know about it. He took 7 for 27 against the South African XI and gave the crowd a rare moment of cricketing joy with some of the greatest fast bowling ever seen at the Wanderers. It would have been better had he been able to bowl out the little dark-haired batsman who showed enormous courage against him and refused to give an inch. This was Tieffie Barnes and he showed a rare brand of fight in combating Lillee and the other International Wanderers bowlers. I wasn't slow to underline again for the local South African officials that there might even be a few D'Oliveiras lurking about, just waiting, like Barnes, to be discovered.

Eddie Barlow came up trumps in the final match in Durban where he had in his side a left-arm spin bowler, Baboo Ebrahim. The Wanderers were set 348 to make in the last innings of the match and he bowled South Africa to victory by a margin of 122 runs. It was a double pleasure for Barlow who had been one of the players, with Graeme Pollock and Mike Procter, to make their protest against the South African Government policies that day in Cape Town some years earlier.

Eddie Barlow was magnificent on the 1976 tour. He was always a fine all-round cricketer, combative sometimes to an extreme, but also generous, even though playing the game as hard as it is possible to play. He came across as one well aware of the problems facing his country in getting back into international cricket and as a man with a fine sense of humour. He needed it!

I had gone on this short tour to see for myself what was happening to and in South African cricket. They had done a great deal from the last time I was there, indeed they had done far more than even their friends had thought possible, but there was still an enormous amount to be done. To try to gain readmission to the international field was going to be a job of near-impossible proportions because by now the politicians were busy fine-honing the Gleneagles Agreement, which was in later years to give the excuse for some of the most laughably hypocritical behaviour we have seen in sport.

I went back to Australia happy with the information I had gained and hopeful that the tour would be a stepping-stone for others like Howie Bergins, Barnes and Ebrahim to make a mark in South African cricket. Happiest moment of the tour? Undoubtedly to see the skill with which Ebrahim bowled under Eddie Barlow's splendid captaincy at Durban.

One of the most interesting moments of the tour was to have a meeting with Prime Minister Vorster, Dr Piet Koornhof and Joe Pamensky in Parliament House, Cape Town, during our stay in that city. It would be an exaggeration to say Mr Vorster made a lasting impression on me because of his general bonhomie and goodwill, though he did deliver a speech to let me know visitors to South Africa were expected to conform to the laws of the land. All I could do was reply that if I found any of my pre-tour conditions were not being adhered to then I would remember his thoughts on the laws of his land and go home, but I don't think I got through at all.

I thought Piet Koornhof was a very solid character with a good deal to him. I'm not sure what he is doing now in South African politics but I am afraid his dream of normalizing sport so he can watch a Test played at Newlands has as much chance of succeeding as one of those outsiders running in the 3.30 at one of the picturesque South African racetracks.

The next significant stage concerning the South African question had as its highlight, or lowlight – whichever way you care to look at it – the ICC meeting at Lord's in 1982. It was at this meeting the South African delegates wished to present a paper setting out what had been done in multi-racial cricket in South Africa in the previous 12 months. With the Gleneagles Agreement very much in mind, the politicians of the cricket-playing countries were taking great interest in proceedings. In Australia Mr Malcolm Fraser, the Prime Minister, was preparing to chair the meeting of CHOGM in Melbourne and his advisers were keeping a wary eye on whether South Africa might be readmitted to the ICC, or even admitted to the pending meeting to put a case.

I don't blame the Australian Government for being edgy over this, nor do I blame the politicians of the other countries for being edgy about it. What I do blame them for though is not having the elementary foresight to understand what would be the effect of refusing South Africa the chance to put their case. They were so terrified of upsetting some of the black nations they were unable to see past the immediate effect, and the sigh of relief they breathed when the news came that South Africa had been given the elbow was typical of the lack of forward thinking.

When the news of the South African rejection was broadcast in the afternoon I just shook my head. There was no question as to South Africa's next move. They would stage their own matches from now on because they had been given a clear indication that until 'one man, one vote' became law in South Africa there would be no international cricket. First of all the South African cricket authorities successfully organised a team of Englishmen to tour and they followed up with the Arosa Sri Lankan tour. That was either a failure or a muted success, depending on the voice to which one listened. That was followed by the signing of the West Indians and that one was a real success.

All this was predictable from that day in 1982 when the International Cricket Conference allowed the politicians of their countries to make the decisions for the future. It also had far-reaching effects on cricket all over the world and will continue to do so in years to come.

Following the tour by English players, under intense pressure from the politicians of India and Pakistan, England banned for three years from Test cricket all the players who had taken part in the 1982 tour. This in itself seemed to be an extraordinary decision, taking into account the fact that the cricketers had broken no law of the land and had certainly broken no existing law of the TCCB. For England to impose these bans on their players seemed to me to be nothing less than capitulation to blackmail. India and Pakistan said they would not tour England if the players were included in a Test team, so the players were banned. It may have been expedient but it hardly made sense.

It made less sense to me having sat through the court case in 1977 when Mr Justice Slade issued his judgement on the attempted banning of those players who wished to play for World Series Cricket. Why the banned English players of 1982 themselves never set up a test case in court will remain one of the mysteries of our time.

No one had been banned after the International Wanderers team visited South Africa in 1976. So why were the England players banned after their tour in 1982? Was it on account of that piece of paper called the Gleneagles Agreement?

The Agreement came into being in June 1977 because there was a chance of a withdrawal by the black nations from the Commonwealth Games in Canada in 1978. (Some black nations had already withdrawn from the Montreal Olympics of 1976 and four years earlier Israeli athletes had been murdered at the Munich Olympic Games, all of which tested one's belief in the worth of the Olympic movement.) The Gleneagles Agreement makes it clear that no Government must necessarily take away from sportsmen and sports bodies the 'freedom' and the right to decide whether or not to play against South Africa. In some countries the word 'freedom' is relatively unknown, whereas compulsion is very much to the fore. How that Agreement could in any way be regarded as justification for banning the English players leaves my non-legal mind in a whirl.

The banning came about not because they had done anything wrong – the cricket authorities were at pains to stress this particular point – but because of money. In a way this is understandable because cricket is only able to exist at first-class level with adequate finance, despite the outraged feelings of many that this should be so. India's politicians allowed the England tour of India in 1981–82 to go on purely for monetary reasons. The TCCB banned the English players to avoid losing money. The Cricketers' Association confirmed the ban on the players and backed the TCCB for financial reasons. The worst part of the banning of the English players was that they had no idea in advance what the penalty, *if any*, would be if they were to go to South Africa as professional cricketers following their trade.

I have no doubt the eventual penalty pleased the politically-minded in some countries but how it could possibly be construed as fair rather than expedient in England, a country which is the bastion of fair play, is totally beyond me. Equally strange is the fact that in 1979 an ICC delegation recommended a strong multi-racial team be sent to South Africa, yet since that date precisely nothing has been done. It requires no abnormally agile mind to see the hands of the politicians in that one.

In the same year, 1979, a group of English women cricketers toured South Africa. In 1983 the Governments of Jamaica and the Bahamas refused to accept another team of women cricketers because some of them were in that 1979 team. This banning occurred around the same time as the West Indian XI, captained by Lawrence Rowe, began their South African tour. The cricket world was in turmoil. The tour was apparently a great success with the matches completely dominating life in South Africa for more than four weeks. The 'Tests' were sold out well in advance, there was live television of the games and the multi-racial matches attracted a multi-racial audience, which was in my experience never notably the case in South African domestic cricket or when South Africa played Test matches.

First Sri Lankan players, now West Indians! The immediate and lasting attitude was one of fury that the South African cricket authorities had done such a thing. Why had they not merely sat back and waited until the other countries handed them a crumb or two at the whim of the politicians?

Sadly I have to assume they simply got fed up to the back teeth with the empty words they were hearing from everyone and eventually it sunk in that they were merely being played along. The mistake made though by the administrators of the game, as highlighted earlier, was that they didn't play them along enough. In 1982 at the ICC they did not have the commonsense to see what an opportunity they were giving South Africa. They were in effect compelling them to go it alone and organize their own cricket tours whereas, by permitting them to present their case, they could have said: 'That all sounds good. We'll spend a year examining what you have said and we'll see you again in 12 months. Of course in the meantime you will not organize any tours to South Africa because that would prejudice your case . . .'

Lawrence Rowe's team and future teams to South Africa need have no fears or ambitions that they will be helping or hindering South Africa's future as a Test match nation. That will never come about. All the players will be doing is making a choice of whether or not they wish to play sport in a particular country, whether it be South Africa, Russia, India, Pakistan, the United States, Australia or Sri Lanka, to name but a few.

The West Indies' tour of South Africa produced many strong reactions, one of which came from the Australian Government. It would appear that very little thought went into their statement on 21 January, 1983, banning for life from Australia all the West Indian players taking part in the tour. At least I hope very little thought went into it. It would be a poor business if that was the best my Government could do after giving the matter mature political thought. I was not in accord with the views of Mr Fraser and the

Government and said so in a column published in the *Melbourne Herald* the following day.

'The announcement from Canberra yesterday was one of the most astonishing statements of our time, even if we make allowances for it being made against a political background.

'Last year when a team of white Englishmen went to South Africa – a tour which was paid for by the South African Cricket Association and a Brewery – no word was heard from our capital. Mr Fraser, so far as I know, did not place a lifetime ban on Graham Gooch, Geoff Boycott and all the other Englishmen who were later suspended by the Test and County Cricket Board. I hope there is not one law in this country for a white cricketer and another for a black West Indian. Now that would be something, even in the politically-discriminating world in which we live.

'I don't have the slightest sympathy for any of our politicians in Canberra if they find themselves in a dilemma over this. When I was in England last year and the International Cricket Conference was on, the two delegates from South Africa asked permission to attend to present a paper on the position of multi-racial cricket in South Africa. The Australian delegates had to refuse even to allow them in to the meeting. A nice piece of political grandstanding but laughable if you worked out the likely consequences.

'As soon as I heard what had happened I knew that down in Canberra there was no one who had the slightest idea about cricket and cricketers. And they certainly knew nothing about South Africa. They might hate them but they know nothing about them.

'If Canberra, instead of orchestrating the refusal to let the South African delegates in to the meeting, had used their brains and allowed them in, they would have effectively stopped the Springboks organising any tours of this kind for at least two years. It was a naive political gesture lacking commonsense. And it was simply asking South Africa to go away and organise their own tours. Which is precisely what they have done.

'It is amusing now to see the same politicians suddenly realising what a nonsense they made of last year's meeting at Lord's. I, and many others, had told them late in July that they had absolutely no idea of what they were doing. But can one tell politicians anything? Now our Prime Minister has come out and banned for life from Australian shores, for life mind you, West Indian cricketers who, in any case, are most unlikely to have wanted to come to Australia. The Englishmen might and so might the Sri Lankans, who were also noticeably absent from the Government's lifetime ban list of yesterday.

'It has been my experience over the years that sport gets along famously until politicians decide to take a hand, other than in countries like the USSR and East Germany where Governments run sport. The July 1982 ICC meeting at Lord's was a classic example. It was Australia's first real political move in cricket and it was mucked up.

'In Adelaide yesterday the Chairman of the Australian Cricket Board, Phil Ridings, was reported as saying, "Whatever Mr Fraser says is Government policy. I can't comment until we have had time to consider it." The members of the Australian Cricket Board do not normally get a great deal of sympathy from me but I now offer them my deepest condolences. I am afraid there is no way out now for the Board because when a Government of any persuasion takes over decision-making that is the end.

'The Australian Cricket Board will have to live with Canberra pulling the strings of cricket for a long time to come, even if some of the actions are as stupidly discriminating as this one.'

Those were my thoughts the day after my Government placed the ban on the West Indian players and I have not the slightest change of mind a year later. It was a weak, thoughtless decision and the Australian Cricket Board and other sports authorities in Australia should be looking with disquiet at any Liberal or Labor Government of the future which tries to do the same sort of thing. Theoretically in Australia we citizens are still able to have freedom of choice. This was the first time I wondered if that were to be only a myth in the future.

After the West Indian tour of South Africa was completed there was no shortage of further controversy on the South African question.

There were moves to have MCC send a team to South Africa and this was defeated at an Extraordinary General Meeting where the voting was approximately 60 per cent against and 40 per cent for. But fewer than 60 per cent of the members voted, an effective way of denying the necessary two-thirds majority without actually going to the ballot box.

Prior to that the West Indies Board of Control had refused to allow their World Cup team to play a match against Yorkshire at Hull because Geoff Boycott and Arnold Sidebottom were in the Yorkshire side. Both had been banned for having taken part in the tour of South Africa. Proceeds from the match were to go towards financing a scholarship for 'deserving West Indians and what they have done over the years for racial harmony'. There was a certain amount of delicious irony about the whole thing.

Then the West Indian Board of Control were given some stiff warnings that their moves to nominate which English players would take part in matches in England in 1984 were destined to fail. It worked for India and Pakistan when they threatened not to come to England in 1982, but now the counties were digging in and I found feelings certainly had changed to a marked degree.

A lot of people now thought that the effect of the TCCB bans had gone on long enough and, whilst some counties, in the normal modern fashion of denigrating the fixture against the touring side, might anyway leave out their 'rebels', others would insist on playing them. West Indies scrambled out of complete capitulation by asking 'that they be given the same consideration as India and Pakistan' the previous year with their tours.

It was announced on 5 August, 1983, that the West Indies tour of England would go ahead but it required quite a climb-down on the part of the West Indian Board for this to be so. This in itself was sad. People like Allan Rae and Jeff Stollmeyer, both fine administrators, had no choice in the fact they had to appear completely intractable on the issue. When the climb-down came it was they who appeared to have buckled under rather than the politicians who had been manipulating the issue.

During the 1983 summer South Africans Allan Lamb and Chris Smith played cricket for England whilst Englishmen Graham Gooch and John Emburey, among others, were confined to county cricket. West Indies, India, Pakistan and Sri Lanka took part in the World Cup and some of their players happily played county cricket against Gooch, Emburey and the rest. Sometimes they were in the same team, sometimes in the opposition.

Hypocritical or merely massive irony? No more ironic and mixed up, I suppose, than that the rebel West Indian players were banned for life from visiting Australia because they played against white South African cricketers who had been barred from international cricket because of the policies of their own Government. When Mr Fraser's coalition Liberal/National Party was defeated at the polls a few months later, a far more sensible and reasonable wording was substituted for the original ad hoc statements.

In June 1983 the International Conference on Sanctions against South Africa took further steps to ban from the Olympic Games any country having sporting links with the Republic. Organizations like the British Amateur Rowing Association were to be 'taught a lesson' for allowing South African oarsmen to compete at Henley, and Britain, the United States and New Zealand as countries were condemned.

Britain were also singled out for their intention to use South Africa as a staging post for the building of the Falklands airport. In vain I looked for some mention of condemnation of one of the most interesting and lucrative pieces of collaboration of our modern times, the joint venture between South Africa and Russia on the establishment of international diamond market prices. Between Russia and South Africa. Can you believe it? To give them the benefit of the doubt, I assume the Conference delegates merely forgot to mention it, even if it is weighing heavily on the consciences of those same members whose organization is sponsored by the United Nations.

To assume otherwise would again be to bring into question the matter of hypocrisy and double standards in dealings with South Africa. The worst of these double standards comes, as in the diamonds affair mentioned above, when countries happily trade and deal with South Africa on one level and on another exile them on the level of sport. As it stands now the right to trade with South Africa to the tune of millions upon millions of dollars has never been seriously challenged. This, so far as I can see, is because it is expedient not to do so but it is a relatively simple matter to beat the hell out of sport.

I should very much like to be in court as a spectator when the first such challenge comes along to hear the definition of sport and trade and other matters, and to hear the verbal ducking and weaving of the plaintiffs as they try to circumvent Mr Justice Slade's judgement of the World Series Cricket case which was won with costs. In the meantime, don't hold your breath for the moment when South Africa will next appear in international cricket. It will never come.

I believe South Africa's cricketers should be brought back into the international sphere because of the tremendous progress which has been made in integrated cricket throughout the country. I am not naive enough to think there is anything in the slightest degree reasonable about apartheid apart from self-interest of the ruling party. In the same way I am not naive enough to think there is anything good about the Soviet Union shooting down an unarmed aircraft carrying 274 passengers or invading countries like Hungary and Afghanistan, murdering as many as they like as they go along. Nor is there much to commend in the racial and religious prejudice in countries like India, Pakistan and Iran. And how could an Australian be other than disturbed by the injustice and repression in his own country, where the Aboriginal rights question has been the subject of such appallingly slow and muddled thinking.

It seems though that we are expected in the cause of expediency to accept all these things and, at the same time, give South Africa, but no other country, the wham-bang treatment. The problem with South Africa as a cricket country, and for politicians like Piet Koornhof and South African cricket administrators like Joe Pamensky and Ali Bacher, is not that they haven't done well but they have done *too* well. The smart ones among South Africa's opponents are not in the slightest interested in progress in South Africa. To recognize progress of any kind would have the appalling effect of eliminating the political weapon they themselves have deliberately manufactured. Full marks to them for being clever! But is it something else as well?

Hypocrisy? Double standards? Whatever you like to call it, it will be with us for a long time and, in cricket, you can forget about South Africa other than as a country which will have bigger and better rebel sports tours in years to come.

10

WHAT AM I OFFERED FOR THIS JOB LOT OF ADMINISTRATORS?

Captaincy of a cricket team is the delight of one's life. It is exciting, nerve-racking, depressing and joyous. It allows for gambling instincts to come to the surface, defensive plans sometimes to be put into operation to save a game, and it brings out the best, and sometimes the worst, in a cricketer. In a sense, one cricket captain is like one cricket administrator. The former is doing the job on the field, the latter off it, sometimes without having had the benefit of ever having been on it at first-class or Test level.

Captains need certain attributes to be successful. Top of the list of these are, I believe:

1. Their thinking should be rational.
2. They should remain calm in the face of the worst of adversity.
3. Whatever decisions they make should be in anticipation of events.
4. All decisions taken should be in the light of winning a match or at the very worst settling for an honourable draw.

That may appear a daunting list but it is not as difficult as it looks. It adds up to commonsense, quick thinking and an ability to behave rationally. Should not the same guidelines apply to administrators who run the game? Administrators are in a unique position. It is not hard for a player to be dropped from a cricket team – thousands can testify to that. It is only a little more difficult for captains to be changed – Cowdrey, Illingworth, Denness, Yallop, Close, Hughes, Brearley and Botham can testify to that. Umpires these days are sitting ducks to be dropped – either temporarily or permanently. But administrators are seemingly with us forever. There may occasionally be a case of a minor official getting the chop but it is rare indeed for the more established ones to feel the touch of cold steel on the neck. It has always intrigued me that this should be so.

I grew up in an atmosphere in Australia where there was a clear division between players and administrators. The administrators ran the game like a private club, with little reference to the players, and there was no one to take them to task for decisions they made off the field, nor is there these days. It is only since World Series Cricket in Australia that the current players there have had any kind of purposeful connection with administration; in England, however, the Cricketers' Association has for many years acted as an excellent bridge between the groups.

In my days the players were never highly regarded by the Board other than as the athletes who took part in the matches . . . and administration was inflexible. Sometimes that inflexibility was taken to farcical extremes, as happened when Pat Crawford's wife was ordered off the ship at Melbourne in 1956.

Crawford had been chosen in the Australian team to go to England in 1956, had married an English lass and was taking her home by boat. The Australian Cricket Board tossed her off. That was bad enough but the most hilarious thing then happened when we were in the Mediterranean. Our ship's captain announced the name of the vessel we could see in the distance sailing parallel to us and it turned out to be the one on which Pat Crawford's wife had been put. So there we were, two ships going in the same direction, husband on one and his wife on the other. The ludicrous aspect of it was that Crawford could have had a mistress on board, but not his wife, and the Board would have said nothing. They were the days when the administrators made absolutely certain that they kept one foot on top of you all the time.

Some Australian administration over the years I played was, to me, quite baffling. Many of the baffling bits were to do with finance, two were 'specials'.

New Zealand, just over the water, were not only ignored for many years, they were insulted by not being offered the chance to play cricket with Australia. It was a travesty that we were not prepared, because of the thought of losing money on a tour, to have a New Zealand team in Australia for a Test series until 1973.

The first time I properly watched a New Zealand Test cricketer in action was in 1957 when Ian Craig's team played three representative matches and other games against Plunket Shield sides. No Tests! That was eight years after I had made my début in first-class cricket in Australia. These days there is a cry that too much Test cricket is played between countries. You certainly could never use that as an excuse in those days when tours came along just often enough for the amateur players and administrators to cope. Australians were never allowed to see such cricketers as Sutcliffe, Reid, Donnelly and Richard Hadlee's father, Walter, in action on a full-scale tour. Our administrators gave them the occasional crumb here and there, with a New Zealand team returning from another tour being permitted to play some matches against the Australian southern states, but it was poor fare for everyone.

The first Test between the two countries took place in 1946 at Basin Reserve, Wellington, where Australia won in only two days by an innings and 103 runs on a wet pitch. It was another 11 years before an Australian 'B' team was to set foot on New Zealand soil. The top team was on tour in South Africa but Les Favell's team was a very powerful combination which included Brian Booth, Peter Burge, Paul Sheahan, Peter Philpott, Norman O'Neill, Barry Jarman, John Gleeson, Alan Connolly and some other players who were fighting at that time to establish themselves in the Australian side.

The Kiwis put up a tremendous performance, winning the first representative match of the four-'Test' series and drawing the other three games. Their win came in a low-scoring match which had been switched from Wellington to New Plymouth because of some doubts about the fitness of the Wellington pitch. The Australians were bowled out for 175 and 191 and it was the spinners, Vic Pollard and Brian Yuile, who between them did the damage for New Zealand, taking 18 of the 20 wickets to fall. A great day for New Zealand but it still took six years for a New Zealand team to make it to Australia for the first official Test between the two countries for 28 years. Can you believe it?

New Zealand's administrators were far from blameless in allowing Australia to get away with it for so long. Their reaction was their players were not good enough and they should wait their time. My reaction was then, and is now, that this 'wet' approach held back New Zealand cricket to a ridiculous degree and, had their cricket officials stood up for their players as they should have done, the upsurge in New Zealand cricket we are seeing now could have come in 1960, not 1980. It would have been within New Zealand's scope to put a powerful team in the field in the late 1960s and early 1970s and the great victory achieved over Australia at Christchurch in 1974 could have been duplicated several times over.

On a par with the administrators' attitude to New Zealand was the internal matter of Western Australia. When the Board allowed them into the Sheffield Shield they made WA pay a subsidy for the privilege. One can only guess at how many years Western Australian cricket was held back because of that attitude, but one thing it certainly did in the West was make them determined!

A kindly way of looking at the Board stand on the Western Australian subsidy would be to call it muddled thinking, certainly from the overall view of Australian cricket. But it was also in many ways clever, in that the other states forced Western Australia to pay for the privilege of being part of Australian cricket. They had to pay a subsidy to all the other states to have the latter travel to Perth to play. That crippling subsidy was kept on for several years until some of us applied enough pressure to have it dropped. New South Wales, Victoria and South Australia, the original members of the Sheffield Shield, hung on for as long as they could without complete embarrassment. But that piece of administration was one of the worst I have ever seen in Australian sport, a real case of administrative bullying, on the basis that if Western Australia didn't like it then they could always go back to playing on a part-time basis.

*　　*　　*

Much of the controversial nature of cricket has stemmed from the Laws of the game and their interpretation. Matters like short-pitched bowling, throwing and other areas which produced publicity and sometimes acrimonious discussion have underlined that over the years cricket has been *the* controversial game. The lbw Law is another area of argument. At different times it has been the utter despair of bowlers and spectators who have seen drawn match after drawn match at county level and then in the past fifty years batsmen have encountered their own problems with it.

The first pads or leg-guards were simple affairs made of two bits of wood with a fastening which allowed them to be attached to the front of the leg. Their purpose was to allow the batsman to avoid being struck painfully on the bare shin, but before long they were being used as a second, or sometimes a first, line of defence for protecting the wicket. Between 1900 and 1934 there was such a prevalence of pad-play to balls pitching only fractionally outside off stump that in the end it was decided something had to be done about it.

The lbw Law at the time required the ball to pitch in a straight line between the two sets of stumps; in the opinion of the umpire, the ball must also have been going on to strike the stumps. In 1934 MCC decided to experiment with an amended lbw Law, which experiment has carried through in much of its original wording to the present day. This permitted a batsman to be out to a ball pitching on the offside of the wicket if, in the opinion of the umpire, it would have hit the stumps and the pad was in a line between wicket and wicket. If all this was done because the batsmen had carried things too far with their pad policy and were thereby giving the bowlers no chance, then I suppose it might have been worth it. But once again, as in so many of the administrative decisions over the years, I doubt if those who framed the Law really thought through to what its side-effects might be.

As a result of this particular Law, the medium-pacer and the quick bowler were encouraged, so too the offspinner and the inswinger. I regard it as the single most important factor in the gradual demise of the bowler who spins the ball from leg to off, or moves it as his natural delivery off the seam from leg to off.

Some people maintain that the new lbw Law should have been extended to include the ball pitching outside leg stump. Although such a move would have benefited me as a leg-break bowler, I believe it would have created even more negative cricket, with bowlers of all types being too good for the batsmen and the game becoming a very low-scoring affair: faster bowlers would have started bowling around the wicket, batsmen would have had to stand more front-on and, in all, it would have been very much to the detriment of the game as a spectacle.

Prior to the amendment to the lbw Law in 1934, there was an interesting experimental rule produced in England in 1929. This was to say a batsman, even if he snicked the ball on to his pad, could still be out lbw, providing the wording of the Law was satisfied. Many umpires – Frank Chester was one – and several prominent players thought it a good idea, and it then continued in 1930 as an experiment and seemed again to create few problems.

The wording of that 'snick' Law was, 'in experimental Laws for county championship matches the striker be given out lbw under Law 24 even though the ball may first hit his bat or hand.' One thing you can guarantee is that it would take a lot of the controversy out of modern Test match cricket where batsmen can be seen tapping the edge of their bat to try to signify to the umpire, the crowd, plus the millions watching on television, that they weren't out lbw but the ball had in fact come off the inside edge. It would have spared us from many exhibitions including the one put on by Sunil Gavaskar in Melbourne when he claimed he wasn't out to Lillee and tried to take his other batsman, Chetan Chauhan, off the field and forfeit the match to Australia.

It is of course much too late for that 'snick' Law to be suggested again, but what a pity it hadn't gone on at the time and perhaps been included as an experimental Law in 1934 when the wording of the lbw Law was changed. What I *would* like to see now is the old Law return with the intent clause retained.

The present lbw Law – Law 36 – states that, 'The striker shall be out lbw in the circumstances set out below:

(a) Striker Attempting to Play the Ball

The striker shall be out lbw if he first intercepts with any part of his person, dress or equipment a fair ball which would have hit the wicket and which has not previously touched his bat or a hand holding the bat, provided that:

(i) The ball pitched in a straight line between wicket and wicket, *or on the off side of the striker's wicket*, or in the case of a ball intercepted full pitch would have pitched in a straight line between wicket and wicket; and

(ii) The point of impact is in a straight line between wicket and wicket, even if above the level of the bails.

(b) Striker Making No Attempt to Play the Ball

The striker shall be out lbw even if the ball is intercepted outside the line of the off stump if, in the opinion of the umpire, he has made no genuine attempt to play the ball with his bat, but has intercepted the ball with some part of his person and if the circumstances set out in (a) above apply.'

By simply deleting my italicised words in (a)i, two aspects of the game would be satisfied. It would continue to penalise the player who makes no genuine attempt to play the ball outside off stump but just shoves his pad at it. It would also mean any batsman who intended to try to play in a negative fashion, as seems to have been the problem in the 1920s and 1930s, would be taking a risk of being out lbw, and yet the batsman who genuinely wants to get on with the game would not have the incessant inswing, inslant and offspin bowling directed at him. If cricket followers and administrators are honest in their desire to reintroduce outswing and legspin and left-arm orthodox spin bowling to the game, then I contend I am offering them a real opportunity to do so with the above suggestion.

I am convinced this revision in the Law would see more emphasis on offside play. The batsman would be denied the chance to pad up to the ball coming in from outside off stump and would therefore be forced to play a stroke. At the same time, he would not be in fear of the ball darting back and having him lbw. I would anticipate more offside back-foot and front-foot attacking play with this revision of the Law.

If I look at that change in the lbw Law as a means of encouraging the bowler who moves the ball from leg to off, it is no great task then to think of legspinners coming back into the game. I make no apology for wanting to see that happen. In some ways it could be looked on as a selfish desire, having been a legspinner myself. But that apart, I believe it would be good for the game of cricket as a whole.

It is impossible to legislate directly to have them return to the game for you simply cannot say to selection committees that their attack must include a slow bowler. The desired effect can, however, be achieved by a sensible introduction of other legislation and a rethink on the standard of pitches. Altering the lbw Law and speeding up over-rates would redress the balance, to some extent, in favour of the legspinner.

*　*　*

I have absolutely no time for negative captains in the game of cricket and I certainly have no time at all for time-wasting and slow over-rates, the latter in my opinion having become the great bugbear of modern-day cricket. There is no question over-rates were consistently higher in the period before the Second World War than is the case in world-wide cricket today. You only have to look back to some of the greatest batting feats of the game to see what a change there has been in the amount of cricket provided for the audience. That is where the standard should begin.

Nowadays the standard is set in England where teams visiting that country to play in Test series are asked if they will agree to bowl 100 balls an hour during the Test series. Astonishingly, the answer to that has generally been 'no', although the New Zealanders agreed to make 100 balls an hour the mark in the summer of 1983. No such agreement had been forthcoming from the Australians in 1981 or from the Indians and Pakistanis in 1982, when the targets were first 90 balls an hour, then 96.

There are various reasons given for this attitude of the modern-day player and administrator, not least of which is the argument that captaincy is so much more specialised and fine-tuned these days that it takes a good deal longer to assess the tactical requirements of the game and set the fielders accordingly. This often-trotted-out excuse is one of the most nonsensical statements I have heard in my life: through my own experience, the skipper should *always* have his finger on the pulse and his field-settings should be as quick and unobtrusive as possible.

Just have a look back to two innings where there were centuries made before lunch in matches in England before the war. In 1929, Owen-Smith hit a century before lunch at Headingley in the second innings for South Africa against England and the English bowling rate then was 138 balls an hour. When Bradman batted at Headingley the following year and made his triple-century, the English bowling rate throughout the day was 140 balls an hour. Both of these bowling rates were remarkable because, when scoring of this kind is taking place, the ball has to be chased to the boundary and returned to the bowler which generally provides a much slower bowling rate than would be the case if a number of maidens were being bowled. In fact, in that innings of Bradman's, when Australia made 556, 30 maidens were bowled and yet the rate stayed up at 140 balls an hour – quite incredible by modern-day standards.

Let's assume for a moment that 140 balls an hour, in an innings where a man makes a triple-century, is inordinately high. Let's also assume that 80 balls an hour is ridiculously low, although you wouldn't really believe it watching some of the Tests in recent years. Take a figure in between, say 108 balls (18 six-ball overs), and you will see what a state of affairs we've reached in modern-day cricket at Test match level: there is no way in the world, playing a normal Test match with a couple of fast bowlers, a medium-pacer plus one or two spinners, you would get anywhere near 108 balls an hour these days. Some of the teams struggle to reach 85 balls an hour and, much as it hurts me to say it, the Australians have been as bad as anyone in this department over the past 15 years.

Slow over-rates are not a recent phenomenon. They have been going for some time and were particularly bad in the two series we played against England in Australia in 1954–55 and 1958–59.

In 1954–55 the excuse for the appalling exhibition of slow over-rates was that the days were hot and the English bowlers were mostly of the pace variety and needed to conserve their energy. In one five-hour day England bowled only 54 eight-ball overs which worked out at 86 balls an hour. In those days that was appalling; today it is only regarded as being slightly on the wrong side of excellent.

In the 1958–59 series it took us until the first day of the Fourth Test match to score as many as 200 runs in a day and those were from 56 eight-ball overs bowled in the entire day. There were only 54 overs in the complete second day of the match in Adelaide and I sometimes wonder how we ever managed to keep the interest of the spectators, or indeed their continued patronage. Perhaps we didn't; perhaps they all went away and did something else and got sick of cricket which was being played at snail's pace.

When I came into first-class cricket and played under Arthur Morris and Keith Miller, and against captains like Lindsay Hassett, Phil Ridings and Bill Brown, there was never the slightest problem about over-rates – they were high and no one thought about slowing the game down. Shortly after I became captain of New South Wales, over-rates had begun to exercise the minds of the players. We even experimented in New South Wales to try and come up with some kind of a reasonable mark.

In one Sheffield Shield match played at the Sydney Cricket Ground, without bothering to tell the administrators what I was doing, I got the team together and said I wanted to find out the proper high-mark for a session of play over two hours in Australian cricket with the eight-ball over operating. I also wanted to find out what was the lowest mark we could achieve by wasting time. This was a Sheffield Shield match which we were in no danger of losing and, without any interference from the weather, we were almost certain to win. It seemed a good opportunity to try an experiment under field conditions.

In the first session we set out to bowl as many overs as possible and we got through 32 in the two-hour session, 128 balls an hour. We used our pace bowlers and our spinners and everyone moved quickly into their positions. In this respect, they didn't need any extra cajoling from me because that was one of the set pieces of captaincy as far as I was concerned. The players knew where they had to go every over once they had originally been told and, if I wanted them moved, I did it with a quick nod or movement of the hand – not through interminable conferences with bowlers or with the fielders themselves.

Having established 128 as the maximum figure we could achieve, we then set out in another two-hour session to give the impression we were moving quickly, but, in reality, to bowl as few overs as possible. Again using pace bowlers and spinners, we bowled 22 overs at 88 balls an hour, which is around the figure that is the accepted norm these days in Test match cricket. I believe it was a most instructive experiment and again, if you were to take a half-way mark between the two, you would come to 108 balls an hour, the figure I mentioned earlier.

Much of the problem has to do with the selection of teams and whether or not there are any spin bowlers in the 11 players to take the field. Even allowing for that though, there are still plenty of ways captains and players could raise over-rates so that an acceptable level of entertainment can be provided for the spectators – and that is what I think is of paramount importance. A quick glance at the mathematics of the situation will give some idea of the way the spectators are being short-changed these days.

Let us assume, for the sake of argument, that 46 runs per 100 balls is an acceptable run-rate for batsmen in first-class cricket in the 1980s, although under certain circumstances, such as a poor playing surface, the rate can be expected to fall. By applying that figure to the three over-rates already discussed, a picture emerges as to the number of runs a spectator is likely to see scored over a typical six-hour day:

128 balls an hour produces 354 runs;
108 balls an hour produces 300 runs;
88 balls an hour produces 244 runs.

The difference in runs scored between the reasonable figure of 108 balls an hour and what seems to be the acceptable figure in Test cricket of 88 balls an hour is quite astonishing. What is even more astonishing is the fact that no one seems to pay proper attention to it. Given 88 balls an hour, the only way batsmen could offer the spectator reasonable value for their money would be to raise their strike rate to 56 runs per 100 balls – an unrealistically high figure in first-class cricket, let alone Test cricket.

One of the problems we face is that there has never been any concerted effort by the media to improve over-rates – indeed the old system of talking about runs per hour prevails at all levels of cricket. In recent years there has been more use made of so many runs per 100 balls as a yardstick, but we are still told a team has made only 74 runs in the pre-lunch two-hour session. In those two hours, however, there might have been only 28 overs bowled, meaning they have scored 74 from 168 balls faced, which is not far short of 50 runs per 100 balls and a very good run-rate. Seventy-four in two hours is diabolical according to the clock, yet 50 runs per 100 balls, or just under that, is perfectly acceptable and, in many cases, desirable. If I had my way, never again would there be any reference made to runs being made in time because I believe in the 1980s it has no relevance whatsoever, certainly not until we get back to 18 overs an hour.

The people who can change all this are, of course, the captains. Nothing can be done without their assistance and, in fact, they can go the other way and make more of a nonsense of things if they so wish rather than improve things for the spectator. It is no trouble for any captain to slow the game down and I would defy anyone not in the centre of the ground to pick up what is going on.

One of the biggest problems everyone faces with regard to over-rates is that there is an insidious campaign to have us believe the players and administrators are doing as well as they possibly can.

You would soon see an entirely different approach to over-rates from administrators and players if Test cricket were to rely these days only on money received at the turnstiles. The administrators would be desperate, because not enough money would be coming in for them to meet their commitments in the game. The players would be even more desperate because such a shortfall in receipts would mean their own salaries, which were rightly increased dramatically after World Series Cricket, would suddenly be downgraded to the dark ages. If a players' superannuation scheme were to be instituted, depending on the number of spectators paying admission money and the excitement generated for them at the ground between the hours of 11 a.m. and 6 p.m., you can bet your life there would be a different approach. You wouldn't have too many teams appearing at the ground with four or five fast bowlers and getting through something like 85 to 90 balls an hour, simply because the spectators would make clear their disapproval of such tactics, as indeed they do on occasions now.

As it is, sponsorship and limited-overs cricket have provided such a back-up for administrators and players that they don't really have to worry too much about the overall entertainment of the paying public. Do they intend to do absolutely nothing about the problem of over-rates?

It has astonished me for years that administrators and players at the top level make quite clear their intent to do absolutely nothing about the problem of over-rates. Instead, we have had comments from captains and administrators from Australia, West Indies and, to a lesser degree, England in recent years setting out the reasons why over-rates cannot be improved past whatever disgraceful figure may have been produced in the previous series. West Indies' administrators have pointed to the fact they have fast bowlers in their side – sometimes all fast bowlers and nothing else – and they keep coming back with the argument that if the cricket is good enough nobody will worry about the over-rates. I believe this is not only a spurious argument but also downright misleading, and I would like to see the future hold something much better for the spectators than the platitudes which at present are bandied about.

In England there are fines for slow over-rates in county matches, with the players and the counties themselves having to pay whatever fines are applied. The counties reaching the required over-rate share in the money paid by those who do not. What I can't understand is why nothing is done by that weakest of all cricket organisations, the International Cricket Conference, to compel touring teams playing Test matches to achieve, or approach, the same high rate as applied in county cricket, 18.50 overs to the hour. There we have a standard which is just about my middle-of-the-road figure and which is certain to provide proper entertainment for the public. It is not outlandish, 108 balls an hour, and if its introduction into Test match cricket were to result in selectors having to consider picking one or two spinners, then you would not find me – nor I suspect the majority of cricket followers – in violent disagreement.

If necessary, I would be prepared to have legislation brought in to ensure that a certain number of overs were bowled in a day and I would draw it up along the lines of the legislation in force in Australia for the Benson and Hedges World Series Cup matches: if they don't bowl their overs in the required time there is a financial penalty of $600 to $1800 per over for the team, the money to be taken out of the prize-money won by that side at the end of the series.

The administrators in England, to their eternal credit, tried to provide for spectators at Test matches by saying a certain number of overs have to be bowled in the day and extra time may have to be played. Even this is not a proper solution because what happens is the fielding side, sometimes containing four fast bowlers, realises very quickly, if they have to play on for an extra half an hour or threequarters of an hour, the batting side will be forced to bat in poor light as the required number of overs is built up.

The solution may well have to be a levy on the players, as already suggested. When the bowling rate for a day, or part of a day, is below 108 balls an hour, it would do wonders for the players each to pay into a fund £100. At £1100 a day, if it happened on all five days, the fund would be worth £5500. For the complete Test series it would rise to £27,500. The fines would be paid out of prize-money, players' payments and by the team's Board of Control. I suspect you would quickly have a vastly different attitude from administrators, selectors and players.

What's that you say? You don't think the fines are high enough? I can only conclude you must have paid your money to see a match where 88 balls an hour was the fare.

In India's spin-bowling heyday, Bishen Bedi, Bhagwat Chandrasekhar, Erapally Prasanna and Srinivas Venkataraghavan accounted for 649 out of the 831 wickets to fall to their side during the 15 Test series which spanned their careers. Conditions might have changed since those days, but the game is ill-served by the undiluted battery of fast and fast-medium bowlers that is the norm in modern Test cricket. By increasing over-rates, selectors will be forced into considering the introduction of more spin into their attacks, enabling spectators to enjoy *more* cricket and *more varied* cricket at the highest level. One need only look to the reception given to the emergence of Nick Cook on the Test arena in England in 1983 to know that that is exactly what the paying spectator wants.

*   *   *

From 1948, when I came into first-class cricket, up to 1960 much of the cricket was dominated by bowlers. MCC in 1946, for some reason best known to themselves, had recommended bonuses for bowlers and had suggested a new ball be available to the fast men every 55 overs (40 in Australia). That of course suited Bradman's side in 1948 when they went to England loaded with pace bowling, and the general result of the rule was further to persuade youngsters, and those not so young, that fast bowling, with the accent on inswing or inslant, was the thing to do.

It is no mere coincidence that from the time the 55-overs new-ball rule came into cricket in 1946, no Australian team for the next 25 years was able to score 50 runs per 100 balls in a Test series against England. Astonishingly, the best effort was in 1954–55 (47.13 per 100 balls) when the over-rates were so slow. Only once in that 25 year period (1965–66) did England even manage 40 runs per 100 balls!

In recent times the administrators, and heaven knows why it took them so long to do it, have gradually changed the availability of the new ball back to 85 six-ball overs. If you think in terms of a run-rate of, say, 46 runs per 100 balls, it means the new ball is not taken until the score has reached approximately 230, whereas under the 55-overs rule the new ball would be taken at 150 runs.

What a difference! No wonder spectators were getting bored with the whole thing by the time the administrators pulled themselves together and started to make the required changes. Who on earth wants to see a new ball taken with 150 runs on the scoreboard?

The 40-overs new-ball rule was an astonishing piece of thinking. In the first match I played against Queensland, New Year 1949, Lindwall, Miller and Walker crashed through the opposition batting. There were four spin bowlers in that match, Vic Emery, Fred Johnston, Colin McCool and Mick Raymer – I suppose I could just about count myself as a fifth. Between us we bowled 39 overs but I didn't have a bowl. I also saw from fine-leg my initial first-class hat-trick when Alan Walker had Colin McCool lbw and bowled Don Tallon and Mick Raymer. The 40-overs new-ball rule, together with a very grassy pitch, produced exactly what the administrators were angling for – more and more pandering to the pace bowler. But once again they hadn't thought the thing through. It did a great deal of damage to the future of spin bowlers and, I believe, to the game itself.

There was a faintly ridiculous look about the whole thing. This was another example of administrators having absolutely no idea of how to plan ahead. If they had had a proper feel for the game, they would have known this would become a real problem in future years and they would not have leapt in with what goes down as one of the worst administrative decisions in the history of the game.

One of the reasons administrators gave for changing the Law pertaining to the taking of the new ball to a number of overs, rather than a number of runs, was that there were times when a batting side would deliberately slow down when moving towards the 200 mark if they didn't want the new ball to be taken. This happened one day in Adelaide, in 1963, when Australia had set a target of 356 to win on the final day at a rate of around six an over. I was without Alan Davidson – he had torn a hamstring muscle after bowling four overs in the first innings of the match – and I had Ken Mackay opening the bowling with Graham McKenzie. After we had knocked over Geoff Pullar and David Sheppard for 3 and 1 respectively, there was a partnership between Ken Barrington and Colin Cowdrey of 94 in only 86 minutes but, although we dismissed Cowdrey and Dexter, there was never any real chance of a result on what was still a pretty good batting pitch.

However, Barrington and Tom Graveney in the course of their partnership, with the total moving on to 190, suddenly realised there was an opportunity looming for Australia if McKenzie were to pick up wickets with the second new ball and they declined to take any singles off three overs from Bob Simpson and myself. I called Bill Lawry in then and had him bowl an over, with instructions to bowl wides so the ball would run away down to the fine-leg boundary and the 200 would be brought up. He did that, much to the dismay of our wicket-keeper who had four byes instead of wides called against him with the first ball Bill bowled, followed by five wides. The least happy fellow on the ground at the time was Arthur Wallace Theodore Grout, even when I patted him on the back and told him to mark it down to experience and team spirit.

There was some criticism of the tactic I used that day, but the batsmen were refusing to give us any legitimate opportunity of taking the second new ball. It was my job for the team to provide it as quickly as possible to see if we could achieve a breakthrough.

Now we also have uniformity in the number of balls to an over. I didn't mind if it were the eight-ball over or the six-ball over which eventually became uniform in cricket, but I'm pleased that at long last Australia and England have been able to agree one or the other will be used. In this case it is the six-ball over and, as far as I can see, it makes very little difference to the pace of the game. All the tests carried out by the authorities of both countries seem to indicate minor saving of time either way, and the main thing now is that bowlers will bowl the same number of balls every over. It was very odd, when totting up the balls bowled by MCC tourists in Australia, that it had to be done on a different basis from their normal matches in England.

So at least in Australia we reached uniformity with the rest of the world and, in Test matches, captains now have the option of taking a new ball after 85 six-ball overs. From the time the original 40-overs new-ball legislation was introduced, to the time Australia adopted 85 six-ball overs, was slightly over 30 years.

* * *

New legislation though is never easy to turn from suggestion into law. There is no more complex game than cricket with its 55 Laws, reduced to slightly more than 40 after Mr S. C. Griffith was given the task of rewriting them. The very first Laws seem to have been the Articles of Agreement covering the conduct of matches between two teams representing the Duke of Richmond and Mr Broderick of Peperharow in 1727. The match consisted of 12 players a side and was played on a 23-yard pitch, with each side appointing one umpire and the home umpire selecting the pitch. Since those days the Laws of Cricket have come into being and not always have they turned out to be in the best interests of the game and those who watch it.

I hated the 55-overs new-ball rule, but quite the worst of my time has been the front-foot Law, which was almost a direct result of some pictures of Ray Lindwall shown in England in 1947, and then some other pictures of Pat Crawford at the Sydney Cricket Ground in 1955, in both cases showing the bowlers with their back foot dragging over the bowling crease at the instant of delivery. There were other bowlers who had drags such as Gordon Rorke, Frank Tyson, Fred Trueman and several minor Australian players in the 1950s, and the sum total of their transgressions brought about one of the most enormous over-reactions I've ever known in the game. The front-foot Law was produced by weak administration as a matter of convenience for administrators and umpires and it causes more wasted time in the game of cricket than anything else, and you can throw into that all your time-wasting players and captains.

In 1947, the pictures shown in England of Ray Lindwall coincided with the fact that he was certain to tour England with the 1948 side. Before Lindwall's arrival in England, there was much conjecture that the Law might have to be changed overnight or a new playing condition added, to the effect that the front foot should be grounded between the batting and bowling creases. From then on it was almost inevitable the Law would one day be changed, even though administrators clearly had never paid the slightest attention to what might be the negative by-products of such change.

There is no better sight than a fast bowler, or a slow bowler of quality, performing against a talented batsman. I had plenty of experience of the old rule and the new one in the time I was playing, and there is no question in my mind that a change back *towards* the old Law would be for the benefit of the game. In short, I regard the front-foot no-ball Law as one of the worst pieces of legislation ever perpetrated on players and public, brought about by a gross over-reaction to those few bowlers who dragged their back foot. Players have snarled at it, umpires have taken the easy way out with it, so too have administrators, and spectators have been, are and always will be, annoyed by it. And administrators are scared now to do anything about it.

After Lindwall had been photographed in 1947–48 and then Tyson in 1954 in Australia, we had Pat Crawford in Sydney playing for New South Wales just before the Australian team were chosen to go to England. My sports editor at the time, Con Simons, sent a photographer out to the Sydney Cricket Ground to get some shorts of Crawford side-on because he had a feeling he was dragging over the line. So he was. From that moment on, until 1961 when I took the team to England, administrators and umpires were pussyfooting around with the Law, unable to come to terms with what was required by the most important people, the players and spectators. In 1962 they decided the whole of the front foot had to be behind the popping crease at the moment of delivery, showing again how administrators would leap in to change a Law without giving any thought to the consequences.

By-products of a changed Law can often be disastrous and I contend that is what has happened in this case. No sooner had the administrators changed the Law and made it arbitrary in 1962 for all of the front foot to be behind the line, than I was able to show an administrator in Australia it was one of the greatest pieces of stupidity ever produced. There was no difficulty in doing this, I simply had to ask him to stand where an umpire would normally stand while I put my front foot just behind the batting crease with my toe an inch from the edge of the line nearest to the stumps. I had a photographer taking pictures at the same time. He took shots from side-on which showed that my foot was behind the line and therefore the delivery was legitimate. He then moved to where the administrator was standing and took a photograph from exactly alongside his eyes. From that point, both by eye and later-developed print, there was no question the ball was a 'no-ball': the umpire's line of sight pushed the foot forward and away from him on to the batting crease.

How, you may ask, could a group of administrators, supposedly the best at their craft, come up with a piece of legislation of this kind? The answer is they simply didn't think it through. If they had used commonsense they would have followed the example of the 1961 Australian tour of England where we had one of the most satisfactory tours ever as regards no-balling. We did it by paying due attention to the bones of the Law they intended to introduce. You may even allege we only paid lip-service to it, but what we did on the tour was prove without any shadow of doubt that the game could be allowed to proceed with co-operation from the umpires, the bowlers and the captains. This was at a time when we all knew something was about to be done regarding the front-foot Law and, as touring captain, I was given a list of umpires who were on the panel for the Test matches in 1961, two of whom were to have our first match at Worcester on 29 April. Sid Buller and Eddie Philipson were the men and they and the other umpires in England came up with a commonsense approach to things which made the game far more pleasant for everyone, whether out in the centre or watching from outside the ring.

The solution was simple: the umpires would use the popping crease as a guide and the bowlers would be permitted to put their foot on the popping crease but, as soon as they went over that popping crease by a margin the umpires thought was 'a bit much', the bowler would be spoken to. If he continued to go over too far he would be called for no-balling. What it meant was the bowlers, instead of having an arbitrary half an inch to play with, had something more like six inches. They were thus able to get through their bowling action worrying only about that and not about the exact spot on which their feet were going to be placed. Remarkably few no-balls were bowled, not only in the Test matches but on the whole tour. No damage was done to anyone, certainly none was done to the game and everyone concerned enjoyed themselves far more.

In our first main match of the tour against MCC at Lord's on 27 May, there were three no-balls bowled by MCC bowlers and none by the Australians. We bowled none in the First Test match at Edgbaston, none in the Second Test at Lord's, none in the Third Test at Leeds, none in the Fourth Test at Old Trafford and none in the Fifth Test at the Oval. England bowled one at Edgbaston, none at Lord's, none at Leeds, none at Old Trafford and none at the Oval. What a contrast with what happens these days with this ridiculous Law in operation. Take the last Australian tour of England in 1981. In the First Test match at Trent Bridge there were 15 no-balls, in the Second at Lord's 57, in the Third at Leeds 42, in the Fourth at Birmingham 51 and in the Fifth at Manchester 27. When we came to the final Test at the Oval 32 no-balls was the mark, and if that is good cricket legislation then I'll take the lead part in the remake of *Tootsie*.

As usual, the spectator is the one who suffers, having to watch endless wasted deliveries, normally by the fast bowlers. Nowadays, even spin bowlers are called for having their foot one quarter of an inch over the batting crease. Could there be anything more ridiculous than that?

Some people say that the late calling of the no-balls by the umpires, because of the use of the front foot, causes an additional problem in that it denies the batsman the chance to score runs. This is quite true but I am sure the Laws were not originally framed to give the batsman the chance to score runs – that was something which came about because he had plenty of time to play his stroke when the 'calling' was off the back foot.

Towards the end of my career, when the front-foot rule was experimental, I was called for no-balling. Ashley Mallett was another to suffer. In 1972, in the latter part of the English tour, he became so frustrated at being penalised he asked for some assistance. He had bowled reasonably well in the final Test against England at the Oval, taking 3 for 80 and 2 for 66, but then against Kent, and in the first of the Prudential Trophy one-day matches, he'd had a ton of problems. He came to me and asked if it would be possible for me to spend some time with him at the Lord's nets and I told him that, providing Ian Chappell agreed, I would see him on the morning of the second Prudential one-day match on 26 August.

This created something of a problem because on the previous night there was a special team dinner at the Waldorf Hotel and it meant, with the normal toasts undertaken by team members, that not everyone was going to wake up the following morning feeling bright and chirpy. 'Could I postpone it?' 'Sorry – no.' To his eternal credit, Ashley made it to the nets and we went through the standard drill I use for spin bowlers if they are having any trouble with this Law.

I was interested to see how Ashley would perform once he got on to the field because I wouldn't have put his concentration level at the nets as precisely one hundred per cent. He did the right thing early on by bowling Dennis Amiss and at the end of a very tidy pre-lunch spell he had to bowl the last over to John Hampshire who was on 10. Ashley was concentrating so hard on trying to dismiss Hampshire he didn't hear the umpire's call of 'lunch gentlemen' and, as he saw Hampshire moving off from the Nursery end crease towards the pavilion, he attempted to run him out. All he managed instead was to miss the ball with his hand, tread on it with his right foot and twist his ankle. At that point, looking up, he realised it was lunch, got up and limped off for the pavilion, forgetting that in his way were the three stumps – by now bail-less of course – which he flattened.

After lunch, he finished with 2 for 24 and brilliantly caught Alan Knott off Bob Massie's bowling when he was fielding at mid-on. There was great interest however among his team-mates who wanted to know how he would cope down at deep third-man after his bowling spell. Tony Greig tested him out very quickly. A vicious cut behind point off David Colley fairly raced away towards Q stand and Mallett took off after it. He did that by putting his head down and racing for the exact spot he thought he would meet the ball but it didn't work out quite that way. As he lifted his head, and reached down on the run for the ball, it belted into the boundary a good 20 feet *behind* him. It was without question one of the more droll things I've seen any cricketer, without trying, do on the field, and I'm afraid I might have had a hand in it by insisting he keep our early morning appointment.

When our firm was acting as sports consultants to World Series Cricket, the front-foot Law was one of the things on which we advised. The rule used in World Series Cricket from 1977 onwards was exactly the one the English umpires had so sensibly suggested in 1961: the bowlers were allowed to cut the popping crease and would not be called unless the umpire considered they were gaining an unfair advantage. They would certainly not be called if they were a millimetre or a half-inch over the line. The rule worked perfectly. It meant the bowlers were not forever having to keep one eye on the popping crease and one on their bowling action. In short, they were allowed much more freedom, the game flowed in better fashion and the batsmen were no less happy than under the normal rule.

That original suggestion about the foot having to be completely behind the popping crease was modified in later years until now some part of the foot must be on or behind the line in delivery stride. It still produces an extraordinary number of no-ball calls, such as occurred on that 1981 Australian tour, and I maintain it is a useless addition to the game of cricket.

Administrators say that the Law was only enforced because umpires voted for it and even insisted on it in order to make their task more straightforward. Spectators in Australia are growing to dislike it intensely, although they've kept their sense of humour about being deprived of a certain amount of play each day. Over Bay 14 at the Melbourne Cricket Ground one day, when Lennie Pascoe was bowling and was being no-balled, floated the poster 'Len "No-Balls" Pascoe'. We didn't manage to show it in our Channel Nine telecast of the match which, in one sense, was a pity because it would have provided another criticism of this piece of administration.

A bowler moves in to bowl at a pace akin to that of an Olympic athlete in the 800 metres. Now whoever heard of an athlete being asked to put his feet within one quarter of an inch of a line every 30 yards or at the end of his run when he is trying to win a race?

I would like to see spectators assist in having this Law modified. A touch of laughter could do wonders every time the count passes ten in a day. The next time you're watching cricket and you get tired of seeing the umpire's arm outstretched, give a minus mark to the administrators who have done absolutely nothing for the game of cricket by its introduction.

*　　*　　*

It doesn't matter in the slightest how many Law changes you make, or what the administrators do to try to make the game more attractive, if the playing surface is not good then the competitors will struggle. It is almost impossible to provide a good Test match if there is so much grass left on the surface of the pitch the pace bowlers are unduly favoured; or if the first day surface is dusty so the spinners turn the ball far more than they should; or if the pitch is so slow and dead it is difficult for the batsmen to play strokes off the back foot. I have been urging for a number of years in Australia that, prior to the start of every summer, there should be a curators' seminar where the head groundsmen of the main centres throughout the country could meet. There would be an exchange of ideas and discussion about the latest advances in agronomy and grass cultivation, plus everything else which goes into keeping a cricket ground in good shape and providing a perfect pitch for the players.

To me the perfect pitch is the one where the grass has been rolled into the surface, instead of sticking up on top, with the roots underneath binding the surface. The pitch should be rolled until it has the consistency of concrete and until there is a shine on the surface. At that point the fast bowlers should be able to get something out of it, particularly in the early part of the match, and there will be enough pace in it for the batsmen to play their strokes. There will also be some spin and it will be quick spin because of the gloss. I am always asked by old-timers of the shiny surfaces on which cricket was played before the war – is it completely out of the question in these days of modern technology that groundsmen should be given the facilities with which to make a shiny pitch? I am sure if administrators really put their minds to it, instead of fiddling around with things which are of little account, the pitches throughout the world could show a marked improvement.

One of the great boons to the development of young cricketers in Australia is the artificial pitch. There used to be, and still are, concrete pitches in Australia and now there are also a variety of artificial surfaces which allow youngsters, for the most part, to bat with the idea firmly in their minds that they are not going to be hit by a ball lifting from just short of a good length.

I believe this is most important in the development of a young cricketer, and I am very much against schools' cricket being played on anything but artificial pitches with a true bounce. So often there is a feeling from schoolmasters and parents that there is something second class about a fixture if it is not played on turf. This is all very well if the groundsman is able or willing to spare the time to prepare a proper turf pitch and it can be protected from rain, but otherwise it is crazy to have kids play on a surface which gives an uneven bounce. Apart from anything else they will finish up not liking cricket, and what is the point of that? Cold showers and being hit on the fingers by a cricket ball are in some quarters regarded as the vital ingredients in making the finest citizens. That kind of thinking was marvellous around the time of Bulldog Drummond, who gave me countless hours of excitement and pleasure. They are now slightly out of date.

The spectators would be better served with good pitches, so too the players of course, and both groups would also benefit from the universal introduction of light meters. Over the years one of the most disputed aspects of cricket in the time I've been playing, captaining and watching has been the fitness or otherwise of the light. I have been delighted to see that, after a considerable amount of prompting, the umpires in England are now permitted to use meters to judge the fitness of the light, and I just wish that happened in every country. I won't say it is foolproof but it is as close as you will ever get to being foolproof and that, surely, has to be the ideal thing in this game. What it needs is for the panel of umpires to test the light on different grounds at different times before the start of a Test series, or they can even use an arbitrary figure on their light meters – say 2.8 – at which point they will offer the light to the batsmen.

One of the best BBC television interviews we have done in England in recent years was with Patrick Eagar, the outstanding freelance photographer who covers cricket matches all over the world. He gave his ideas on light meters and his thoughts should be used as a standard work for umpires in every country. The great benefit to come from the use of light meters is that this side of the game would be standardised and spectators would know, once the players went off the field, the light had reached the point where both umpires and light meters considered it to be unfit for play. It would, in my opinion, reduce the chance of nasty incidents and crowd behaviour where spectators in one section of the ground might believe the light to be perfectly playable.

It astonishes me that proper sightscreens are not in use on every ground in England. There are makeshift productions or there are painted seats, sometimes with dark-clad people sitting in them, their heads peeping out to merge with the cricket ball. But still on some grounds, when a Test match is being played with some of the fastest bowlers in the world in action, ground members' wishes take precedence over players' needs.

There should be written into the playing conditions of every tour that a proper sightscreen, either on the fence or inside the playing arena, be provided for the players. Surely, if you have a cricket tour where players travel 12,000 miles for the games, the best possible facilities must be provided. The finest example of proper sightscreens in England is at Old Trafford, but the one at the Nursery end of Lord's is also excellent – just about perfect for an Ashes' battle.

* * *

Sometimes cricket administration can be frustrating because of the pace at which it moves. There is nothing about it of the old quickstep dance routine – quick, quick slow. It is based on slow, slow, slow. But one area where administrators did have to take their time to solve a difficulty was in the contentious area of throwing. I was playing in the era where throwing posed enormous problems for administrators. This was no modern trend – since overarm bowling had become fashionable there had been many players who, either accidentally or deliberately, exploited the chance to bend the elbow. It was always a difficult thing for umpires, particularly the umpire at the bowler's end, to judge, but the one at square-leg did have the chance of seeing if the bowler bent his arm and then straightened it.

A real catastrophe was avoided in 1960 when the ICC Throwing Conference found a temporary solution which later on was to become permanent. It was said at the time by Sir Donald Bradman that throwing was the most complex question he had known in cricket because it was not a matter of fact but of interpretation and opinion. And even when the agreement from the 1960 Conference was made public he added, 'It still has to run the gauntlet of time. Integrity, good faith and judgement will be essential.'

Way back in 1898, James Phillips, the Australian umpire, was one of those who held the opinion that, to have a fair ball bowled, it was immaterial whether the arm be straight or at an angle, so long as there was no perceptible movement in the elbow joint at the precise moment the ball left the hand. That was a very sensible interpretation, and even more sensible when you think it wouldn't have caught out quite legitimate offspinners whose arms were bent throughout their bowling actions.

Hopefully the throwing problems are behind us now, though occasionally I do see a bowler who makes me raise my eyebrows. From what I can see though, any bowlers with the slightest doubt about their bowling action have little chance these days of making it on to the Test arena.

My retirement by coincidence happened about the same time as the end of the throwing problems and, as I pointed out elsewhere, the season was not without its moments of light and shade. There were plenty of runs to be had, not many wickets to be taken and a few farewell functions to be attended around the country. Mostly they went very smoothly, were convivial affairs and I was able to remember everyone's name. Or almost everyone's.

Not everybody has a retentive memory for names. Keith Miller has – he is quite extraordinary – but I certainly haven't and, despite having tried all those American ideas of associating names with specific things, they just don't work for me. Although concentration is one of my strong points when working on television it certainly isn't when faced with someone who says, 'We met in 1956 at a Mayoral reception at Parramatta ... you must remember me.' Nowadays my answer generally is, 'No, but if you could tell me your name, it's going to save a lot of guessing and fooling about ...'

I had a certain sympathy then for Roy Middleton, the chairman of the South Australian Cricket Association, when he made the farewell speech to your correspondent early in 1964 on the occasion of my last Sheffield Shield match in Adelaide. I had made a century and shared a partnership with

Brian Booth, who was in tremendous form at that stage of the season, and the SACA had been kind enough to lay on a cocktail party to mark the day. In the course of the speech Mr Middleton continually referred to me being a household name in Australian cricket, a great name in world cricket and, more particularly, a name indelibly imprinted in the minds of cricket lovers the world over.

He then proposed the toast. The whites of his eyes suddenly showed . . . there was a slight hesitation . . . 'To Richie *BENNY* . . .'

The roar which greeted this toast was muted by the fact that the guest of honour was having to support himself on the ivy on the wall, tears welling in his eyes, not through emotion but at one of the funniest unconscious sequences I'd heard. The aftermath came the following week in the Test in Sydney when, pinned up behind the dressing-room door, was a newspaper story of the impending arrival of the great American comedian Jack Benny. In Sir Donald's handwriting were the words, 'Your brother I presume . . .?'

11

THE BENAUDS – JUST ONE OF MANY CRICKETING FAMILIES

The Mohammad brothers are the most famous family of cricketers. Four of them represented their country, three in the one Test in Karachi against New Zealand in 1969–70. All three Grace brothers played against Australia at the Oval in 1880 and there have been ten sets of brothers who have played cricket for Australia, some like the Chappells at the same time, some like the Benauds in different eras. Often there is a fatherly figure behind the scenes, as is the case with Walter Hadlee of New Zealand – a Test player himself prior to his sons Dayle and Richard representing their country.

The Benauds cover three eras. My father, Lou, a descendant of a French settler, coastal sailor and newspaper owner of the 1790s and 1800s, played his cricket from the early 1920s to 1956. I played mine at first-class level from 1948 to 1964 and John played his from 1966 to 1973. In many ways our cricket was in similar vein. My father was an attacking bowler and strong hitter and he transmitted those desires to his two sons with a certain amount of success.

He was one of the casualties of that awful era known as the Depression. Young people now understand little of it but it must have been a harrowing time. Like today the world over, the lucky ones had a job.

Named Louis Richard, he was born at Coraki on the Richmond River on 28 February 1904. The only cricket he played there was on a grassy area between the main street and the river where the kids shaped their own bats from the branches of willow trees and even used broom handles or pick handles. Each set of 'stumps' consisted of two kerosene tins, one on top of the other. They used a tennis ball or a solid rubber ball and there was no coaching. Cricket was only one of many games they played and it had no special appeal.

When he was 13, the Benaud family moved to Grafton where my father spent four very happy years at Grafton High School and a school-mate, Max Johnston, showed him how to bowl leg-breaks. Four years later the family moved to Penrith where I was born, but that event was not until 1930. My father attended Fort Street High School for a week but then was told he was to attend Parramatta High which was closer to Penrith. It was a fortuitous choice as Parramatta won the High Schools cricket competition and he was chosen in the Combined High Schools cricket team.

During his first season at Penrith he played second-grade junior cricket and, in one match, took all 20 wickets. On the first Saturday the match was played on Penrith Showground but, on the second Saturday, play continued at St Mary's. The first Saturday he could do nothing wrong with the ball and took 10 for 30. The second week he took the first seven wickets very quickly ... 'and then the medium-pacer at the other end bowled so wide the batsman could hardly reach them. I realized what was going on and told our captain I wouldn't bowl any more if the wide bowling at the other end continued. He spoke to the medium-pacer, I went on to bowl and captured the remaining three wickets.'

Penrith won the second-grade competition and he was promoted to Penrith first grade at the beginning of the next season. I'm not surprised – after taking all 20!

'One day some representatives from Central Cumberland District Cricket Club came to Penrith and asked my father if he would allow me to play for the club. It was a great thrill for me. I played second grade during the season but then had one game in first grade at the SCG Number One, scoring 13 not out and, off two overs, taking none for 11. When I started training at Sydney Teachers' College, we played inter-section cricket and I played against Bill O'Reilly who, even in those early days, bowled with wonderful accuracy. On 28 July 1925 our section assembled at the Education Department building to receive our appointments. I was first on the list and heard, "Benaud, Louis Richard, to One Tree Farm Provisional School."'

Six hundred miles from Sydney! He tried to have the appointment changed, in the light of having recently played a first-grade cricket match, but the Education Department refused all his entreaties.

It was a great time for Australian cricket. England, led by Arthur Gilligan, had been beaten out of sight by Herbie Collins's team, with Bill Ponsford, Vic Richardson, Clarrie Grimmett and Alan Kippax making outstanding débuts during the series. Interest in the game for a young man having just turned 21 could not have been greater. He was able to see first-class cricket in the Christmas holidays and played for North Casino, then for the district team to represent the Casino area. When Alan Kippax took a team from Sydney to Lismore, he had figures of 3 for 65 and made 39 not out. At the end of the day he was called into the opposition dressing-room and congratulated on his performance. A Cumberland man, 'Gar' Waddy, had saved the Combined side with 65 not out and Kippax said, 'Gar tells me you bowled extremely well out there. If you are thinking of coming to Sydney, contact me and I'll arrange for you to play for a district club.'

Whilst at North Casino my father was selected in the *Daily Guardian*'s 'Quest for Bowlers' and was also chosen twice in the North Coast Country

Week team. On each occasion leave of absence was refused by the Education Department. After the fourth such refusal he took two vows: if he ever married and there were any sons in his family he would make sure at least they had a chance, and there would be no more schoolteachers in the Benaud family.

My father got married during the Christmas vacation and was transferred to Warrandale Public School near Koorawatha in January 1930. It was during the Depression and there was no cricket team there, but towards the end of 1930 he was asked to start up a team. Most of the players were young and keen, they responded well to coaching and captaincy and they won most of their matches. The school closed in May 1932 and we transferred to the public school at Jugiong where we remained until August 1937. At that time, aged 33, there would, of course, be no belated call for my father from the state selectors, but there was a call from the headmaster of Burnside School, 'Banna' Edwards, a former Cumberland cricketer who had a hand in the appointment of his staff. He contacted my father and made the point that if he would like a transfer to Sydney, Burnside to be exact, it happened to be in the Cumberland area and the club could do with another legspinner. The chance would be there for him to try out for selection in the three grade teams.

As far as my own cricket was concerned, I started off as an allrounder at the age of six in the cement-walled storeroom at Jugiong. I was O'Reilly, Fleetwood-Smith and Ward as well, the latter having come into the Australian side to replace Grimmett after the 1935–36 tour of South Africa. I was in those days the complete allrounder because I was McCormick too, and McCabe, and, when it came to batting, I was Fingleton, Bradman and Brown combined. I used to dream of one day playing for Australia but at that young age couldn't see how it was going to happen because, although I had reached the mature age of six and had been playing 'Test cricket' for some years, we were stuck away in the country nearly 300 miles from Sydney.

I used to pick my own teams from a list my father had given me, written out in capital letters, from the 1934 Ashes battle in England. Later at Parramatta I had the 1936–37 *New South Wales Cricket Association Year Book* from which to choose my teams and, although I had never seen any of these players, I chose my teams because of their names, some because they were well known and others because they sounded pleasant. On that basis, Worthington and Fagg were always listed in one side and so was Jim Sims, the Middlesex slow bowler, whose name would roll off the tongue of any aspiring six-year-old. With the teams chosen, I would bowl the ball against the wall and play it on the rebound. Coming from only 15 feet and bouncing, it could be a reasonably difficult assignment. It certainly improved my eye!

When I was seven years of age, and my father moved to Burnside School in Sydney, I bowled gentle off-breaks because he had decided, quite rightly, my fingers were too immature to attempt at that age the difficult business of legspinning. We played our primary school competition on a concrete pitch with a composition ball made of cork and rubber and, because it bounced a lot, it provided plenty of problems for opposing batsmen.

Twice we were in the final of the competition – the first time meeting a school called Canley Vale – and we rather fancied ourselves to carry off the trophy. In fact, a big left-hander who seemed about seven feet tall, and was probably only five feet four inches, hit 160 against us. I can't remember his name – 'Slammer' perhaps, or 'Slasher' – but I can recall he gave us an almighty belting and his team made over 300. The following year we were more fortunate and, playing outside Cumberland Oval where I was later destined to play inside for the Cumberland Club, we scored enough runs to beat the opposition outright and win the competition for the first time.

It is a long while ago but all sorts of things stick in the mind, the most memorable of which was I couldn't use my own bat when making 50 not out in the second innings. I used to have a bat for Christmas every year to replace the broken one and it was always a Sports Master brand – I haven't seen those around for 20 years. When this final took place I had made nearly 400 runs in the competition for once out and, after being dismissed cheaply in the first innings, agreed to allow one of the other boys to use my bat, so long as I could have it when I batted. But when I got to the centre he was playing so well he wouldn't come near me and said I'd have to use another one.

They were great days at Sutherland road and they were also formative years. It was drilled into me over meal tables at home when I was a child that cricketers who do not set about trying to win the game from the start of the match would never be successful. This meant that right from the time I was old enough to play the game I had a positive attitude on the field whether as a batsman, bowler, fielder or captain. Be positive, but be fair, was the stricture. If captains don't start with the aim of winning the match from the time the first ball is bowled they have little chance.

Being brought up in a cricketing house had a great number of advantages and, as far as I can remember, no disadvantages, unless it was the fact I was never allowed to go out and play cricket before I'd eaten my vegetables. Just as my father had vowed that I had to be given the chance to be a good cricketer, my mother was quite determined that I would have the strength to be able to bowl many overs and bat for a long time out in the centre in the very hot sun.

As it happened, I wasn't too keen on eating vegetables. I especially hated choko which ran alongside and over our fence and, I suspect, given half an opportunity, would have eaten the fence itself. In those wartime days choko was regarded as being almost a weed but it was cheap and we didn't have much money. Now chokos sell for 25 cents each in Australia in the greengrocers' shops but then, when I was nine or ten years of age, I hated the taste of choko more than anything in the world. Unfortunately my parents liked it. It was usually on the menu when in season – which seemed 12 months long – together with squash, pumpkin and turnip, all of which I hated to varying degrees. But there was no bargaining: to get out there to the bottom paddock where we had manufactured a pitch, albeit a fairly rough one, those vegetables had to be eaten.

There was much to be learnt in the home about cricket and life and much to be learnt in the schoolroom as well. And then there were the weekends . . . After watching my father play in first grade for a couple of seasons, at 12 years of age I was allowed to go around with the Cumberland second grade as there was no permanent scorer available for the wartime one-day matches. Most of the time was spent scoring but just occasionally, if one of the chaps on army duty hadn't been able to turn up for the match, I was permitted to go out to field as substitute. What joy! How tempting it was to hope that the commanding officer would have put one of our players on some kind of fatigue, or stop him catching one of the army trucks along to the railway station to make his way to the ground . . . just so I might again be able to get out on the field! There were several occasions on which I managed 15 or 20 minutes and they were marvellous moments for a youngster in white shirt, white shorts and sandshoes to be out there with the men who were his heroes, despite them only playing second grade.

Jack O'Donoghue was captain of the Cumberland second grade, a magnificent attacking batsman who played a lot of first grade and then decided he was happy to play in the lower grade as skipper. My father played some matches in second grade that year before it was realised legspinners could still be match-winners in first-grade one-day matches. I used to go to the matches either on the train with Jack O'Donoghue, or in Arthur Howell's big truck which would take two or three other players as well, or with my father, and, when we arrived at the ground, I would get my score-book ready and then go out and have some fielding practice with the team when they hit up before the start of the match.

Sadly for me, more often than not, every player would be there in time for the start of play, but in that 1942 season there were two occasions when I was able to get on the field for some time. The first was when we were playing Petersham at Petersham Oval. When the local side batted, I managed to catch Jack Rowley off my father's bowling and then had to go in, batting at number 11 of course, with 4 runs needed for Cumberland to win. I had only the final ball of the over to face and at the other end, looking 12 feet tall, Milton Jarrett smashed the first ball of the next over straight out of the ground for six. There was no happier 12-year-old in the whole of Sydney as I marched off the field. Later that summer Cumberland were two men short in a match against North Sydney at North Sydney Oval. Not only was I called on to play, but also a friend of mine, Doug Milner, who was at the match with me. We fielded and batted and both of us edged a few runs. As a childhood dream, it was like going through the same things Kimpie did in Hugh de Selincourt's marvellous story of *The Saturday Match*. Minimum runs, no turn at the crease to bowl, but a lot of heart-thumping excitement – and the afternoon teas were absolutely magnificent. Gauvinier's captaincy was no better than that of Jack O'Donoghue and they were great days for a 12-year-old.

By 1945 I was playing lower-grade cricket for Cumberland, bowling legspinners and batting down the list with inconspicuous success. I started my first match in third grade, making 12 runs and watching from cover while a left-arm bowler named Jim Russell ripped through the opposition so quickly that next match he was taken straight into first grade. I managed to get into second grade at the end of the season – there were lots of players dropping out with football starting – and had one game against Gordon on Cumberland Oval before the season ended.

There was a good topspinning legspinner named Jack Prowse playing with Gordon at the time, a man who in years gone past had been a fine first grade cricketer and was still a useful bowler in the lower grades. A square-built cricketer, his topspinners zipped off the surface at a pace sufficient to make one wonder about the scientific theory that a ball cannot gain pace off the pitch. Jack Hill, who played for Australia, always seemed to make pace off the pitch and, to a 15-year-old second-grader, this fellow Jack Prowse appeared to do the same.

Before I went to the game my father, who was playing first grade at another ground at the time, gave me a word of advice. 'As he brings his arm over, you play forward and don't move your bat off a straight line,' he said. Jack Prowse gave me a pleasant nod as I walked nervously to the crease this day and then ran up and flipped at me a ball which was obviously going to turn sharply from the leg. Dutiful son disregarded the obvious turn and the fact the ball was short, and played forward with an impeccably straight bat. 'Ah!' came a voice from the other end. 'Who's been talking to you?' 'My father said I had to play straight at you,' I piped timorously. 'He says you can't turn them.' Perhaps it was the sun which had turned Mr Prowse a slight shade of puce but he was kind enough to pat me on the shoulder and say, after I had made a dozen, 'Well played son – give your Dad my regards.'

I played a match in third grade the following year and made 90 against a side which included Phil Tresidder, now a journalist and good friend, and then one game in second grade before being promoted to first grade to play in the same side as my father. It doesn't often happen that father and son play together in first-grade cricket in Sydney and it was a tremendous thrill to walk out alongside him the following week after selection, though the performances were nothing to write home about. In the second match I managed to get some wickets and then made 98 when Cumberland batted against what was a useful bowling attack, being dismissed whilst father was standing at the non-striker's end. I was out stumped to New South Wales offspinner Vince Collins with whom I had been having some trouble. He bowled a beautifully flighted topspinner, and one of the papers next day ran a story that nervousness at having my father at the other end had cost me my initial century in first-grade cricket.

There was varying success for the remainder of the season, probably more with bat than ball because in those days I was primarily regarded as a batsman – a fact which will no doubt bring a half-smile to the lips of many bowlers the world over. It was much the same story in 1947–48 when I made plenty of runs but found wickets rather elusive, at the same time doing well enough to give myself a chance of playing in the State Colts' fixture in October 1948. In this fixture, the first one of a representative nature in which I took part, I was only the second legspinner, and was not really needed anyway because of the run-getting of the early batsmen and the tremendous fast bowling of Alan Walker, who was making his initial moves towards going to South Africa the following year with the Australian side.

The number-one legspinner in the colts side was Brian Flynn who went on to play for the second XI but whom I eventually beat for a place in the state side, not because I could bowl better but because I could bat better. Brian was the finest legspinner I ever saw in the nets, almost unplayable on the most perfect practice pitch, and the dread of my life at the Sydney Cricket Ground Number Two was to have to bat against him with the state selectors present. His length never varied, his direction was perfect and he spun the ball sharply and dropped it into whatever breeze was blowing at the time. He later played successfully for Queensland, taking eight wickets in his first innings against New South Wales, but eventually lost his bowling action and rhythm and, after a season in Lancashire League, his bowling confidence low, retired to a successful business career.

The colts side to Queensland contained players like Jimmy Burke, who made a hundred and later played for Australia, as well as eight other eventual state representatives and the game was easily won. That injury to my head, sustained in Melbourne, followed soon after and, having already played in one state match against Queensland, I made what amounted to a come-back in 1949–50.

* * *

Looking back now at the late 1940s it is remarkable how many leg-break bowlers there were in Australia prior to the introduction of that previously mentioned 40-over new ball rule. They were everywhere. Now they have almost been exterminated. I keep on hoping to see some more emerge from the humdrum groups of pace, medium pace and inslant. Is it just wishful thinking?

It is not only the orthodox legspin bowlers who ply an interesting method in the game. There have also been some captivating bowlers of unusual style who have made the headlines in years past.

Eighty years ago the development of the 'Bosey' gave the impetus to three South African bowlers, Faulkner, Schwarz and Vogler, to develop the art. They had striking success and it is sad now to think that in England, the land where the leg-break and googly bowler first flourished, there will never again be a legspin bowler play Test cricket.

Australia produced variations of the over-the-wrist-spinner, great bowlers like O'Reilly and Grimmett, and then two even more unorthodox variations came from J.B. ('Jack') Iverson and John Gleeson. Iverson was the first: he was a tall, solidly-built man and was a great bowler, though he was by no means a great exponent of the art of bowling and he didn't know much about bowling. He came into the game when I was playing my second season with New South Wales and the full Australian team were in South Africa. Later the same summer he toured New Zealand and took 75 wickets at seven apiece. That season in Australia he had previously taken 46 wickets costing 16 runs each and it is no exaggeration when I say he was a sensation.

He played for Australia in 1950–51, taking 21 wickets at 15, and, if he were allowed to bowl as he wished, he could be almost unplayable. The NSW batsmen got to him in the match in Sydney the following year and ankle injuries then restricted his cricket. I have no doubt that, had he been fit and available for the 1953 tour of England, there would have been no celebrations for the home side that year.

Whether or not 'Jack' liked cricket very much is a debatable matter and it needed Lindsay Hassett to be there to set the fields for him and tell him, perhaps, to shift his line another three inches towards middle stump. He was as accurate as that. He adopted his bowling style in New Guinea during the Second World War, using a table-tennis ball and holding it between a bent middle finger and his thumb. He was basically an offspinner, but one who gained a tremendous amount of bounce from the pitch and he bowled, as well, a topspinner and leg-break without a discernible change of action. His Victorian team-mates would jealously guard his right to bowl only to them when the Australian team were practising in the nets.

John Gleeson bowled with the same bent-middle-finger style as Iverson, after starting his cricket career as a batsman and wicket-keeper. Gleeson was, and is, one of the quiet men of sport and no one enjoyed his cricket more, whether at country town, interstate or Test level.

I first saw him play, in fact played against him, when I went with Jack Chegwyn's team to the north west of New South Wales in 1965. I went around behind the bowler's arm with a pair of binoculars after a time because the batsmen seemed to be having an extraordinary amount of trouble in 'reading' him. We had heard he was unusual, but surely not this unusual?

It seemed easy enough from the car. When it came to my turn to bat, he ran up and bowled me what was obviously an off-break pitching on middle-and-leg and I turned it behind square-leg. Or rather I would have done that, other than for the fact the 'keeper had taken it outside off stump and thrown it back to Gleeson.

That was my first sight of him on a cricket field and I always enjoyed watching him bowl. He had a genuine feel for the game and a deep love of a contest, no matter who the batsman may have been; the better the batsman, the more enjoyable the contest and the greater the prize. Having finished at first-class level, he decided to take up lawn bowls where he is applying himself as assiduously as he did earlier to become only the second bowler in the history of the game to bowl in that extraordinary style.

It is a fascinating apprenticeship, that of legspin bowling, and one that takes years to master. In 1960 I went to South Africa with Ron Roberts's Commonwealth touring team and Ken Barrington was in the side. In the course of the tour Ken, who was a keen legspin bowler, prevailed on me to show him how to bowl the 'flipper', a ball which is literally flipped out underneath the bowling hand and 'fizzes' off the pitch, often cutting back at the right-hand batsman.

It is not an easy delivery to control, but I showed Ken and he practised it as much as possible. When he returned to England he went to the Surrey nets and confided to Tony Lock that he had been taught by Benaud how to bowl the 'flipper'. 'Locky' had a wealth of bowling experience and knew how difficult it was to learn a new delivery and how much time it took to perfect it. He said nothing.

It wasn't until the third match of the season against Northamptonshire, having reminded everyone day after day about the 'flipper', that Ken was called in to bowl by skipper Alec Bedser on a rather cold day at the Oval. He bowled one over and then told Tony Lock, who was fielding at leg slip, that the last ball of the next over would be the 'flipper' . . .

The opening night, as it were.

A combination of cold fingers and nerves saw it slant shoulder-high at the batsman who smashed it to the boundary past Tony's left ear. Tony said nothing, but walked down the pitch to meet Ken, full of apologies, coming in the opposite direction. 'Locky' didn't break stride. 'Bloody marvellous,' he said, looking straight ahead. 'Benaud couldn't get it right in seven years and five thousand overs and you've perfected it in one week.'

All cricketers need to have a good sense of humour, legspinners perhaps more than most. One such bowler was Eric Hollies who achieved immortality by bowling Bradman at the Oval in 1948 with his second ball, thus denying the great man a Test average of 100. The crowd were stunned.

Hollies had taken 8 for 107 against Australia when Warwickshire played the tourists a week before the final Test. When it came to the Oval Test his figures in the one innings were 56-14-131-5, one of those five being the great Bradman playing in his last Test match. He therefore had every right to be proud of his achievements. There he was, 36 years of age and, in spin-bowling terms, still with plenty of time left to master his craft, and there was the world's greatest batsman walking back to the pavilion with the crowd on their feet applauding him every inch of the way. Hollies, straight-faced, walked across to Middlesex left-arm spinner Jack Young and said, 'Marvel-lous, isn't it? It's the best ball I've bowled all season and they're clapping *him*.'

Not only the legspinner showed his sense of humour that day. Back in the pavilion when Bradman came through the door and, with a half smile, tossed his bat on to his cricket bag, Sid Barnes, still with the pads on, and also a Hollies victim three balls earlier caught by Godfrey Evans for 61, was able to say to him, 'Bad luck "Braddles", but don't worry about a thing. I managed to get the whole of your innings on film.'

I only ever played against Hollies twice, once in 1953 on my first tour of England when we played Warwickshire at Birmingham in early August, and the other time in Sydney in 1950 when he toured Australia with MCC under Freddie Brown's captaincy. In that 1953 match, Australia were almost beaten by the county in what was one of the most exciting matches of the tour. We were set 166 to make in just under three hours on a pitch allowing enormous spin. Hollies had bowled us out in the first innings, taking 5 for 45 from 33.3 overs and, in the second, we watched with some trepidation as he spun his way through over after over and nonplussed every one of our batsmen. Lindsay Hassett, who opened the innings, batted through the full time for 21 not out and I had the pleasure of being in with him for the last ten minutes, in the course of which Hassett managed to let me have as little of the bowling as possible. It was a fantastic performance from Hollies and one which confirmed what Australians already knew, that he was one of the finest English legspinners ever to play on English pitches.

One of the greatest problems for legspin bowlers has always been that of ripping skin off the two knuckles of the spinning fingers. It could be agonizing, bowling with torn fingers, and it was extremely difficult to perform at one's peak. It could also take a lot out of the pleasure of bowling. Occasionally though luck plays a great part in the career of a cricketer and being in the right place at the right time is all part of that luck. Nothing better could possibly have happened to me than the exchange of views I had with a chemist in New Zealand during Australia's short tour of that country in 1957.

I was still having problems with the dengue fever I had contracted in Bombay at the end of the 1956 tour, although the fever attacks were being more widely spaced at this stage. Even so, I had run out of Sulphanilamide tablets by the time we reached Timaru on the eastern coast of New Zealand, just below Christchurch in the south island. If forced to nominate in order the places likely to have a beneficial effect on my future cricket career, I must confess that, at the time, Timaru would have been well down the list. But Ivan James, the chemist who organised the prescription for me, happened, as I handed over the papers, to notice my spinning fingers on my right hand were absolutely raw. I explained the problem, telling him how the stitches on the ball were constantly ripping them to pieces, and he suggested that his own treatment for leg ulcers might be able to do me some good. 'But,' he added, 'It's not an orthodox treatment and you will have to try it and see.'

The treatment was simple, involving the use of boracic acid powder and oily calamine lotion. The combination of the two used in the correct manner produced a waxy substance which filled the hole, crack, or split in the finger and toughened the skin, as indeed it apparently did for patients of his who were suffering from leg ulcers. The injury wasn't hardened or softened, as was the case with other things I'd used – merely toughened, and it made an enormous difference to my bowling from that time on.

There was nothing new in slow bowlers having trouble with their spinning fingers. Colin McCool, who played for New South Wales, then Queensland and Australia, used to have terrible problems. Had Colin still been playing when I found my remedy, I reckon it would have added years to his playing life.

I was able to pass this remedy on to other bowlers and, for the most part, it served them well but it could not have come at a better time as far as I was concerned. If I hadn't had the remedy on hand I would have had real trouble in South Africa in 1957–58, which is where I started to improve as a bowler. I would have spent most of my time trying to avoid having my fingers torn to pieces instead of concentrating on the art of bowling. It was after I discovered the remedy that my bowling came on apace, so I am in no doubt when I say it was one of the luckiest things ever to happen to me.

*   *   *

Family sporting groups are never easy. There are always comparisons to be made of the skills of the father, son, brother or cousin, and everyone has their own ideas on which player was better. We still hear, for example, that Les McCabe was a better player than Stan, and there are arguments at the local club over whether Ian or Greg Chappell was the finer batsman.

In India they discuss now the virtues of the Amarnaths and, in Pakistan, how could you decide which of the Mohammad brothers was the more outstanding? In New Zealand there are the Hadlees and Howarths, and in South Africa the Pollock brothers had it right when one became a great batsman and the other a very good pace-bowler.

I started out as a batsman and finished up as an allrounder, with an accent on legspin bowling and captaincy. My brother John concentrated on batting and, at one stage, captaincy.

While the Australian team were away in India and South Africa in 1969–70, he was made captain of the rebuilt New South Wales side. He exhibited plenty of flair as a captain, was never scared to take a risk and played some very useful, hard-hitting innings for the state. But it can, as I say, be extremely difficult being a brother or son following on some other member of the family who has played cricket for Australia – sometimes you are credited with ideas which are not really yours.

When Victoria were playing New South Wales in Melbourne in December 1969, the Victorians won by one wicket. It was a great match, with New South Wales knocked over for only 131 in the first innings and bowling out Victoria for 278. Then John hit 134 in the second innings, leaving Victoria 181 to win. He was in the centre of the Melbourne Cricket Ground trying every tactic he could think of whilst I was watching the game on television back in Sydney, living every moment of it as well. Victoria were coasting along very smoothly. Dave Renneberg, John Martin and David Colley were the pace bowlers and Kerry O'Keeffe was the spinner in the New South Wales side.

Sitting back in the living-room, which is always much easier than being in the centre, I reckoned the tactics were to keep pace going from one end and O'Keeffe from the other. All of a sudden, with O'Keeffe on at one end, John called up Geoff Davies to bowl and I was up out of my chair saying, 'Oh no, not two spinners at the moment – two overs from Davies could cost you the match.'

At that instant the television commentator said, 'Ah yes, you can see here John Benaud has picked up some of the captaincy flair of his brother. That is precisely the kind of bowling change Richie would have made. A real gamble. Richie will be pleased at this.' I subsided sulkily into my chair and Geoff Davies proceeded to take four quick wickets at a time when it seemed Victoria had the game made and although, in the end, they scrambled in by one wicket, 182 for 9, it was a close-run thing.

It was only last year I had someone come up to me and say, 'You know, I remember watching on television that match in Melbourne when your brother pulled one of your tricks with that great bowling change.' I had the commonsense to smile knowingly and say nothing.

At the end of the 1969–70 season John Benaud's forthright nature and very, very inquiring mind got him into trouble. The chairman of the New South Wales executive at the time was Mr S. G. Webb who had been my manager on the 1961 tour of England and who had achieved some publicity during the tour by slapping a 'gag' on me. This was after he stated he had received a letter from the Australian Cricket Board suggesting he, rather than the captain, should make press statements in future in the light of one or two newspaper stories which had appeared back in Australia. We managed to get around that all right with a few smiles and eventually, as the records show, came out of the tour with a victory in the series, although Syd and I were still having our discussions on a variety of matters at the end of the tour.

In the 1969–70 season a lot of cricketers in Australia were wearing a new type of cricket boot, the one which is almost universally worn now, with spikes in the soles and ribbed rubber in the heel. It was then, and is now, widely regarded by sports-medicine experts as being ideal for cricket, in that it puts far less stress on the knee and certain muscles. It was very popular with the players.

By coincidence, I was at the SCG standing at the back of the New South Wales executive room when the trouble started. New South Wales were in the field and a ball was snicked to second slip who dropped a 'sitter'. One of the New South Wales executive members, a long-time administrator in Australian cricket, said, 'Look at that. That's all to do with those boots. How can they possibly stand up and catch if they don't wear proper, sturdy boots?'

I raised my eyebrows and, as the discussion went on, shook my head and walked out. I reckoned I had stood about as much of that as I could from people who had no idea whether the boots were good or not and hadn't pulled any on for 20 years. As the season went on though the argument gathered pace and the Cricket Association actually turned around and, in an astonishing directive, banned the boots from being worn by the New South Wales state team.

There were two home matches still to be played for New South Wales and, a few days prior to one of these Sydney matches, John Benaud wore, under the directive, a new pair of boots he'd been forced to buy and finished up with blistered feet. He went to the executive and asked permission to use his old boots for the remainder of the match and in future, but this was refused. He then told them not only was it painful for him to wear boots which had given him blistered feet but it seemed to him as well to be absolutely ridiculous.

New South Wales won those two matches – the first one by 171 runs and the second on the first innings by 95 runs – and the executive suspended him after the second game. His lasting memory is of fronting the executive chairman and being called 'Richie'. Memories die hard!

The upshot of this was I ceased to be a life member of the New South Wales Cricket Association. The story is interesting, even though my decision had nothing at all to do directly with the fact my brother had been suspended. That kind of sacking one would take with a certain amount of equanimity, merely putting it down as another example of odd administration in Australian cricket.

What happened however was entirely different. There was quite a lot of publicity about the boots business and Pat Farrell, racing editor of the Sydney *Daily Mirror*, was at Randwick racecourse on the Saturday when he happened to run into Syd Webb who, by now, had probably had enough of the anti-publicity to last him a long time. Farrell published a column on the Monday, going deeply into the question of the suspension and quoting Syd Webb as saying at some length that in any case the whole thing didn't matter very much because everyone knew Benaud wasn't a good captain. The team was better off without him and it had been said at an Australian Cricket Board meeting he shouldn't be captain of the New South Wales side.

I was rather intrigued by this because I knew a lot of the members of the Board of Control and I was surprised to hear that they would have concerned themselves with the domestic affairs of New South Wales. It also struck me as odd that they would have been so fierce in their criticism of John's captaincy because this was his first effort at the job: up to then he had done fairly well and had shown much attacking flair.

I made two telephone calls interstate to two members of the Board, asking them if the extremely critical aspect of the article with regard to my brother was correct. I was assured the matter had never been brought up at any Board of Control meeting, nor could they care less who captained New South Wales. That put an entirely different complexion on things and I waited with interest to hear the result of the meeting of the delegates to the New South Wales Cricket Association, where a statement was to be made on the boots matter. Particular attention was to be paid to this article which had appeared in Farrell's column. I also rang Pat Farrell who had in his race-book his notes of the interview quotes. He read them back to me. They were word for word as they had been printed. The following Tuesday the Cricket Association delegates' meeting were told Farrell's story was absolutely untrue and no one had spoken to Farrell about cricket.

In view of this, I dropped a note to Alan Barnes, secretary of the Board, to intimate that, as a result of my knowledge that the article was completely correct in its quotes, I would like his Association to strike my name off their list of life members. It was impossible to belong to an organization which would permit something of this nature to be said at a meeting when, in fact, the delegates had made not the slightest move to talk to Farrell to check the story. Alan Barnes's letter came back to me on 9 March, 1970, letting me know it was my entitlement to resign and that the resignation had been noted.

A lot of people said to me they couldn't understand why I resigned over the fact my brother had been suspended. I didn't. I resigned because the delegates of the Association had accepted that Pat Farrell had deliberately published something he knew to be false. It was a curiously weak piece of administration.

The New South Wales Cricket Association went through a rough patch from around that time until 1983. It took 17 years for the Sheffield Shield to be won again and it must have been a well-deserved moment of delight for Rick McCosker and his men when they defeated Western Australia in Perth in March 1983 in the first-ever Sheffield Shield final. There were many old NSW cricketers back in Sydney, myself included, who raised a glass to the players when that final wicket was taken.

* * *

With all our extensive overseas touring at the moment, there is not much opportunity for the Benaud family to talk cricket at first hand as a threesome around the kitchen table, but it was interesting recently to chat to both my father and John to obtain some idea of their feelings about various aspects of the modern-day game. The three faces of Benaud do not always mould into one but, as it was over the years, the discussion was amicable and very much to the point.

New South Wales, once the stronghold of cricket in Australia, has only just regained the Sheffield Shield after a 17-year drought. I know we lost some good players in 1962, 1963 and 1964, but to wait until 1983 for a win seems a bit much.

John New South Wales got out of the habit of winning. We lost a lot of good players in one batch and that is always a problem. I wonder though, in the era when we weren't winning the Shield, whether or not the selectors were at fault. I think it's only in the last few years selectors have come to grips with what I always thought Western Australia did well, and that was give well-performed grade players a chance at Shield level. WA, when they started winning the Shield, would always have a few unknown players in there who would perform well. New South Wales's tendency was to hang on to state players for a long time but they weren't making hundreds and taking five wickets. Too often New South Wales gave the mediocre performers at Shield level a much higher standing than they deserved and I think a lot of good grade players missed out over the years because of that selection style in the 17 years when the Sheffield Shield was gone.

Lou Could it be there has been too much generalised and theoretical coaching and not enough practical work? With all the coaching they have, why are they unable to develop 12 or more very good players for an Australian team and the Sheffield Shield and grade teams? Instead, they look to players from overseas. Now I've no objection to overseas players – they do a fine job. But if our coaching is to cost thousands and thousands of dollars, I think it should be able to produce the local goods so we don't necessarily have to import people to play for the states.

Now between you, you can cover the period 1904 to 1984 – father for a longer period than John. In all that time current players have rarely been regarded as being as good as those of the past. How do you rate the players of today?

Lou I don't see much difference in the standard of cricket. A player like Don Bradman was exceptional. He was the only one mind you. In my opinion, there are as many good cricketers around today, batsmen, bowlers and fieldsmen, as there ever were in my time. One thing I don't like about the fielding is the fall-over fieldsmen. I don't mind a fellow diving for a ball but you'll see them now field the ball and then fall over. That's a bad habit. It's not that they have to do it to field the ball – some correctly dive to field the ball – but then you watch others who stop the ball, hold it and then fall over. In the Test sphere, Hobbs and Sutcliffe would have relished such fieldsmen in the opposition, while in grade cricket in Sydney, Mort Cohen and Jim Brown, and other great runners between the wickets and stealers of singles, would have shown them up.

Batting technique seems to have changed, many batsmen playing cross-bat strokes in defence. Some, in fact, for back defence, seem so obsessed with being side-on they forget footwork and hold out a tentative bat. They would do much better stepping across and back and playing from only a semi side-on position. If that were done we would see much more offside driving off the back foot. The square-cut technique these days has all but disappeared.

On the whole, Australian batting style has changed from being closely related to the West Indian back-foot natural-ability type to the more staid, purist style used by English batsmen. The blame for this backward step can be placed squarely on the shoulders of the 'build an innings' coaches who have forgotten it is better to play every ball on its merit. If the ball is there to be hit – then hit it!

The batsman who impressed me most was Bradman, who was so good they couldn't set a field for him. The poem *Abou Ben Adhem* ends with 'And lo Ben Adhem's name led all the rest'. In any batting poem, the last line should end, 'And lo Don Bradman's name led all the rest'. Why was Bradman so much better than other batsmen? His eyes weren't better, his footwork was good . . . but maybe it was because he possessed a super-speedy analytical mind which, if he misjudged the ball, enabled him instantly to take remedial action.

Next to Bradman for me was Charlie Macartney, who possessed the fleetest of footwork and was a scintillating stroke-maker, whilst the spirit of absolute acceptance of a challenge oozed from every pore. His placing of the ball was magnificent. A marvellous batsman, with his attacking nature a model for any young cricketer. One look at Macartney and you had something to paste in your cricket bag and remember for evermore. 'Learn to move your feet on all occasions and they will lead you to batting brilliance, otherwise you will never move beyond miserable mediocrity,' Macartney once said. He was absolutely right.

John It's always difficult to make comparisons unless you played in the two eras. It seems to me cricket all round is probably stronger now – that may have something to do with the aggressive nature in which it's played and there, I think, lies a fault with modern-day cricket. It is probably over-aggressive and I don't think players these days have the same subtlety and may not even enjoy the game as much as they did 15 and 20 years ago. It has that coliseum touch about it, perhaps a sign of the times; people's lifestyles generally have become more aggressive.

Fielding now is streets ahead of what it used to be. I would have to put it down to the modern-day training methods where they have baseball gloves, and baseball pitchers come along and coach players who do so many more exercises their fitness is probably greater than at any other time. You only have to look at the Classic Catches segment in the Nine Network TV cover to realise what players are capable of these days – it's magnificent.

You have seen umpiring in New South Wales now for a long time and you have watched a lot of television. How would you solve the problems which seem to exist at the moment in umpiring?

Lou The ACB should arrange, at the end of each cricket season, a meeting of umpires so they can discuss umpiring and all problems associated with it. The umpire–player relationship ought to be like that of schoolteacher and pupil – friendly but slightly aloof, with a line drawn by the umpire to discourage familiarity and undesirable conduct by players. An umpire must keep his dignity on all occasions. It should be remembered an umpire is part of the match being played, just as the players are part of it. An umpire is chosen on ability, in the same way as a player is chosen on ability. Over a period any umpire or player who cannot perform well should be dropped.

At present there seems to be some strange panic with statements that television replays of umpires' mistakes are driving umpires from the game. Those making the statements appear to forget there are replays showing the mistakes of batsmen, bowlers and fieldsmen. Are those players being driven from the game because the replays worry them? I would hope they have more temperament and courage than that.

Over a season of replays of umpires' decisions, a picture emerges of good umpires who perform well, have the right temperament for Test umpiring and who will remain in the game at first-class level. The remainder, as in any competitive arena, will have to go back to grade cricket or retire if they find they do not possess the necessary courage. We should, in fact, be grateful that an aid like television is provided for all to appreciate the problems of umpiring as well as playing.

With regard to the demand for neutral umpires, can anyone answer the question: 'Will neutral umpires be any better in another country than they are in their own?' One must sympathise with umpires as there is much pressure applied by players, such as 'altogether appeals', disappointment displays and bat-pad 'bawling' performances.

Who were the finest players in each department of the game in your years of watching?

Lou It was good to see Dennis Lillee capture the greatest number of Test wickets. He deserved the honour as a reward for the tremendous courage he showed in overcoming his back problems and then making his remarkable come-back. A great bowler.

The bowler of fast-medium pace who impressed me most was Maurice Tate. He had everything – maximum bodyswing, with front foot hitting the pitch very hard; well disguised movement in the air and off the pitch; pace combined with lift off the pitch; and almost perfect control of length and direction.

The legspin bowling spot goes to Clarrie Grimmett. He used wonderfully well all the legspin bowling skills and was a master at out-thinking batsmen. Why was he not chosen earlier for Test cricket? His arm action seemed to be almost round-arm so I reckon the purists, the theory men who abound in cricket, would have nothing to do with him until his continuous success forced them to recognise his great talent. A remarkable bowler.

The three fieldsmen who have impressed me most were Neil Harvey, Jack Gregory and Vic Richardson. As an away-from-the-wicket fieldsman, Neil Harvey had uncanny anticipation, extremely safe hands and a throw which never seemed to be off target. He always appeared to be in position waiting for the ball. He also became a magnificent slip fielder when needed by Australia.

As a slip fieldsman, Jack Gregory was wonderful. To the slow bowlers he fielded almost on the bat and plucked catches out of the air with either hand or with both hands while, for fast bowling, he stood back and caught equally well.

Before and after Vic Richardson, I've never seen any cricketer approach the skill he displayed in suicide catching positions. At silly-point or short-leg he was quite magnificent and absolutely fearless.

Bert Oldfield as a great wicket-keeper possessed an uncanny sense of anticipation which enabled him to be in the right position to handle the ball. He was the best I saw from any country.

Garry Sobers was the finest allrounder I've seen. A great batsman, a great fieldsman and a great bowler, whether he bowled pace or spin. Almost two men in one for a captain.

The boots drama in 1969–70. It seemed such an unnecessary piece of heavy-handed administration. Looking back on it now, how do you see it?

Lou Ah well, that rocked me completely to think a man could be kicked out of a New South Wales cricket team because he wore a certain pair of boots – nowadays worn by everyone. I was amazed at that and I was terribly hurt to think the Cricket Association would treat one of their players that way. I've never been to watch a match at the SCG since then and I won't go again. It was a childish action by the Association, where delegates were weak enough to allow themselves to be dominated by one man.

John Quite obviously the ripple-soles affair was a sign of the times – it was a boot with a difference, spikes and rubber heel, and it showed something could be done in the way of cricket equipment. It was a light-weight boot compared to the normal boot and was revolutionary. Everybody wears *sandshoes* these days and, whilst they could be a problem in wet conditions, certainly they're more comfortable than heavy clod-hopping boots. Anybody who's been to the West Indies, India or Pakistan and played on the concrete conditions there would appreciate rubber-soled shoes.

In a way we have all been mixed up in the media over the years. Louis Ferdinand Benaud with the Richmond River Times, *John and I with newspapers and then radio and television. How do you both see the difference in media coverage of cricket over a time span of 60 years?*

Lou Well, it was straight reporting before the war. In earlier years when I was at Grafton, we used to get the Sydney papers once a week. They'd come up by train and Sydney grade cricket was reported in full detail, entire scores for first, second, third and fourth grades – the full scores mind you, not only for first grade. There was a big coverage in the Sydney papers then and they covered the game from many different angles, giving a description of the match right down to the final detail. In those days, there was no scrambling for an angle on this or that, less personal reporting about individuals and more Tom Goodman style [*Sydney Morning Herald*] – Tom Goodman used to report the game and did it in delightful fashion. But it's good for the game to have plenty of media coverage and I've no objection to what they write in these modern times.

John It has improved greatly. Television coverage is magnificent. Newspaper cover has changed – as pointed out by Australian cricket-writer, Phil Wilkins, in an article for the 1983–84 National Nine Tour Guide – the newspaper these days, because of television, has to change its tack and therefore we are getting more and more behind-the-scenes stories. Whilst that isn't necessarily greeted with favour by the players, it does show cricket is being reported in greater depth. I think in Australia now we may lack some expert cover on cricket from a writing point of view. Some of the fellows going around these days haven't played the game at the level I think would help them make valid comments. Some of the comments on tactics are often naive. Someone who has played first-class cricket senses some of the cricket writers are struggling and that's probably the only disappointing side of the media today. Otherwise I think it is excellent.

Let's be more specific then. Cricket has become a great spectator sport nowadays, with millions watching television and one million spectators at the matches in 1982–83. What's your opinion of the television coverage available?

John I think it's great – I prefer to sit in front of the television and watch the game these days than actually go out to the ground. One of the things I find particularly disappointing about going to the ground is that you are always looking for the instant replay, and whilst that's available in the bars at, say, the Adelaide Oval, it's not available everywhere, which can become frustrating – but the television coverage itself is brilliant.

I think the ads on television are necessary. If you don't have commercial breaks then you're stuck with looking at a screen where nothing is happening. Players are changing ends which is pretty boring and, if you're at home, it's a chance to get up and go and do something and I think there has to be a place for commercial breaks. The other thing you have without ads is talking heads and if you have 100 overs bowled in a day that's 100 changes of ends and 100 talking heads. Nothing could be worse than that.

Lou Now I no longer attend Test matches, I rely on the Australian television coverage, or sometimes BBC if it is an overseas tour, to provide me with a picture of the play and anything else of interest at the game. I have one slight regret concerning the telecasts and that is there seems to be no lens capable yet of providing a full picture of the ground precisely as I would see it from behind the bowler's arm when I attended the matches. That is a small debit and on the whole I thoroughly enjoy the television coverage. The pitch analysis and the unique Weatherwall information are extremely interesting to viewers like me who are settling down to watch a whole day's play and want comparisons with previous days. I enjoy the close-up of the toss and the chat between the interviewer and each captain.

The camera work these days is absolutely outstanding. Coverage of batting, bowling and especially the fielding is marvellous. Nothing seems to be missed. The picture presented on the screen is superior to the view one has as a spectator using the naked eye at the ground. Missing of course is the tremendous atmosphere of being part of a 45,000 crowd!

Commentators all have their own method of describing the play – a good thing because it adds variety and interest to the telecast. But, a television cricket commentator should employ a minimum of talk to convey a maximum of information. Now and again some commentators seem to talk too much. I don't at all mind the ads. In fact, I think they are better than chat where a commentator describes the over and then, as soon as the over finishes, another commentator comes on and again tells you what happened. Now that's boring!

I believe replays of dismissals should be continued but they should be screened without pronouncing judgement. The viewer can make up his own mind. Replays showing the action from different angles are excellent. Sometimes I have difficulty deciding where the ball is going after it leaves the bat and I am not sure of the distance the players are from the pitch. We don't always receive enough information on these matters. But the inset pictures of the batsmen running between the wickets and the score ticking over is wonderful. Television commentators should give the name of each fieldsman as he gathers the ball, in the same way as a light identifies the fielder on the ground scoreboard. The information on players' performances displayed on the screen is excellent and should be continued. Most diagrams are good but I cannot summon up much interest in the ones showing the strokes of certain batsmen.

Changes in the structure of the game. How about an increase or decrease in playing time for Sheffield Shield? What about limited-overs matches?

Lou Limited-overs matches are popular because they exemplify the part of cricket which makes it so wonderful to watch and to play: on most occasions spectators and players are never certain as to which side will win a closely-contested match. Perhaps my enjoyment of this game is because of my early upbringing where one-day cricket was all we played.

I would though like to see legspinners given a chance and I would definitely like the field-restriction circle to be retained. I'm sure if good quality legspinners were playing the limited-overs game would become even more attractive.

I have been astonished that Australia expect to produce cricketers able to compete in international one-day matches without sufficient grounding in the fundamentals of this kind of game. When I look through *Wisden* each year, it seems to me the English first-class cricketers play, in their summer, something like 250 limited-overs matches in four domestic competitions. No wonder they are good at it. Australians don't appear to play more than a handful.

At first-class level I would like to see the Sheffield Shield matches finish on the Saturday and then the Sunday be given over to an interstate limited-overs fixture, as in the McDonald's Cup. The states should play each other twice in Sheffield Shield and twice in the McDonald's Cup. This would mean a fixture list whereby, say, New South Wales would fly to Brisbane on the Monday of a week, practise on Tuesday, play Sheffield Shield on Wednesday, Thursday, Friday, Saturday and the McDonald's Cup match on the Sunday. Spectators would be able to watch, in particular, the final day of the Sheffield Shield match, which is generally the most exciting, with a result in prospect, and then the one-day match with a result guaranteed. The suggestion is geared to the fact that these days cricket should be provided for the public at times when they are able to watch.

I believe the Sydney grade competition, from the first week of October to the third week of March in each state, should consist of 16 matches over 24 weeks: eight of these matches to be limited-overs fixtures of 50 overs a side and eight to be two-day fixtures. The latter would be the nursery for Sheffield Shield and the one-day fixtures would introduce young players to the problems of limited-overs tactics.

In Australia the present concept of the international three-team limited-overs competition seems ideal for spectators. To continue to play old-style cricket all the time in grade clubs is to say, in effect, limited-overs cricket at international level does not exist. Some administrators, blind to modern-day requirements, may even believe that.

John I think five-day Sheffield Shield matches are probably not a bad move, in terms of Test match preparation of players. I'm not too sure though about the effects on players. I know we used to have a problem, and probably it still exists, of players who are not paid by their firms. It's never easy to get away for practice – I know a couple of blokes around Sydney now who have difficulty finding a job and getting to practice, so five-day Shield matches could be troublesome.

Cost could be another factor – might it mean an escalation in expense of running the game, and could cricket afford it? But I think the inaugural five-day Final showed there can be a lot of value there. You would certainly get a result most of the time and, in terms of the abandonment of bonus points, it's probably the right way to go.

There will never again be a legspin bowler play for England. In my opinion, the lbw Law, the 40-over new-ball rule and modern pitches made for fast bowlers almost guarantee there will never again be a legspin bowler play for Australia.

Lou Yes, you might well ask 'Where are the great legspinners of yesteryear?' Cautious captains, together with 'axe 'em' administrators, 'sack 'em' selectors, the lbw Law change and 'green-top' groundsmen, have all helped to produce the present pattern where much pace and some fingerspin, mostly offspin, have taken over from legspin. In doing so, they have lessened the variety, challenge and joy which makes for better cricket. Great legspinners, if handled positively, would more than hold their own in Test, Sheffield Shield and limited-overs cricket wherever cricket is played today.

It's time to have a quest for legspin bowlers in New South Wales, aged from 18 to 25 years of age, give or take a year or so, and the first quest should be staged for players from the five country cricket zones. Any grade or junior clubs which think they have an outstanding leg-break bowler should be able to have him judged at state cricket practices at the SCG so he can be checked out by the state selectors. The best way would be for each zone to nominate four leg-break bowlers to total 20 aspiring Test players.

In New South Wales there are a handful of batsmen, bowlers and captains who are good judges of what it takes to be a leg-break bowler, and they could be put in charge of the exercise. Peter Philpott, Richie Benaud, Ian Chappell, Alan Davidson and Arthur Morris leap to mind, but there are others as well.

Maybe this is the fault of one-day cricket or the great fast-bowling era. Maybe we'll see legspinners again, but it seems to me none are coming on at the moment and it's a very sad thing because it's taken away a great part of the game.

Do you like the new trend of people other than captains having a say in the running of the team?

John I think at Test level a manager is a good idea because a captain can be protected. Managers though should be careful they don't overstep the mark. Physiotherapists are important because there is such a high emphasis placed on fitness these days. Psychologists, outside motivators and hypnotists I'm completely against – I don't think they can serve any purpose a good captain cannot perform.

At Penrith, *team* psychology and *team* motivation played a big part in us winning a premiership in Sydney grade cricket. We went from last to first on the table – and we did it with a team of rejects, some of them from lower grades in other clubs. We used to put on barbecues and movies, such as Sobers's 254 in Melbourne, and this was an important motivational thing. It gave batsmen the feel of scoring runs and the excitement of the crowd. Motivation is a player thing, in the heart and mind, not an outside thing. I think if a player has his own motivation then he has a great start on those who lack it. You can't bring in people from outside a team to manufacture motivation.

Lou I'm not in favour of it at all. I think any player who needs psychological treatment or hypnosis does not have good enough nerves to play Test cricket. I think a player should approach the game in a natural way and, if you need to 'psych' yourself up, you can do it by means of what I would call 'inward anger'. In other words, if the batsman is on top of you, you produce a little bit of anger as you come up to bowl at him and that gives you a lot of extra strength to attack – I don't think you need anything more than that. Commonsense is the best psychology.

Right. What about changes to the Laws? How can the game be improved for player and spectator?

John Quite obviously, Rich, you would like to see the no-ball Law changed and also the over-rates improved. We disagree on the first. I fear, if you change the no-ball Law, you might, with lax umpiring, get back to the old situation where somebody would be cribbing a couple of yards and you'll then have inconsistencies in umpiring, which is what led to the old Law falling down – certain umpires would allow a six-foot drag and others would only allow one foot.

I would certainly like to see something done about over-rates, otherwise you will lose spectators and spectators keep the game afloat as much as sponsorship.

And what of the way the players react to this modern age?

John Player behaviour these days is often boorish and some of the antics are ridiculous. This business with dismissing someone and pointing to the pavilion – that's rubbish. It's brought about by the coliseum atmosphere, the one-day game where it's all go-go-go, together with the fast-bowling era we are in, but I feel it should be eliminated. Take a bowler like Trueman. He was a fast bowler but he didn't go in for this rubbish – things he did were often funny but I'm afraid fast bowlers don't have much sense of humour these days.

Penalties for bad behaviour are not strong enough. If you increased your penalties for bad behaviour, then you would instantly eliminate some of the boorish performances we see. I think the fines should be heavily increased – I'm talking about thousands of dollars – and suspensions should be strongly considered. I would like to see an independent arbitrator – like the Rugby League have Jim Comans the solicitor – and players should be made to appear before a judicial committee. This business about players working their own fines out is the greatest load of nonsense I have heard.

Are they then expected to work too hard?

John No, I don't think the players' work-load is too much. They like to regard themselves as being professional, they want to accept proper remuneration and I think, provided their pay-rates keep pace with their workload, they should be well satisfied with their programmes. Fitness these days is such that there are few breakdowns and here you go back to the physio aspect. As long as the masseur is always there and players know what they can do, there shouldn't be any problems.

Pitches – how can they be improved?

Lou The Australian Cricket Board should arrange, at the end of each cricket season, a meeting of curators to enable a policy of preparing excellent pitches to be formulated. For several years, Australian cricket pitches have favoured fast bowlers because each prepared pitch has had a thick cover of grass left on it. They have played like 'green-tops' and close up on the television screen they look somewhat like coir mats. For want of a better name, we could call them brown green-tops. The grass is there but it's gone brown with rolling and the ball has only to hit on a certain spot and it does something unexpected. That's how these fast bowlers have been so terrifying to the batsmen. Give them a flat pitch and they wouldn't be able to do that.

The only way they'll get back to normal is to shave the pitches, get the grass off and yet still have them concrete hard and therefore still allow the bowlers some bounce. It is the roots of the grass which bind the pitch, so why on earth leave a lush growth of grass on top for the fast bowlers? Let the grass be cut very short so fast bowlers have to work and we can once again see legspinners in action.

I played on many different types of pitches – dirt pitches, concrete pitches without mats or with coir and Kippax mats, polished concrete without mats or with coir and Kippax mats, antbed pitches with and without mats, malthoid, original Bulli soil pitches like a solid block of black glass, turf pitches of a very different type and not nearly as good, and composition pitches. I never found a pitch on which it was impossible for a leg-break bowler to turn the ball.

John Pitches at grade level in Sydney are shocking. You have enthusiastic Parks and Gardens' workers preparing them, unfortunately knowing little about the job – they know about the nature strip in the middle of the highway, and camellias and snapdragons, but not about cricket pitches. At first-class level there is disappointment, including at the SCG, MCG and WACA Ground in Perth in recent years. I find it incredible the Western Australian Association won't take notice of suggestions from their curator to dig up the square. It seems to me he must know more about the pitch now than the Association delegates or those concerned in making the decision. Seminars for groundsmen are a great idea but, looking at that WA situation, it mightn't be a bad idea if you had a seminar for groundsmen and, as well, for cricket authorities.

How much influence can a captain have these days?

Lou There is no royal road to being a cricket captain. One very important factor an aspiring captain should develop is an analytical and inquiring mind. When playing in a cricket match, or watching a cricket match, the aspiring captain must study the actions of both captains and take note of all happenings on the field during each game. After the day's play has been completed, the aspiring captain, on his own at home, should analyse all that went on in the day's play. Then he can decide what he would have done had he been captain. That, in my opinion, is the best preparation for any young cricketer who aims to become captain. It is the preparation I set both of you.

There is though one thing captains must remember. The game is an entertainment. Push, prod and deflect, and a refusal to get through the bowling of overs, holds back the entertainment for the spectators. Captains control the game. If they play it in the right spirit and keep in mind the spectators, then there will be no problems.

Finally, all aspiring cricketers should play cricket, practise cricket, get fit for cricket, watch cricket, read about cricket and analyse the game as well as learning the Laws.

We hear a lot about motivation these days – is it something new?

Lou Love of the game of cricket is the major motivation; from it will spring all minor motivations. The seeds of learning to love cricket should be sown when a young boy plays naturally with bat and ball and gets pleasure from so doing. Only if he has that love of cricket will he have the incentive to improve his game so he can progress through all stages until he reaches Test standard.

Do properly motivated teams need coaches?

Lou Why should Sheffield Shield and Test cricketers need a coach? They need a captain but surely they should be regarded as being good players already or they would not be selected to play at first-class level.

When states employ coaches who are unable to produce a team of cricketers capable of winning at top level and then the states have to use overseas players, is there not something wrong with the system? Is it possible our first-class players are being spoon-fed so much they are beginning to lack initiative and self-reliance? More important, if the answer is yes, are they prepared to do something about it for the good of Australian cricket?

What about the aftermath of World Series Cricket and current administration?

John World Series Cricket was good for the game. It led to changes in schedules so good teams like West Indies can come to Australia more regularly, and Australia had Pakistan tour while they were on top. I think it's good to have some flexibility in tours.

WSC was good for the game because it showed it could be played in a modern and constructive way. It was an alternative to the other cricket and I think it established cricket as a much greater game than it had been previously in terms of a spectacle.

Night cricket obviously is a tremendous success – it's a product of WSC and it showed cricket could cater for a different type of crowd. Night cricket is real entertainment. There is something incredible about going to the SCG under lights – it's so different, a whole new world – there's a magic about it – and you can see it will never stop attracting crowds. It stands as the game's outstanding development in our country, probably the great thing for cricket in Australia since Bradman.

Current administration seems to me to have improved considerably but we are still hassled by some of the lesser administrators being light-weights — I think the McDonald's Cup fiasco in Sydney at the end of the 1982–83 season showed cricket administrators still live to some extent in their own little beehive, and haven't come to grips with how important to the game is sponsorship and keeping sponsors happy. Otherwise I don't see anything too much wrong with the administration. It's just that every now and again they show signs of having not quite moved out of the 1800s.

Any regrets over the years?

Lou When you think that only a few more than 300 men have ever played Test cricket for Australia, how could one really have regrets if two have come from this family? It has been a very interesting time and of course both players had different styles and lived in different eras. There were set-backs for everyone but no regrets. My only personal regret is that I might have succeeded in breaking into first-class cricket if I'd had the chance to try out with a Sydney club when based at North Casino in the 1920s. But when the economic depression then hit Australia it was a matter of being able to eat rather than becoming a first-class cricketer.

I was almost 34 when, after being posted back to the city in 1937, I tried out for Central Cumberland. I played to the age of 46 in first grade, then had another four seasons in second grade and two in third grade. I took 360 wickets in first grade, the level below Sheffield Shield, but it was all too late with World War Two intervening from 1939 to 1945.

Central Cumberland was a marvellous club, ideal for giving two sons the opportunity to reach the top of the cricket ladder.

* * *

It can be seen from the above that the three of us do not see eye to eye on all matters in the game, but that is as it should be. I would, in fact, think there may be something amiss if this were the case. Cricket is that kind of game. It is also a game where, because your deeds cannot be measured in seconds and minutes, as on an athletic track or in a swimming-pool, you never actually deteriorate in the minds of the followers of the sport.

As I sit sipping a glass of 1982 Yalumba Pewsey Vale, I am grateful that is the way of the world. The watching public recall only the good things and the player himself is inclined to discard the 'nasties' as though they were of no consequence. Human nature being what it is, we accept this and try not to correct those who consider the players of today to be inferior to those of years past.

But, for heaven's sake, don't try to relive the glories of yesterday. It never works!

I do not play any cricket these days owing to a legacy from a back injury sustained through bowling. But, when I did make a come-back at different times after 1964, I knew I had made the right decision in retiring. I went on a tour to Pakistan with Alex Bannister's team in 1968 and found no trouble in batting but bowling was almost impossible. A combination of back and shoulder posed real problems for most of the time and then, when I played some matches six years later in Australia, the injuries came thick and fast.

These were limited-overs games in a Channel Ten promotion in Brisbane, and each of the grade clubs there was permitted to ask two southern state players to make guest appearances. All but one of the clubs chose the current New South Wales Test and Sheffield Shield stars but one club, Valleys, asked Alan Davidson and me to turn out for them. It was my first limited-overs competition so I was eager to play, providing either Alan or I, or preferably both, could field at slip.

Valleys won the competition the first year and we couldn't have disgraced ourselves too much as we were asked back again the following season. That was where we made our mistake. We accepted. The young opponents who had treated the odd grey-haired couple with a certain mixture of levity and awe in the first year now got stuck into it. And our muscles were finding new muscles we didn't know existed. We managed to survive the preliminary round, then the quarter-final and then the semi . . . or almost through the semi. Going for a quick single to mid-on, I suddenly had this sensation of someone having pinged me in the back of the leg with a rifle bullet – not that I was any authority on people loosing off the occasional burst of gunfire on the cricket field and laying low a few of the participants.

At any rate, when I arrived at the non-striker's end and said to the umpire, 'What the hell's happened here? – my leg feels as though someone has put a knife through it,' he said, 'You've torn a hamstring, son.' He was right. Much of the next week in Sydney was spent jogging gently with my wife around the park below our flat, with an ice-pack strapped to the back of my thigh so I could be ready for the final.

As it turned out, we won it. I bowled the last of my six permitted overs with Alan Davidson at slip and he took two marvellous catches from outside edges – but at what cost it is difficult to determine to this day. That incredibly competitive streak in him somehow got him parallel to the ground, with his arm outstretched behind the 'keeper to pull the ball out of thin air. I swear on each occasion I could feel the thud from 22 yards as he hit the ground. When we were having dinner that evening, me unable to walk properly because of the hamstring and him unable to reach comfortably for the pepper-mill because of the muscles startlingly lengthened by the catches, we drank a toast. *To permanent retirement.*

I have almost managed to stick to the pledge too, though I was undone once, but not of my own volition. Some years after that match my wife, Daphne, and I went to Kenya to take part in fund-raising for the Variety Club of Great Britain. The charity was a crippled children's home in Thika, near Nairobi. The second year we were there one of the requests was that Bobby Charlton and I should, respectively, referee and umpire a football and cricket match. In return, a prominent sports club would pay into the charity something like £3000. I pointed out that recent manipulative work on my back meant I couldn't do anything more strenuous than umpiring and this was accepted.

When I arrived in Nairobi the posters advertising the game had me as the star performer against the team limbering up to represent East Africa in the World Cup to be played in England in 1979. I taxed the club's president on the fact that this was misleading advertising. 'Not at all,' he said, looking at the sky. 'It was merely a printer's error. But all the people in Nairobi know you will not let them down.' 'Well,' I replied, rather shortly, 'I can't play and that's that.' 'And,' he said, in his most urbane fashion, 'the great thing is the Australian High Commissioner and his wife will be there and they are so looking forward to seeing you play. They've already bought their tickets and made a donation.'

It was approximately 30 degrees Celsius when we won the toss and batted. The captain thought it a good idea if I batted at number three as the opposition had a young and very fast bowler on whom they would like my opinion. He was fast . . . he was also keen because a good match here would guarantee him a place in the World Cup squad. I was fortunate there was a good left-hand opening batsman in our team who went on to make a century.

I made some runs, enough to avoid embarrassment, but my biggest problem had been in running between the wickets. Despite taking it as easily as possible, I was already seizing up by the time I arrived back in the pavilion and began to bandage myself for the task of fielding and bowling.

The High Commissioner said he had never seen me look fitter and he was reminded vividly of the great days of the past. He was enthusiastically hoping to see from me a long stint at the bowling crease. Happily the playing conditions of the 30-overs-a-side game meant a maximum of six for any one bowler.

I gave thanks to the organisers and to the almost non-existent twilight. With the adrenalin trickling rather than flowing, I picked up a couple of wickets, but in front of my eyes all the time I was bowling was the image of a long, foaming glass of ice-cold Foster's lager. My mouth, to coin a phrase, was as dry as an Emu's instep. Daphne is very good at organising drinking matters of this kind and had been left in charge.

As we came from the field I looked for her. She was there but . . . no glass, no ice-cold lager? 'Where is it?' I managed to croak from a parched throat. She pulled down her sunglasses a fraction and looked at me. 'You haven't done your homework on overseas countries,' she said. 'This is a Muslim sports club. No one drinks.' She pushed her sunglasses back. It was also 30 degrees where she was sitting.

There was a reception arranged at the home of a sports administrator for half an hour after the match and, when we arrived, there was this magnificent swimming-pool and, at the side of it, an even more magnificent bar serving ice-cold lager. I reached out my hand for one . . . and promptly fell on the floor. My back had collapsed and I spent the next two days hobbling around the hotel. I kept well away from the High Commissioner so as not to spoil his image of the great days of the past.

* * *

Jugiong, catching fish in the Murrumbidgee, and going to practice at Cumberland Oval with my father are a long time gone. It's delightful though to recall those times and, as well, be able to keep pace with the jet age of the game. Well almost anyway!

No one really can keep up with cricket.

From the time the game began to the present moment, it has produced more conversation points than any other recreation. Perhaps it is because everyone looks at the game with such passionate seriousness. And I am able to predict, with a reasonable amount of certainty, that the happenings to take us into the 1990s and up to the year 2000, will be just as thrilling, boring, pleasant and decidedly controversial as those of the past century.

It will be part of the excitement of life to watch it all unfold.

INDEX

Abdul Qadir 97, 169
Adcock, Neil 58, 85, 86, 161
Alexander, Gerry 50, 51
Allen, G. O. 'Gubby' 69
Alley, Bill 131
Amarnath, L. 100
Amiss, Dennis 35, 212
Archer, Ken 20
Archer, Ron 174, 175
Arlott, John 109, 110, 124, 129
Armstrong, Warwick 34, 180
Asif Iqbal 94, 95
Atkinson, Colin 134
Atkinson, Denis 51
Australian Broadcasting Corporation
    109, 110, 137
Australian Cricket Board 16, 17, 20, 25,
    28, 32, 35, 37, 47, 48, 54, 59, 64, 106,
    119, 124, 127, 143, 144, 147, 150,
    166, 167, 171, 179, 193, 197, 198,
    230, 231, 234, 242

Bacher, Dr Ali 195
Badcock, C. L. 153
Bailey, Noel 120, 121
Bailey, Trevor 80
Bannister, Alex 128, 246
Barber, Bob 134
Barlow, Eddie 55, 187, 188
Barnes, Alan 119, 231
Barnes, S. F. 75
Barnes, Sid 13, 131, 175, 227
Barnes, Tieffie 188
Barrington, Ken 208, 226
Bates, Barry 23, 24
Bedford, Ian 134
Bedi, Bishen 206
Bedser, Alec 226
Bell, Ronnie 163
Benaud, Daphne 18, 121, 247
Benaud, John 32, 33, 218, 229–44
Benaud, Lou 218, 232–44
Benson and Hedges Company 139
Benson and Hedges Cup 18, 133
Benson and Hedges World Series Cup
    143, 144, 150, 206
Bergins, Howie 188
Birkett, Lord Justice 25, 148

Blythe, Colin 75
Booth, Brian 53, 55, 146, 198, 217
Borde, Chandu 94, 166
Border, Allan 42, 67
Botham, Ian 39–44, 66, 67, 75, 89–93,
    95, 100–03, 126, 155, 196
Bowley, Bruce 171
Boycott, Geoff 192, 193
Bradman, Donald 13, 34, 53–61, 69, 70,
    75, 80, 93, 99, 153, 155, 202, 207,
    216, 217, 220, 227, 233, 234
Bratchford, Jim 170
Brearley, Mike 37–44, 49, 69, 72, 90,
    126, 155, 172, 176, 196
Brearley, Walter 75
British Broadcasting Corporation 10,
    112, 119, 121, 156, 215
Brooks, Tom 171
Brown, Bill 14, 153, 203, 220
Brown, Jim 233
Bright, Ray 41
Bryant, Bert 70
Buller, Sid 211
Burge, Peter 20, 53, 163, 170, 175, 198
Burke, Jim 75, 120, 224
Burke, Perry 177
Burnside School 220, 221
Butcher, Basil 178

Callaghan, James 185
Cambridge University 38, 135
Cardus, Sir Neville 129, 152
Carew, Joey 45
Carter, 'Sammy' 180
Cartwright, Tom 184
Chandrasekhar, Bhagwat 206
Channel Seven 110
Channel Nine 95, 106, 111, 114, 119,
    121, 137, 234
Channel Ten 110, 246
Chappell, Greg 26, 28, 60, 66, 73, 88, 90,
    96, 101, 106, 150, 157, 167, 228
Chappell, Ian 25–38, 47, 48, 69, 83, 84,
    88, 98, 116, 134, 157, 184, 212, 228,
    240
Chatfield, Ewen 172, 173
Chauhan, Chetan 164, 200
Cheetham, Jack 181, 182

Chegwyn, Jack 83, 225
Chester, Frank 200
Chilvers, Hughie 131
Chipperfield, Arthur 13
Christ, 'Chilla' 153
Clark, Jack 20
Clinch, Lindsay 119, 120
Close, Brian 44–46, 196
Cohen, Mort 233
Colley, David 28, 212, 233
Collins, Herbie 219
Collins, Vince 131, 224
Compton, Denis 110
Congdon, Bev 37
Connolly, Alan 56, 198
Considine, Bernie 173
Cook, Geoff 153
Cook, Nick 207
Cornhill Insurance 139
Corrigan, Dr Brian 57
Cotter, 'Tibby' 179, 180
Cowdrey, Colin 35, 44–47, 175, 178, 196, 208
Cowgill, Bryan 112
Crafter, Tony 166
Craig, Ian 20, 23, 63, 85, 86, 171, 197
Crawford, Pat 23, 93, 174, 197, 209, 210
Cumberland CC 57, 83, 219–24, 245
Cunis, Bob 124

Daily Mail, London 128
Daily Mirror, Sydney 105, 121, 123, 231
Daily Telegraph, London 121
Daily Telegraph, Sydney 110
Daniel, Jack 173
Davidson, Alan 30, 51, 59, 61, 76, 84, 84–88, 97, 106, 146, 165, 171, 173, 208, 240, 246
Davies, Geoff 229
De Selnicourt, Hugh 223
Dell, Tony 27, 31
Denness, Mike 35, 37, 49, 179, 196
Dev, Kapil 89, 94, 97–103, 155
Dexter, Ted 63, 123, 128, 208
Dilley, Graham 40, 41
Donnelly, Martin 197
D'Oliveira, Basil 183–85
Dooland, Bruce 161
Dwyer, Brian 157, 173

Eagar, Patrick 215
Eastwood, Ken 26, 27
Ebrahim, Baboo 188
Edmonds, Phil 172
Edrich, John 35
Edwards, Ross 29, 32, 98
Egar, Colin 56
Ellis, Jack 153
Elphiston, Herb 171
Emburey, John 42, 194

Emery, Vic 207
Evans, Godfrey 80, 227

Fagg, A. E. 220
Fallowfield, Les 131
Farrell, Pat 58, 231
Faulkner, Aubrey 225
Favell, Les 23, 24, 54, 64, 75, 149, 198
Fazal Mahmood 64, 94
Fender, Percy 69
Fingleton, Jack 220
Fleetwood-Smith, L. O'B. 220
Fletcher, Keith 65
Flynn, Brian 224
Ford, Doug 81, 146
Ford, John Social History of Cricket 9, 11
Fraser, Malcolm 183, 189, 191–94
Fuller, Eddie 86

Gavaskar, Sunil 100, 155, 164–66, 200
Gibbs, Lance 45
Gillette Cup 132, 133, 139, 149
Gilligan, Arthur 125, 219
Gleeson, John 28, 83, 198, 225, 226
Goddard, John 51
Goddard, Trevor 55, 85, 86
Godman, Tom 237
Gooch, Graham 39, 192, 194
Gower, David 66, 67, 157
Graveney, Tom 44, 208
Gray, Bob 121–23
Greig, Tony 10, 18, 37, 38, 116, 135, 179, 212
Gregory, Jack 235
Gregory, Syd 181
Griffin, Geoff 54, 123
Griffith, Charlie 30, 45
Griffith, S. C. 44, 209
Grimmett, Clarrie 13, 102, 161, 219, 220, 225, 235
Grout, Wally 51, 63, 76, 80, 88, 165, 208
Gulliver, Ken 130
Gunn, George 75
Gupte, Subash 78, 79

Hadlee, Richard 89, 101–03
Hadlee, Walter 197
Hall, Wes 30, 45, 51, 84, 85, 156
Hammond, Jeff 28, 34
Hammond, Walter 49
Hanif Mohammad 94, 95
Haroon Rashid 95
Harlequins CC 135
Harris, Lord 69, 157
Harris, David 23
Harvey, 'Mick' 168
Harvey, Neil 55, 63, 64, 67, 75, 76, 78–80, 128, 146, 147, 156, 235
Haseeb Ahsan 64

Hassett, Lindsay 13, 20–24, 74, 75, 157, 158, 181, 203, 225, 227
Hastings, Brian 36
Hawke, Lord 49, 69
Hawke, Bob 183
Hayward, Tom 75
Hazare, Vijay 100
Heine, Peter 85, 161
Hilditch, Andrew 168
Hill, Clem 180, 181
Hill, David 111, 113, 114–18
Hill, Jack 223
Hirst, George 75, 157
Hobbs, Jack 75, 233
Hobbs, Robin 134
Hogan, Tom 88
Hogg, Rodney 88, 168
Holding, Michael 156
Hollies, Eric 226, 227
Holt, J. K. 177
Hong Kong CG 58
Howarth, Geoff 37, 98, 101, 172
Howell, Arthur 222
Hughes, Kim 38, 39, 41, 43, 60, 80, 96, 97, 127, 155, 167, 196
Hunte, Conrad 50
Hunter, Nick 111–13, 118
Hurst, Alan 168
Hutton, Len 14, 25, 46, 49, 59, 75, 153, 177
Hutton, Richard 38, 73–75

Ijaz Butt 95, 166, 167
Illingworth, Ray 25, 29, 30, 37, 45–49, 176, 177, 196
Imran Khan 74, 89, 91, 94–96, 99, 100, 102, 103, 178
Ingleby-Mackenzie, Colin 73
International Cricket Conference 10, 54, 189–93, 206, 216
Intikhab Alam 94, 134
Inverarity, John 29
Iqbal Qasim 172, 174
Iredale, Frank 180
Iverson, J. B. 225

Jackson, Leslie 119
Jardine, Douglas 53, 69
Jarman, Barry 38, 184, 198
Jarrett, Milton 222
Javed Miandad 95, 166–68
Jenkins, Dan 11, 127
Jenner, Terry 27, 31, 176
Jessop, Gilbert 75
John Player League 18, 49, 132, 133
Johnson, Ian 12, 19, 59, 67, 174, 175
Johnson, Mel 166
Johnston, Bill 207
Jugiong 12, 220

Kanhai, Rohan 51
Kelleway, Charlie 180
Kenning, David 111–13, 118
Kenyon, Don 110
Kippax, Alan 219
Kischenchand, Hari 100
Kline, Lindsay 76, 86, 165
Knott, Alan 30, 42, 178, 212
Koornhof, Dr Piet 188, 189, 195
Kunderam, Buddy 165

Laker, Jim 39, 67, 79, 119, 155, 161
Lamb, Alan 194
Latchman, 'Harry' 134
Laver, Frank 179, 180
Lawry, Bill 25–28, 31, 44, 47, 54, 55, 57, 114, 146, 147, 176, 208
Lawson, Geoff 88
le Roux, Garth 96
Lever, Peter 172
Lewis, Phil 112, 118
Lewis, Tony 49
Lillee, Dennis 27–30, 32, 34, 35, 37, 41, 83, 84, 88, 91, 94, 98, 102, 106, 109, 114, 127, 150, 156, 164, 166–69, 187, 188, 200, 235
Lindwall, Ray 20, 22–24, 34, 84, 93, 110, 156, 169–71, 174, 207, 209, 210
Lloyd, Clive 50–52
Lock, Tony 79, 80, 161, 226
Loxton, Sam 77–79

Macartney, Charlie 234
McAlister, Peter 179, 180
McCabe, Stan 220
McCool, Colin 100, 207, 228
McCormick, 'Goldie' 220
McCosker, Rick 232
McDonald, Colin 34, 63, 67, 75, 80, 86, 165, 166, 169
McGilvray, Alan 109, 130
McGlew, Jackie 86
Mackay, Ken 54, 55, 59, 75, 76, 80, 88, 165, 174, 208
McKenzie, Graham 55, 88, 123, 208
McLachlan, Ian 146
MacLaren, A. C. 75
Majid Khan 94
Mallett, Ashley 28, 33, 34, 36, 83, 88
Mankad, 'Vinoo' 94, 100
Manning, James 128
Marsh, Rodney 26, 30, 31, 37, 83, 84, 88, 98, 158
Martin, Johnny 76, 170
MCC 47, 122, 132, 179, 193, 199, 207
Massie, Bob 28, 29, 32, 33, 83, 212
May, Peter 49, 66–68, 80, 81, 155, 175, 176, 178, 179
Meckiff, Ian 53, 54, 56, 75, 86, 146
Melbourne Herald 121, 192

Menzies, Badge 175
Menzies, Robert 183
Merchant, Vijay 110
Merrimann, Bob 167
Middlesex CCC 38, 43, 199
Middleton, Roy 216, 217
Miller, Keith 13, 14, 19–25, 30, 34, 85,
    89, 91–93, 100, 103, 119, 156, 170,
    171, 175, 203, 207, 216
Milner, Doug 223
Minnett, Roy 180
Minney, John 38
Misson, Frank 76, 146, 147
Mohammad Munaf 64
Monger, Dennis 119
Monteith, Bob 36
Morelli, Brian 114–16, 118
Morris, Arthur 19–22, 131, 148, 203,
    240
Morris, Mel 109
Mosman CC 57
Mudassar Nazar 174
Murray, John 44
Mushtaq Mohammad 32, 94, 95, 134,
    168

Nadkarni Bapu 73, 74
Nash, Malcolm 176
NatWest Bank Trophy 18, 139
New South Wales CC 13, 19–24, 50,
    53–55, 57, 60, 81, 84, 87, 109, 128,
    131, 146, 148, 169, 229–32, 236
New South Wales Cricket Association
    Year Book 106, 129, 130, 220
New Zealand Board 36
Noble, Monty 75, 180
Norfolk, Duke of 128
Nurse, Seymour 73

Oakman, Alan 163
O'Donoghue, Jack 222, 223
O'Keefe, Kerry 27, 31, 33, 134, 229
Old, Chris 41, 42, 126
Oldfield, Bert 236
O'Neill, Norman 53, 56, 64, 75, 198
O'Reilly, Bill 13, 131, 161, 219, 220, 225
Owen-Smith, 'Tuppy' 202
Oxford University 135

PBL Marketing 106, 143
Packer, Kerry 15, 18
Pamenski, Joe 186, 188, 195
Parkin, Cecil 125
Parks, Jim 178
Parramatta 13, 18, 85, 107–10, 124, 129,
    137, 216, 218, 219
Pascoe, Lenny 213
Patel, Jasu 77
Patherya Mudar 167
Peebles, Ian 169

Pepper, Cec 13, 14, 161, 162
Phadkar, Dattaray 99, 100
Philipson, Eddie 211
Phillips, James 216
Philpott, Peter 198, 240
Pollard, Dick 175
Pollard, Vic 198
Pollock, Graeme 188
Ponsford, Bill 155, 219
Prasanna, Erapally 206
Prideaux, Roger 184
Priestley, John 128
Procter, Mike 10, 83, 188
Prowse, Jack 223
Pullar, Geoff 208

Queensland CC 13, 14, 20, 30, 53

Rae, Alan 194
Ramadhin, Sonny 51, 60, 73
Ransford, Vernon 180
Raymer, Mick 207
Redpath, Ian 26, 31, 32
Reid, John 101, 197
Renneberg, Dave 229
Rest of the World XI 38
Rhodes, Dusty 58
Rhodes, Wilfred 75
Richards, Viv 52, 157
Richardson, Peter 175
Richardson, Vic 181, 219, 235, 236
Ridings, Phil 171, 193, 203
Roberts, Andy 156
Roberts, Ron 58, 226
Robertson-Glasgow, R. C. 130, 131, 152
Robbins, Derrick 186
Rodriguez, Willy 45
Rorke, Gordon 24, 55, 209
Rosenwater, Irving 115
Ross, Alan 124
Rothmans Company 14, 47, 132, 139
Rowan, Lou 176
Rowe, Lawrence 191
Rowley, Jack 222
Russell, Jim 223
Russell, Philip 176
Ryder, Jack 53, 55, 69

Sadiq Mohammad 32, 33
Sarfraz Nawaz 94
Sargent, Les 23
Sargent, Murray 23
Saunders, Warren 23
Schwarz, Reggie 225
Schweppes 139
Seddon, Dudley 53, 55, 69
Sheehan, Paul 30, 33, 198
Shepherd, Barry 53, 54
Sheppard, David 208
Shiell, Alan 31

Sidebottom, Arnold 193
Sikander Bakht 168
Simons, Con 210
Simpson, Bob 25, 30, 53, 56–58, 76, 146, 208
Sims, Jim 220
Sincock, David 146
Singh, C. K. 177
Sismey, Stan 13
Sloan, Tom 118
Smith, Cammie 84
Smith, Chris 194
Smith, M. J. K. 44
Smith, Syd 181
Snow, John 10, 26, 27, 30, 31, 48, 176
Sobers, Garfield 45, 51, 73, 89, 91, 103, 184, 236
Solomon, Cyril 14
Solomon, Joe 51, 84
Somerset CCC 90, 101
South Australia CC 13, 22–24, 54, 55
Spofforth, F. R. 28
Spooner, R. H. 75
Stackpole, Bill 25
Stackpole, Keith 25, 26, 29, 31
Statham, Brian 80, 153, 177
Steele, Ray 84, 122
Stephenson, Harold 58
Stevens, Gavin 64
Stollmeyer, Jeff 51, 194
Sutcliffe, Bert 197
Sutcliffe, Herbert 233
Swanton, E. W. 73, 121

Taber, Brian 139
Tallon, Bill 13, 14, 74, 153, 207
Tayfield, Hugh 85, 86
Taylor, Bob 66, 67
Taylor, Ken 73
TEST SERIES
England v Australia (1909) 75,
  (1911–12) 75, 179, 180, (1930) 202,
  (1932–33) 53, 155, (1936–37) 129,
  (1948) 175, 227, (1953) 74, 75, 154,
  158, 227, (1954–55) 59, 75, 153, 154,
  203, (1956) 67, 93, 119, 129, 131, 154,
  155, 174, 175, 197, (1958–59) 59, 67,
  68, 75, 80, 81, 155, 203, (1961) 45, 63,
  70, 73, 82, 123, 124, 145–47, 154,
  163, 164, 211, (1962–63) 53, 123,
  128, 208, (1964) 30, 121, 122,
  (1965–66) 44, (1968) 24, (1970–71)
  24, 26, 27, 30, 31, 46–48, 176, (1972)
  28–31, 83, 212, (1974–75) 33–37,
  109, (1975) 178, 179, (1977) 39, 70,
  (1978–79) 38, 43, (1979–80) 38, 43,
  114, (1981) 38–43, 80, 99, 126, 155,
  202, 211, (1982–83) 65–67, 90, 91,
  103, 137, 138, 150, 151, 155
England v South Africa (1924) 125,
  (1929) 202, (1960) 54, 131, 132
England v West Indies (1953–54) 25,
  177, (1959–60) 177, 178, (1966) 44,
  (1967–68) 45, 178, (1980) 39,
  (1980–81) 39
England v New Zealand (1983) 67, 101,
  102
England v India (1946) 109, 110, (1967)
  44, (1981–82) 98
England v Pakistan (1967) 44, 45,
  (1968–69) 178, (1979) 172, (1982) 94,
  97
Australia v South Africa (1949–50) 157,
  (1952–53) 181, (1957–58) 85, 86,
  154, 228, (1963–64) 53–58,
  (1969–70) 24, 83
Australia v West Indies (1951–52) 51,
  (1954–55) 154, (1960–61) 50, 59–61,
  76, 84, 85, 146, 153, 154, (1964–65)
  30, (1972–73) 32–34, (1981–82) 137,
  138
Australia v New Zealand (1973–74)
  34–37
Australia v India (1947–48) 99, 100,
  (1959–60) 77–79, 154, (1980–81) 164
Australia v Pakistan (1959–60) 63, 64,
  76–80, 154, 165, (1972–73) 32, 33,
  (1976–77) 94, 95, (1978–79) 168,
  (1981–82) 95, 137, 138, 166–68,
  (1983–84) 150
Pakistan v India (1982–83) 100, 178
TCCB 10, 126, 147, 176, 190, 192
Thomas, Bernard 173
Thomas, Grahame 53
Toms, George 169
Thomson, Ian 163
Thomson, Jeff 34, 88, 94, 98, 109, 156, 169
Titmus, Fred 35
Toohey, Jack 120
Toshack, Ernie 99
Tressider, Phil 223
Tribe, George 161
Trueman, Fred 80, 156, 209, 242
Trumper, Victor 180
Tucker, Dick 105
Turner, Alan 94
Turner, Glenn 36, 37, 149
Turner, Mike 46
Twistleton, Frank 186
Tyldesley, Richard 125
Tyson, Frank 80, 153, 156, 209, 210

Umrigar, 'Polly' 94
Underwood, Derek 29, 30, 35, 114

Valentine, Alf 51, 84
Veivers, Tom 56
Venkataraghavan, Srinivas 206
Victoria CC 54, 57, 60

Viljoen, Ken 181
Viswanath, Gundappa 43
Vizianagram, Maharaj Kumar of 77, 78, 110
Vorster, John 184, 185, 188

Waite, Johnny 86
Walcott, Clyde 51
Walker, Alan 171, 207, 224
Walker, Max 32, 34, 88, 94, 98
Walmsley, Wally 170
Walters, Doug 26, 34, 36, 57, 83
Ward, Francis 220
Warner, Pelham 75
Watkins, John 32, 33
Watt, Bill 171
Wazir Mohammad 94
Webb, S. G. 229, 230
Wellham, Dirk 42
Westcott, Dick 86
Western Australia CC 34, 53, 54, 60, 123, 198
West Indies Board of Control 50, 193, 194
White, Crawford 124
White, J. C. 169

Whittington, Dick 153
Wilkins, Phil 237
Willis, Bob 40, 42, 49, 65–67, 99, 126, 156, 172, 174
Wisden Cricketers' Almanack 106, 130, 132
Woodfull, Bill 155
Wooldridge, Ian 127, 128
World Cup 98, 99, 100, 193
World Series Cricket 10, 15–18, 37, 38, 43, 58, 62, 64, 69, 107, 110, 135, 156, 190, 195, 197, 205, 213, 244
World Series Cup 101, 137, 143, 144, 150, 206
Worrell, Frank 50, 51
Worthington, T. S. 220
Wright, John 101

Yardley, Bruce 88
Yallop, Graham 41–43, 196
Yorkshire CCC 44–46, 49, 126
Yuile, Brian 198

Zaheer Abbas 33, 94–96